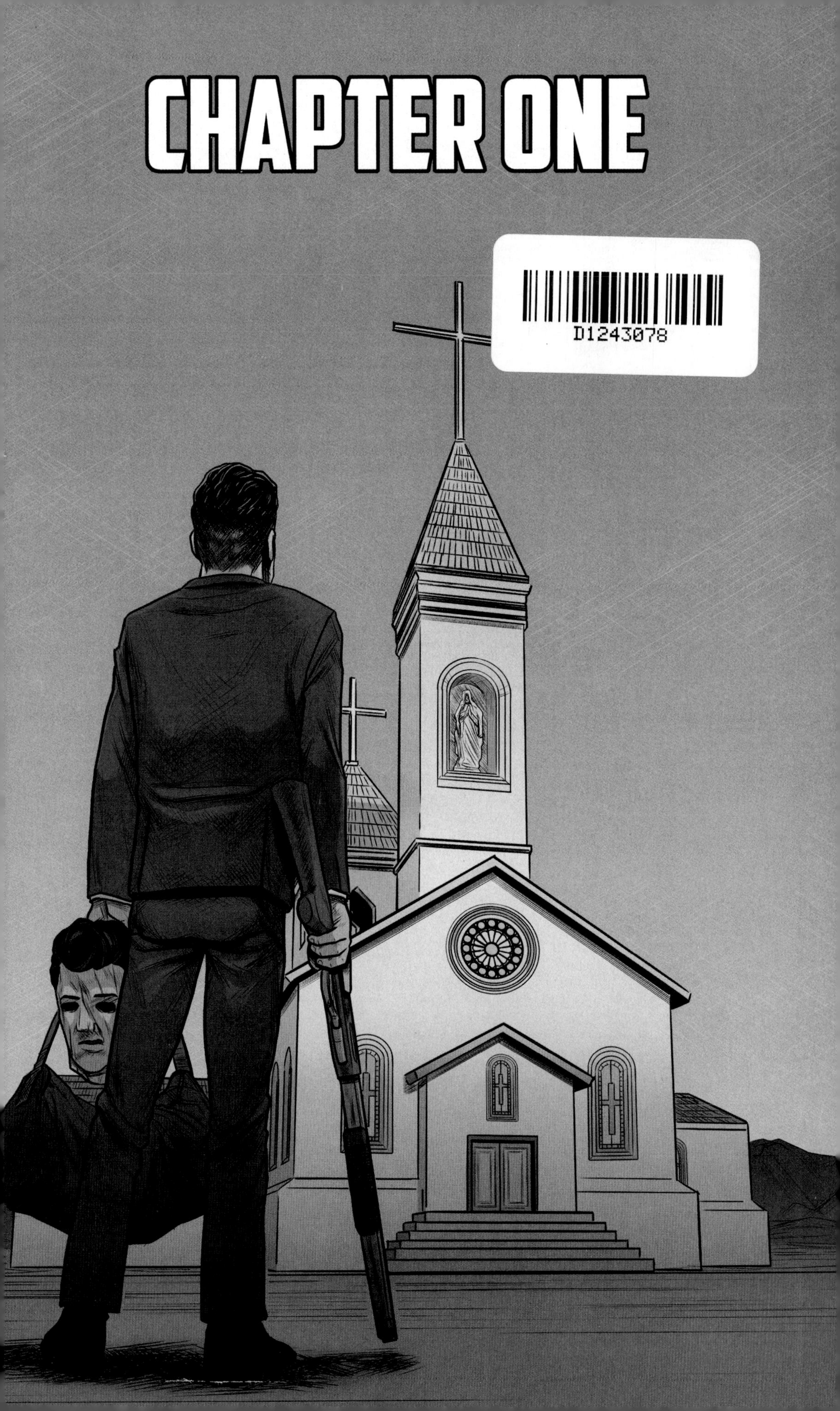
CHAPTER ONE

Going to the CHAPEL

1

Written by
DAVID PEPOSE

Art by
GAVIN GUIDRY

Colors by
ELIZABETH KRAMER

Lettering by
ARIANA MAHER
WITH COLIN BELL

Covers by
LISA STERLE, MAAN HOUSE AND GAVIN GUIDRY

Chapel Of Love
Words and Music by Phil Spector, Ellie Greenwich and Jeff Barry
Copyright (c) 1964 UNIVERSAL - SONGS OF POLYGRAM INTERNATIONAL, INC., TRIO MUSIC
COMPANY and MOTHER BERTHA MUSIC, INC.
Copyright Renewed
All Rights for TRIO MUSIC COMPANY Administered by BMG RIGHTS MANAGEMENT (US) LLC
All Rights for MOTHER BERTHA MUSIC, INC. Controlled and Administered by EMI APRIL MUSIC INC.
All Rights Reserved Used by Permission
Reprinted by Permission of Hal Leonard LLC

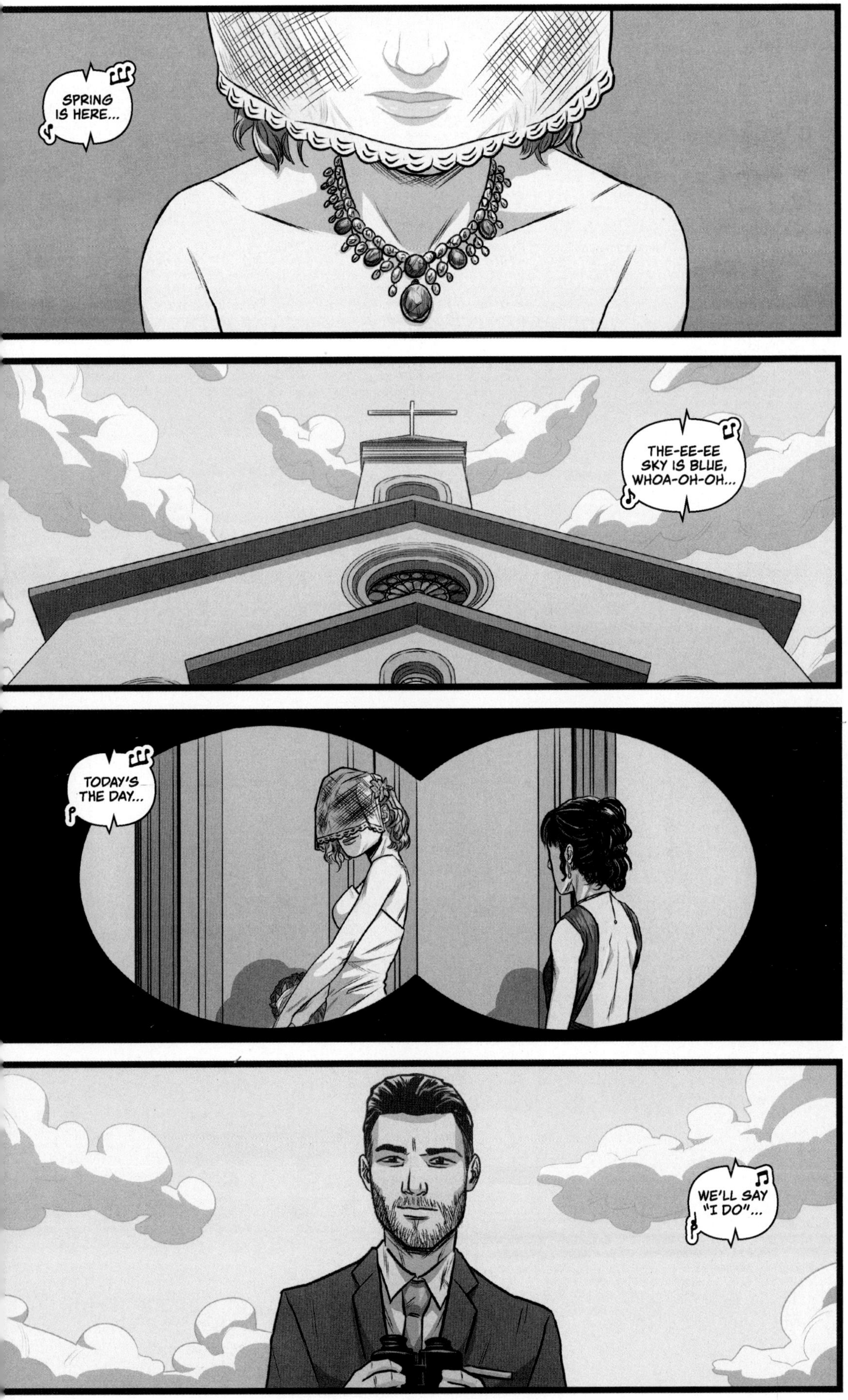
SPRING IS HERE...
THE-EE-EE SKY IS BLUE, WHOA-OH-OH...
TODAY'S THE DAY...
WE'LL SAY "I DO"...

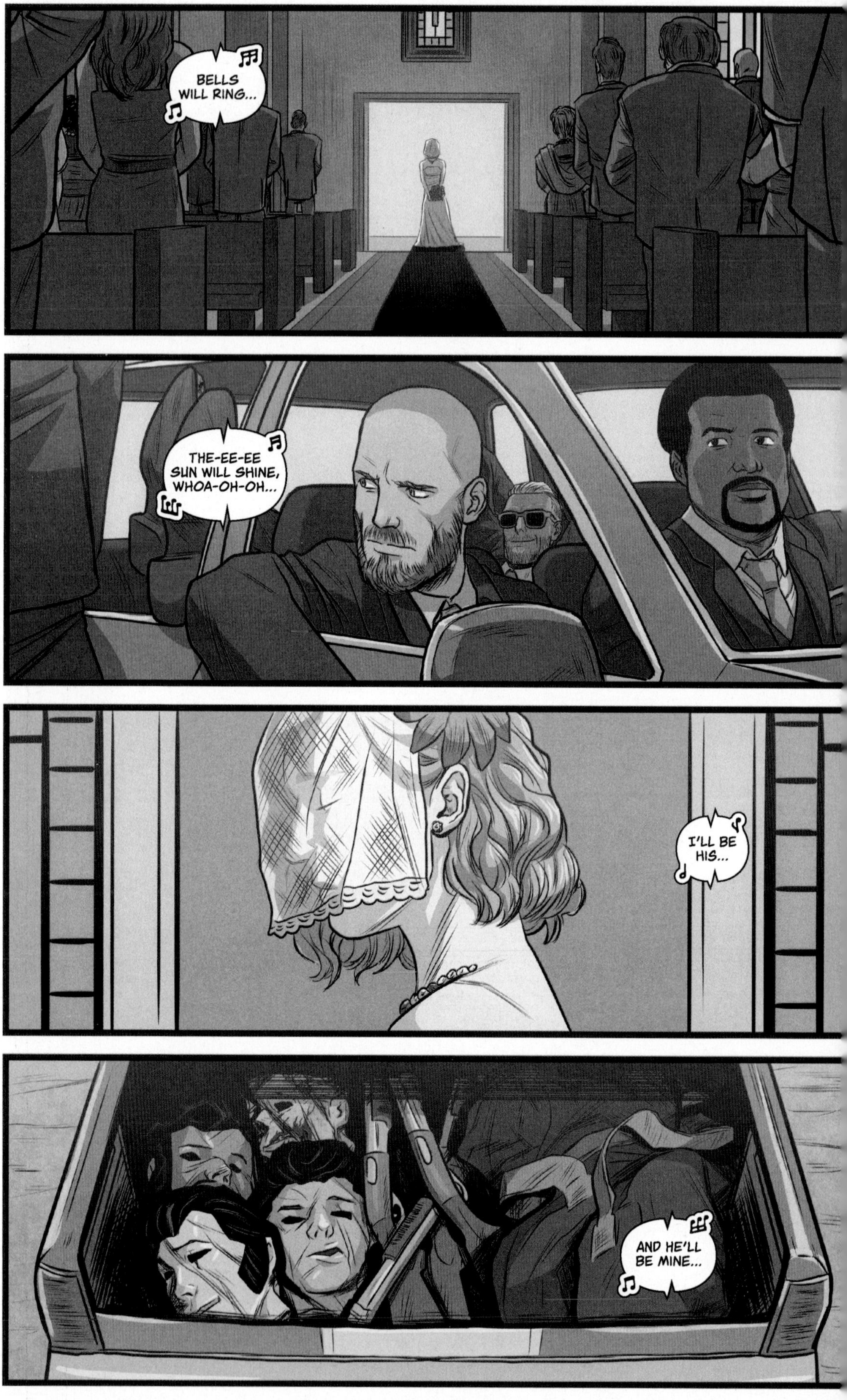
BELLS WILL RING...
THE-EE-EE SUN WILL SHINE, WHOA-OH-OH...
I'LL BE HIS...
AND HE'LL BE MINE...

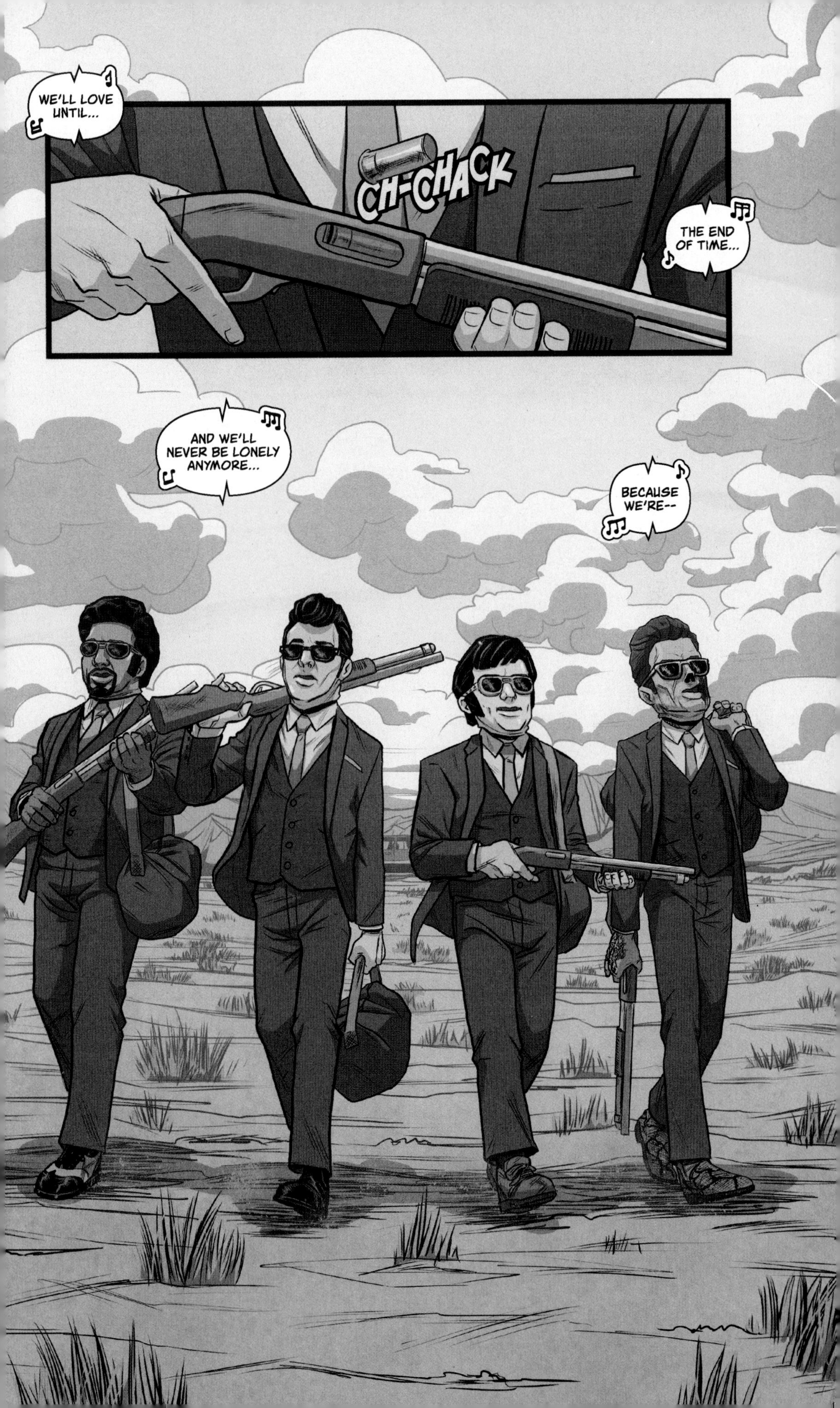
WE'LL LOVE UNTIL...
CH-CHACK
THE END OF TIME...
AND WE'LL NEVER BE LONELY ANYMORE...
BECAUSE WE'RE--

Going

CH

WRITTEN BY DAVID PEPOSE
COLORS BY ELIZABETH KRAMER

to the PEL

ART BY GAVIN GUIDRY
LETTERS BY ARIANA MAHER

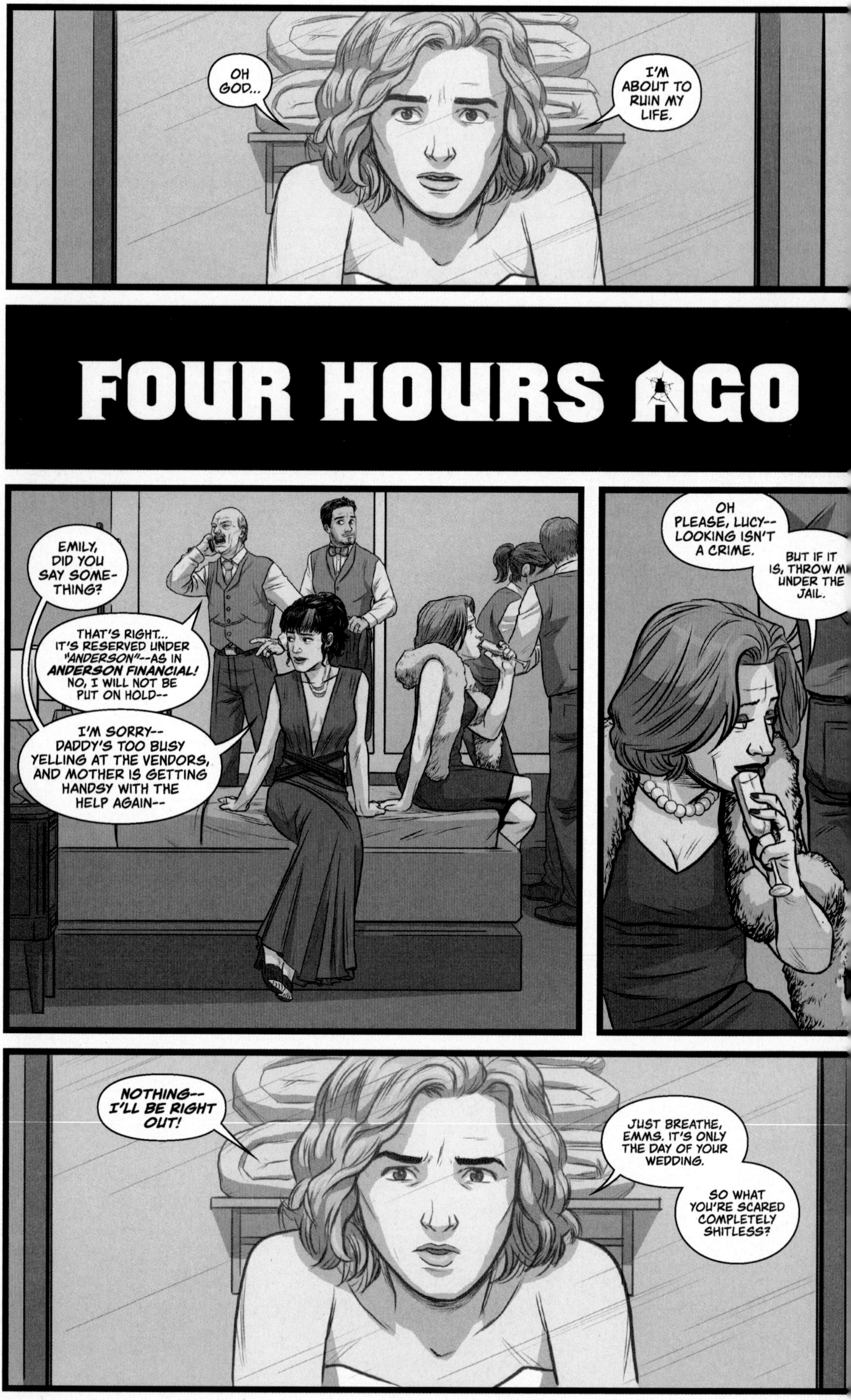
OH GOD...
I'M ABOUT TO RUIN MY LIFE.
FOUR HOURS AGO
EMILY, DID YOU SAY SOME-THING?
THAT'S RIGHT... IT'S RESERVED UNDER "ANDERSON"--AS IN ANDERSON FINANCIAL! NO, I WILL NOT BE PUT ON HOLD--
I'M SORRY-- DADDY'S TOO BUSY YELLING AT THE VENDORS, AND MOTHER IS GETTING HANDSY WITH THE HELP AGAIN--
OH PLEASE, LUCY-- LOOKING ISN'T A CRIME.
BUT IF IT IS, THROW M UNDER THE JAIL.
NOTHING-- I'LL BE RIGHT OUT!
JUST BREATHE, EMMS. IT'S ONLY THE DAY OF YOUR WEDDING.
SO WHAT YOU'RE SCARED COMPLETELY SHITLESS?

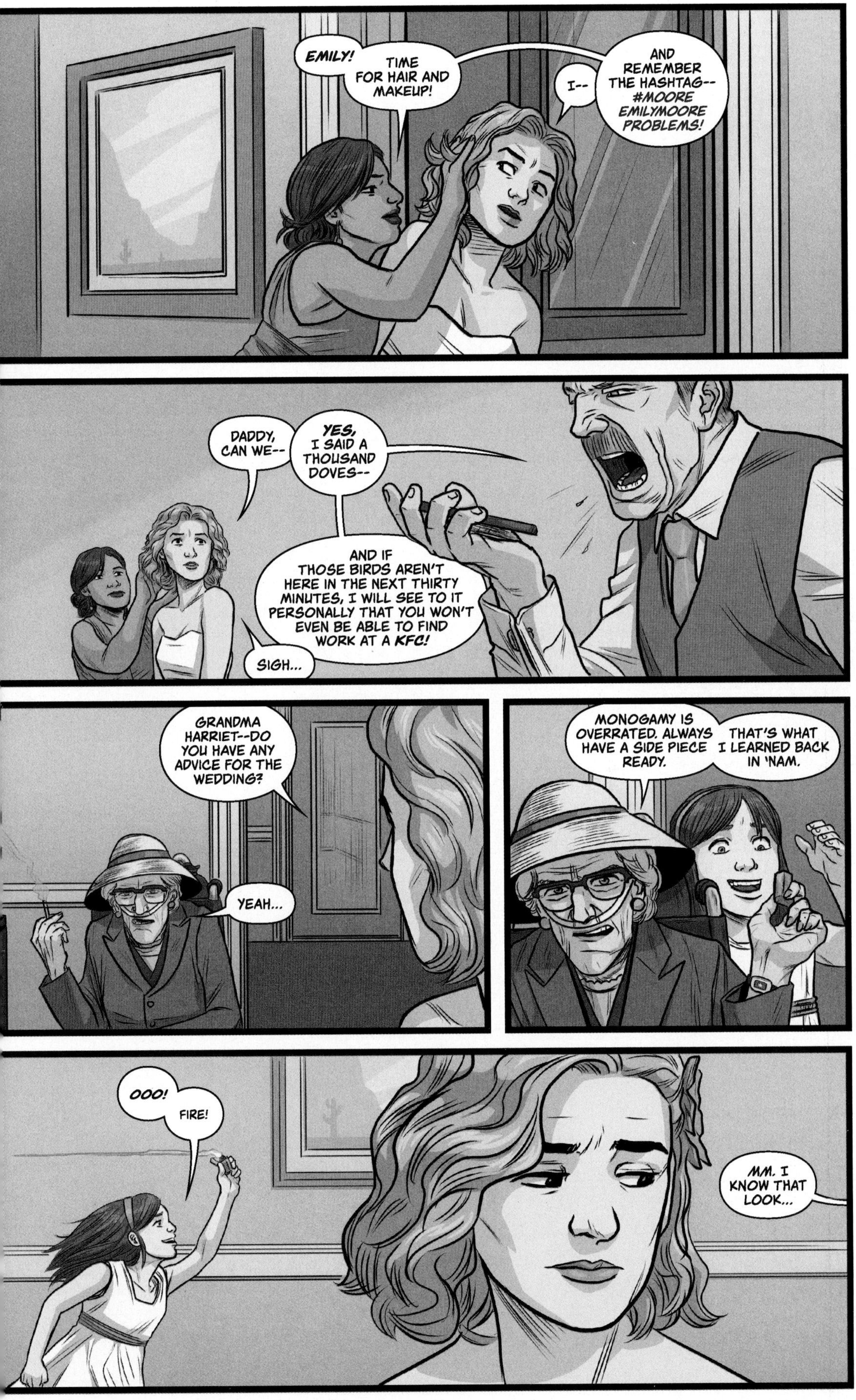
EMILY!
TIME FOR HAIR AND MAKEUP!
I--
AND REMEMBER THE HASHTAG-- #MOORE EMILYMOORE PROBLEMS!
DADDY, CAN WE--
YES, I SAID A THOUSAND DOVES--
AND IF THOSE BIRDS AREN'T HERE IN THE NEXT THIRTY MINUTES, I WILL SEE TO IT PERSONALLY THAT YOU WON'T EVEN BE ABLE TO FIND WORK AT A KFC!
SIGH...
GRANDMA HARRIET--DO YOU HAVE ANY ADVICE FOR THE WEDDING?
YEAH...
MONOGAMY IS OVERRATED. ALWAYS HAVE A SIDE PIECE READY.
THAT'S WHAT I LEARNED BACK IN 'NAM.
OOO!
FIRE!
MM. I KNOW THAT LOOK...

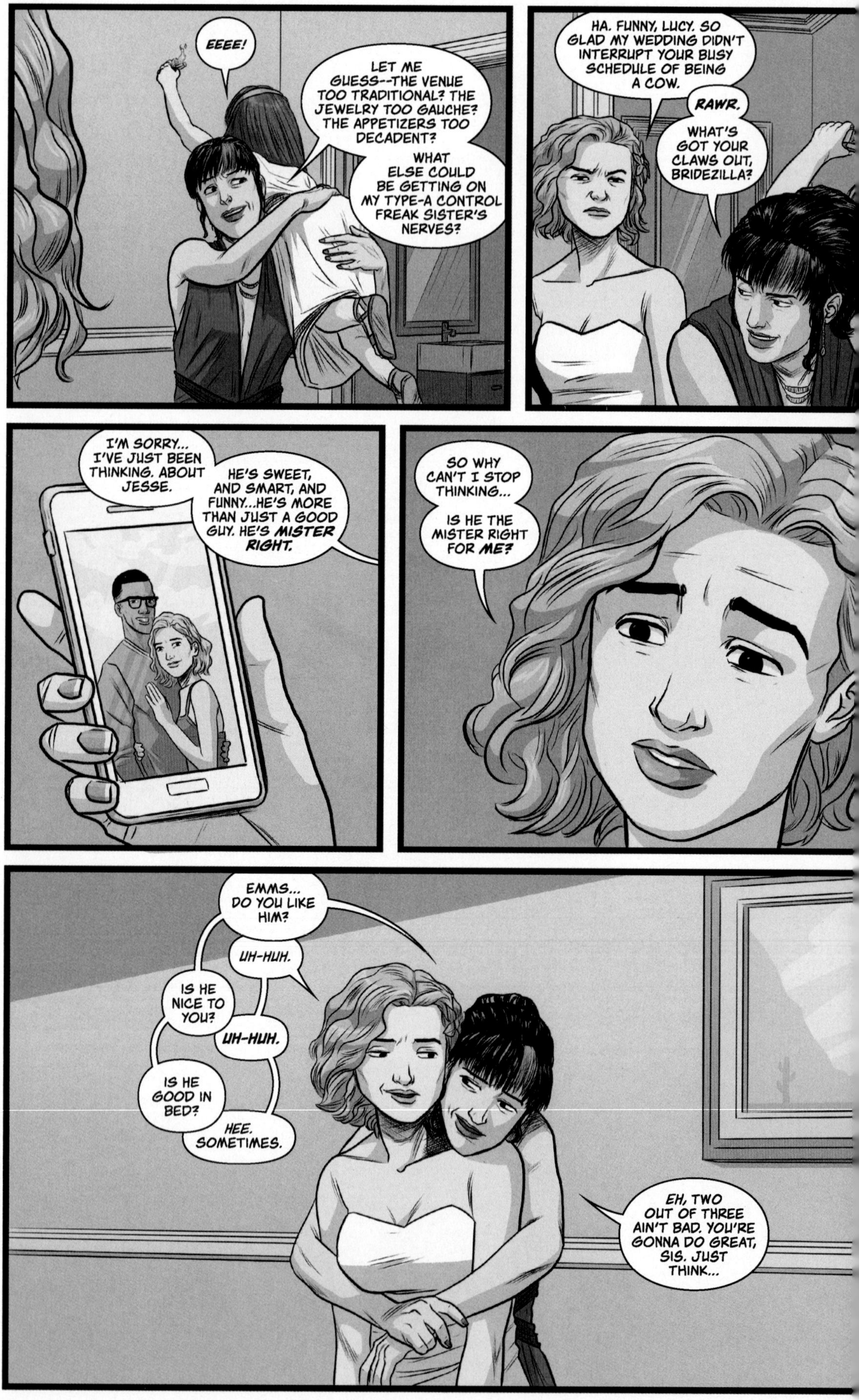
EEEE!
LET ME GUESS--THE VENUE TOO TRADITIONAL? THE JEWELRY TOO GAUCHE? THE APPETIZERS TOO DECADENT?
WHAT ELSE COULD BE GETTING ON MY TYPE-A CONTROL FREAK SISTER'S NERVES?
HA. FUNNY, LUCY. SO GLAD MY WEDDING DIDN'T INTERRUPT YOUR BUSY SCHEDULE OF BEING A COW.
RAWR.
WHAT'S GOT YOUR CLAWS OUT, BRIDEZILLA?
I'M SORRY... I'VE JUST BEEN THINKING. ABOUT JESSE.
HE'S SWEET, AND SMART, AND FUNNY...HE'S MORE THAN JUST A GOOD GUY. HE'S MISTER RIGHT.
SO WHY CAN'T I STOP THINKING...
IS HE THE MISTER RIGHT FOR ME?
EMMS... DO YOU LIKE HIM?
UH-HUH.
IS HE NICE TO YOU?
UH-HUH.
IS HE GOOD IN BED?
HEE. SOMETIMES.
EH, TWO OUT OF THREE AIN'T BAD. YOU'RE GONNA DO GREAT, SIS. JUST THINK...

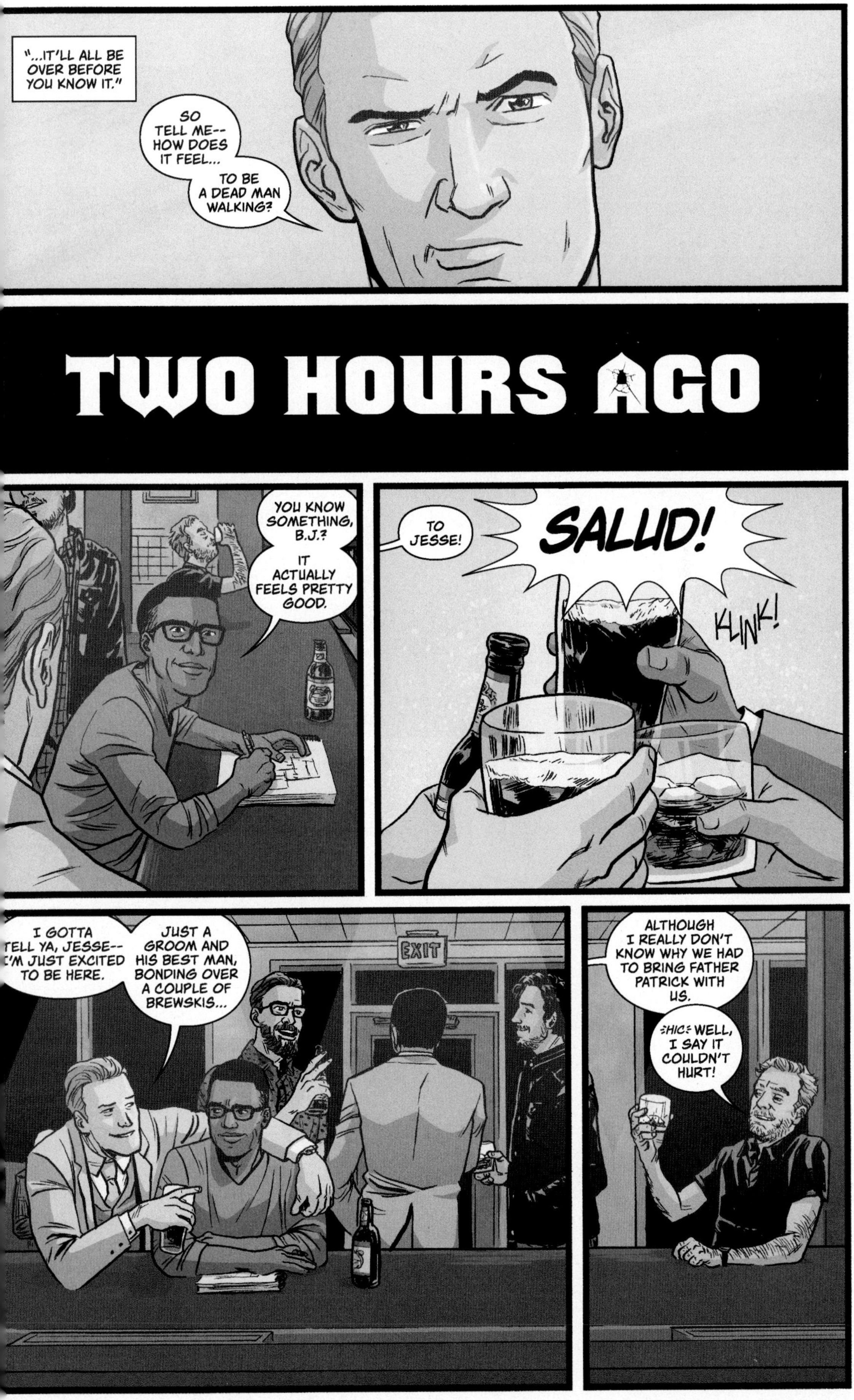

"...IT'LL ALL BE OVER BEFORE YOU KNOW IT."
SO TELL ME-- HOW DOES IT FEEL...
TO BE A DEAD MAN WALKING?
TWO HOURS AGO
YOU KNOW SOMETHING, B.J.?
IT ACTUALLY FEELS PRETTY GOOD.
TO JESSE!
SALUD!
KLINK!
I GOTTA TELL YA, JESSE-- I'M JUST EXCITED TO BE HERE.
JUST A GROOM AND HIS BEST MAN, BONDING OVER A COUPLE OF BREWSKIS...
EXIT
ALTHOUGH I REALLY DON'T KNOW WHY WE HAD TO BRING FATHER PATRICK WITH US.
HIC WELL, I SAY IT COULDN'T HURT!

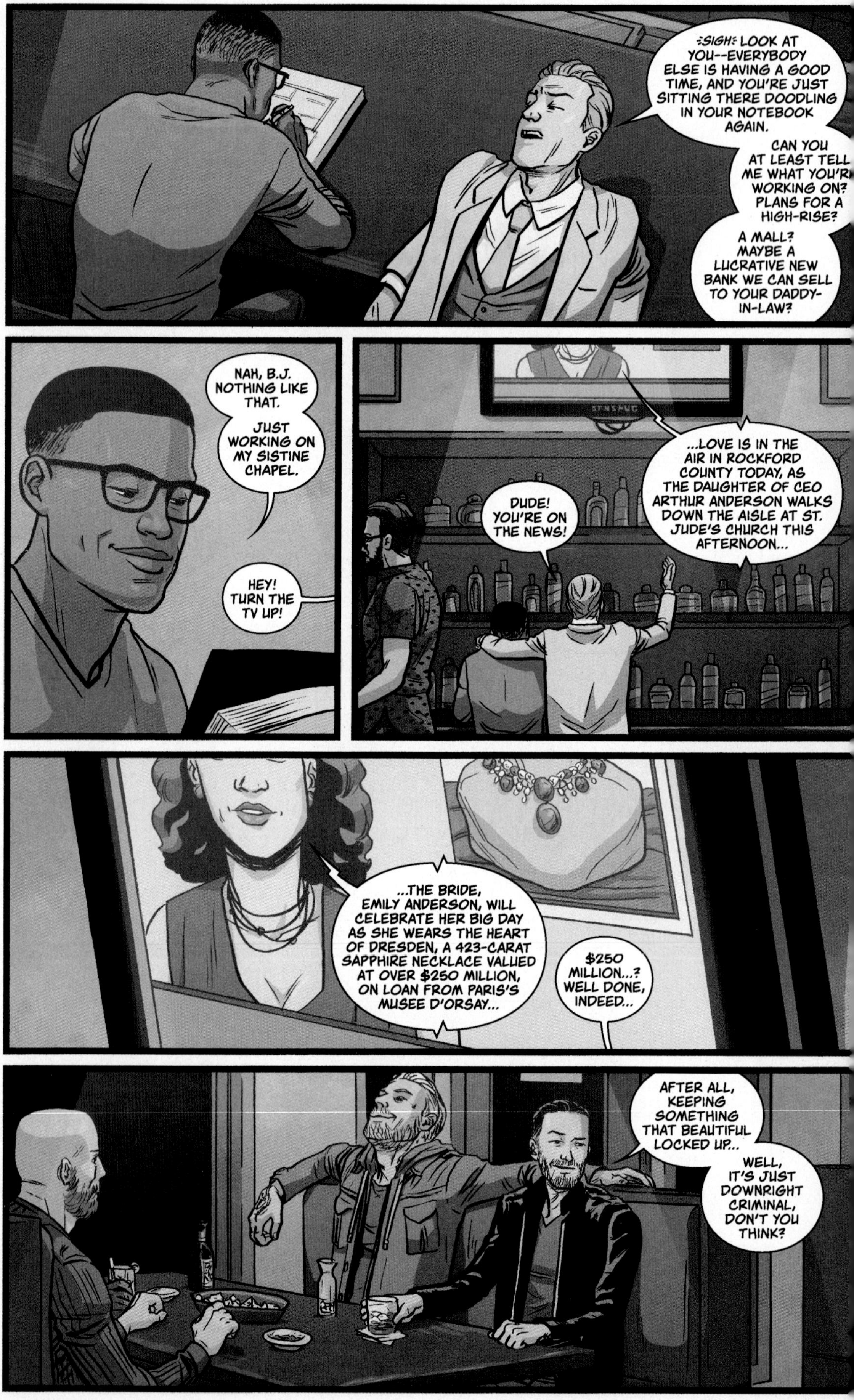

:SIGH: LOOK AT YOU--EVERYBODY ELSE IS HAVING A GOOD TIME, AND YOU'RE JUST SITTING THERE DOODLING IN YOUR NOTEBOOK AGAIN.
CAN YOU AT LEAST TELL ME WHAT YOU'RE WORKING ON? PLANS FOR A HIGH-RISE?
A MALL? MAYBE A LUCRATIVE NEW BANK WE CAN SELL TO YOUR DADDY-IN-LAW?
NAH, B.J. NOTHING LIKE THAT.
JUST WORKING ON MY SISTINE CHAPEL.
HEY! TURN THE TV UP!
DUDE! YOU'RE ON THE NEWS!
...LOVE IS IN THE AIR IN ROCKFORD COUNTY TODAY, AS THE DAUGHTER OF CEO ARTHUR ANDERSON WALKS DOWN THE AISLE AT ST. JUDE'S CHURCH THIS AFTERNOON...
...THE BRIDE, EMILY ANDERSON, WILL CELEBRATE HER BIG DAY AS SHE WEARS THE HEART OF DRESDEN, A 423-CARAT SAPPHIRE NECKLACE VALUED AT OVER $250 MILLION, ON LOAN FROM PARIS'S MUSEE D'ORSAY...
$250 MILLION...? WELL DONE, INDEED...
AFTER ALL, KEEPING SOMETHING THAT BEAUTIFUL LOCKED UP...
WELL, IT'S JUST DOWNRIGHT CRIMINAL, DON'T YOU THINK?

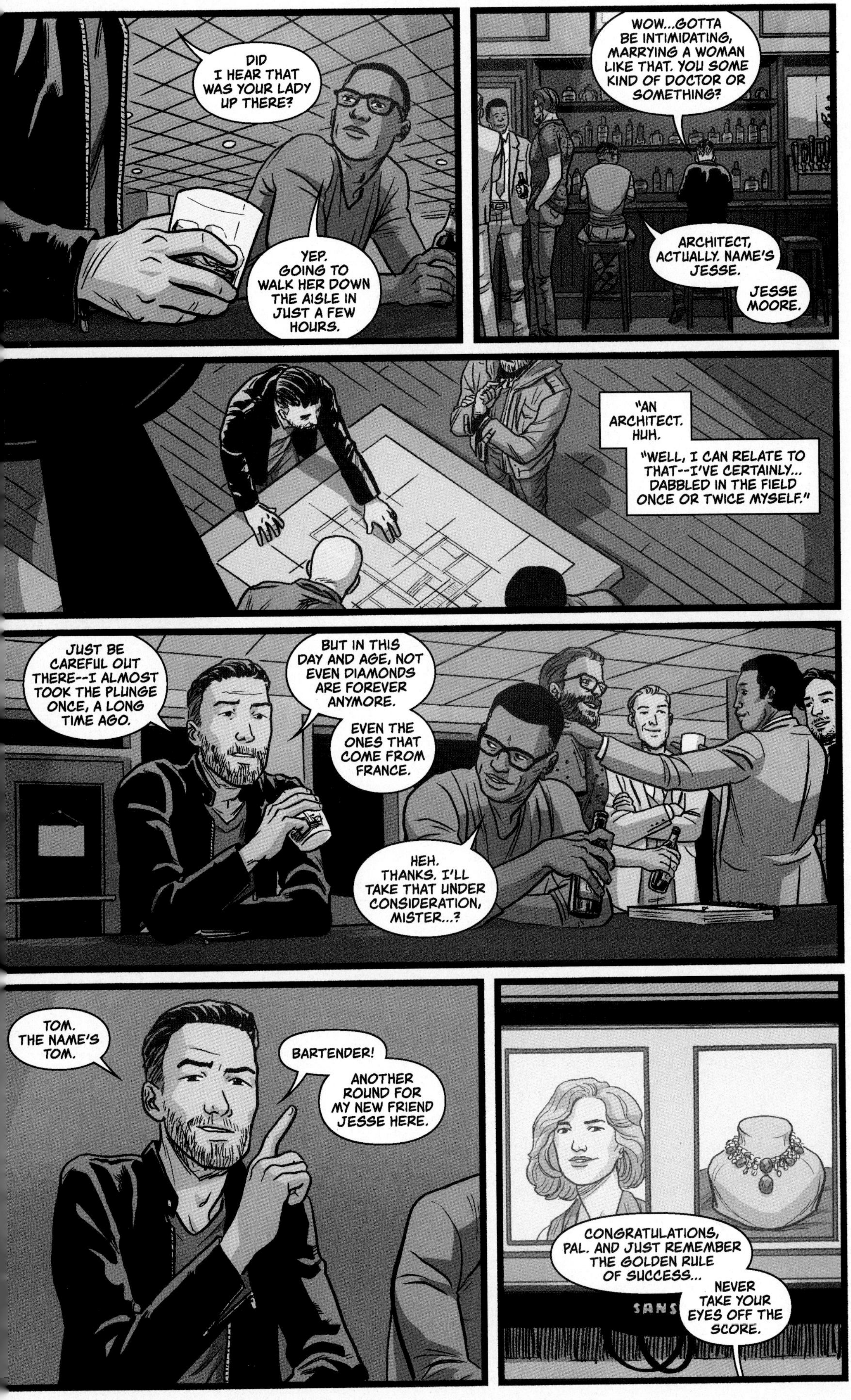
DID I HEAR THAT WAS YOUR LADY UP THERE?
YEP. GOING TO WALK HER DOWN THE AISLE IN JUST A FEW HOURS.
WOW...GOTTA BE INTIMIDATING, MARRYING A WOMAN LIKE THAT. YOU SOME KIND OF DOCTOR OR SOMETHING?
ARCHITECT, ACTUALLY. NAME'S JESSE.
JESSE MOORE.
"AN ARCHITECT. HUH.
"WELL, I CAN RELATE TO THAT--I'VE CERTAINLY... DABBLED IN THE FIELD ONCE OR TWICE MYSELF."
JUST BE CAREFUL OUT THERE--I ALMOST TOOK THE PLUNGE ONCE, A LONG TIME AGO.
BUT IN THIS DAY AND AGE, NOT EVEN DIAMONDS ARE FOREVER ANYMORE.
EVEN THE ONES THAT COME FROM FRANCE.
HEH. THANKS. I'LL TAKE THAT UNDER CONSIDERATION, MISTER...?
TOM. THE NAME'S TOM.
BARTENDER!
ANOTHER ROUND FOR MY NEW FRIEND JESSE HERE.
CONGRATULATIONS, PAL. AND JUST REMEMBER THE GOLDEN RULE OF SUCCESS...
NEVER TAKE YOUR EYES OFF THE SCORE.

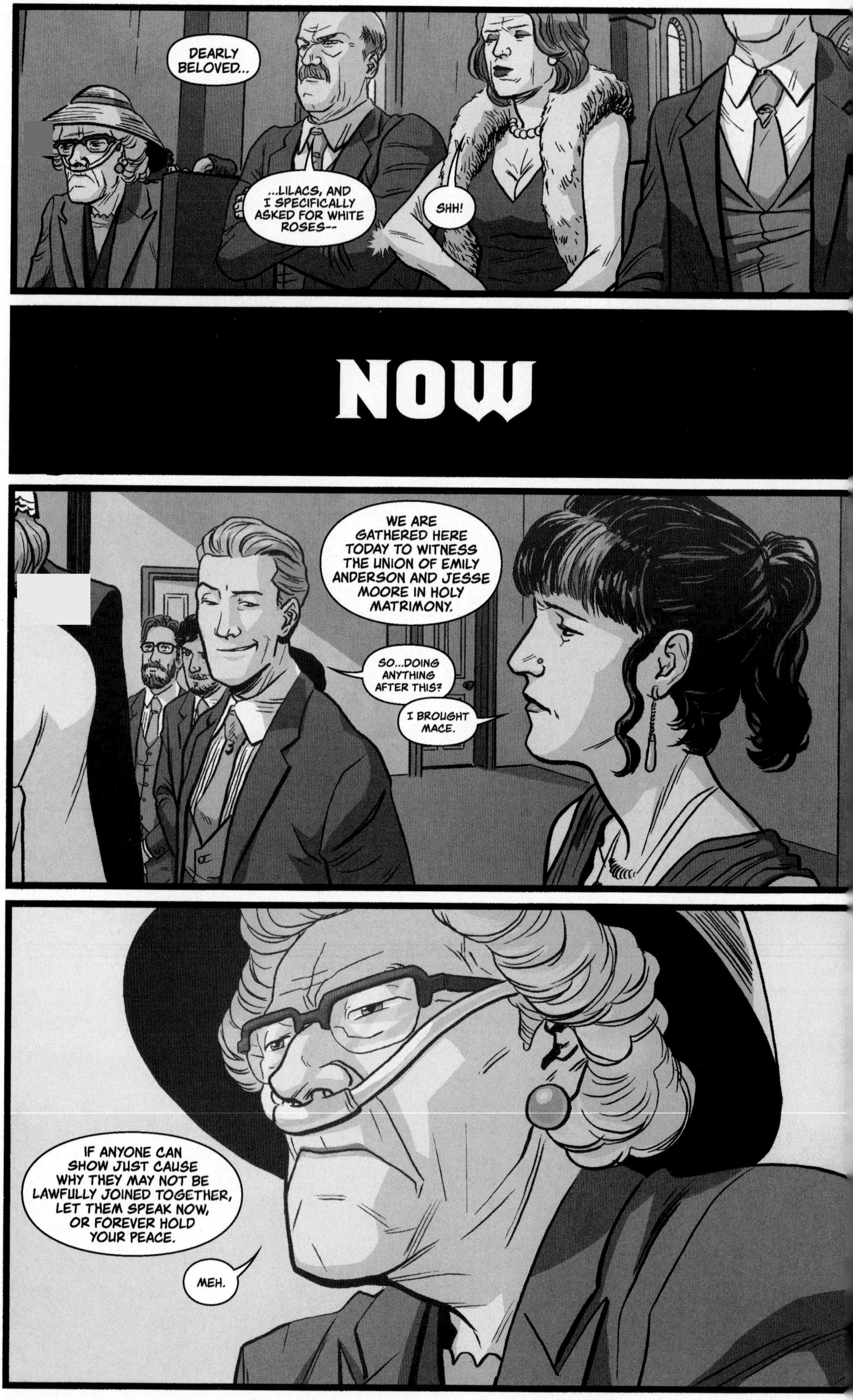
DEARLY BELOVED...
...LILACS, AND I SPECIFICALLY ASKED FOR WHITE ROSES--
SHH!
NOW
WE ARE GATHERED HERE TODAY TO WITNESS THE UNION OF EMILY ANDERSON AND JESSE MOORE IN HOLY MATRIMONY.
SO...DOING ANYTHING AFTER THIS?
I BROUGHT MACE.
IF ANYONE CAN SHOW JUST CAUSE WHY THEY MAY NOT BE LAWFULLY JOINED TOGETHER, LET THEM SPEAK NOW, OR FOREVER HOLD YOUR PEACE.
MEH.

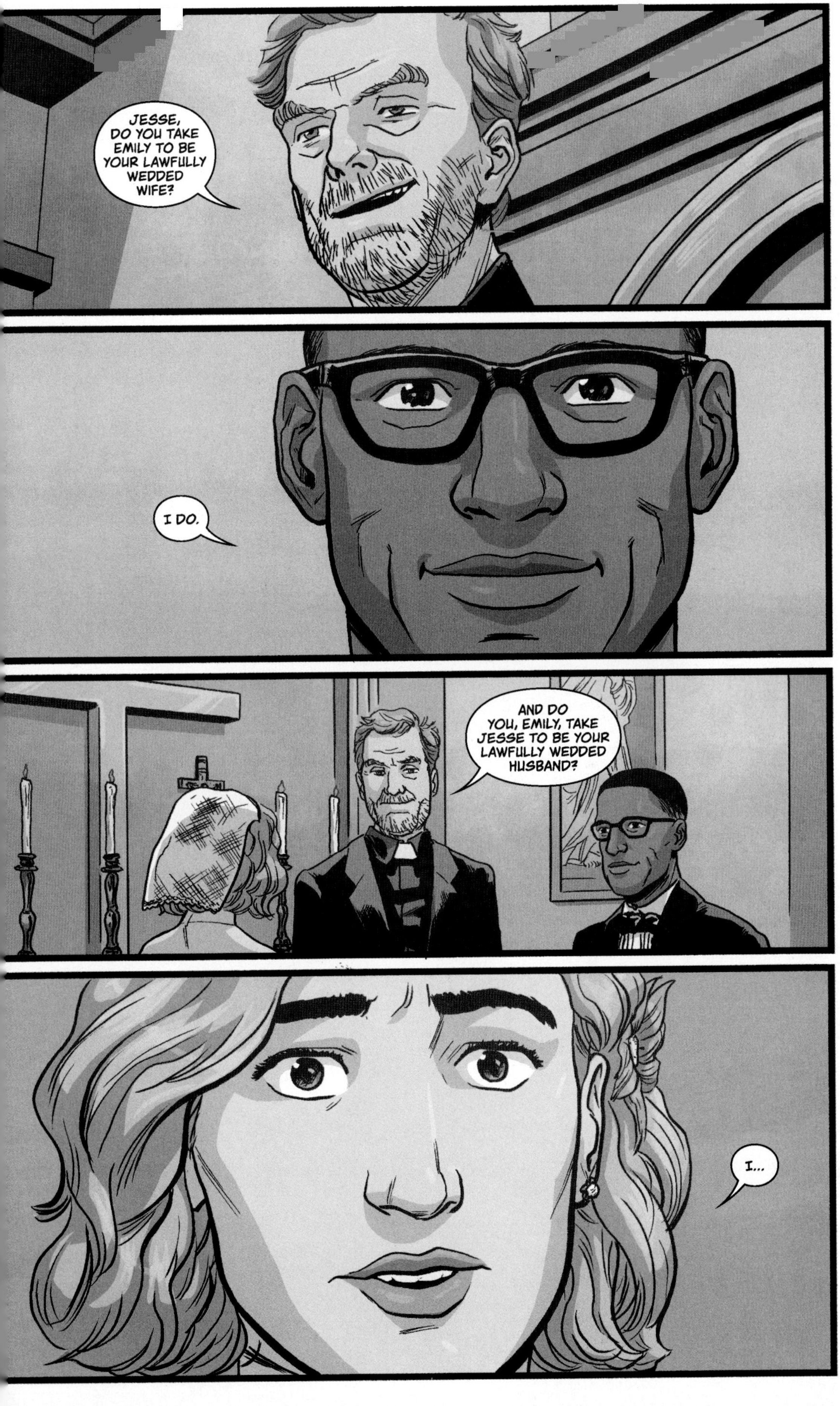
JESSE, DO YOU TAKE EMILY TO BE YOUR LAWFULLY WEDDED WIFE?
I DO.
AND DO YOU, EMILY, TAKE JESSE TO BE YOUR LAWFULLY WEDDED HUSBAND?
I...

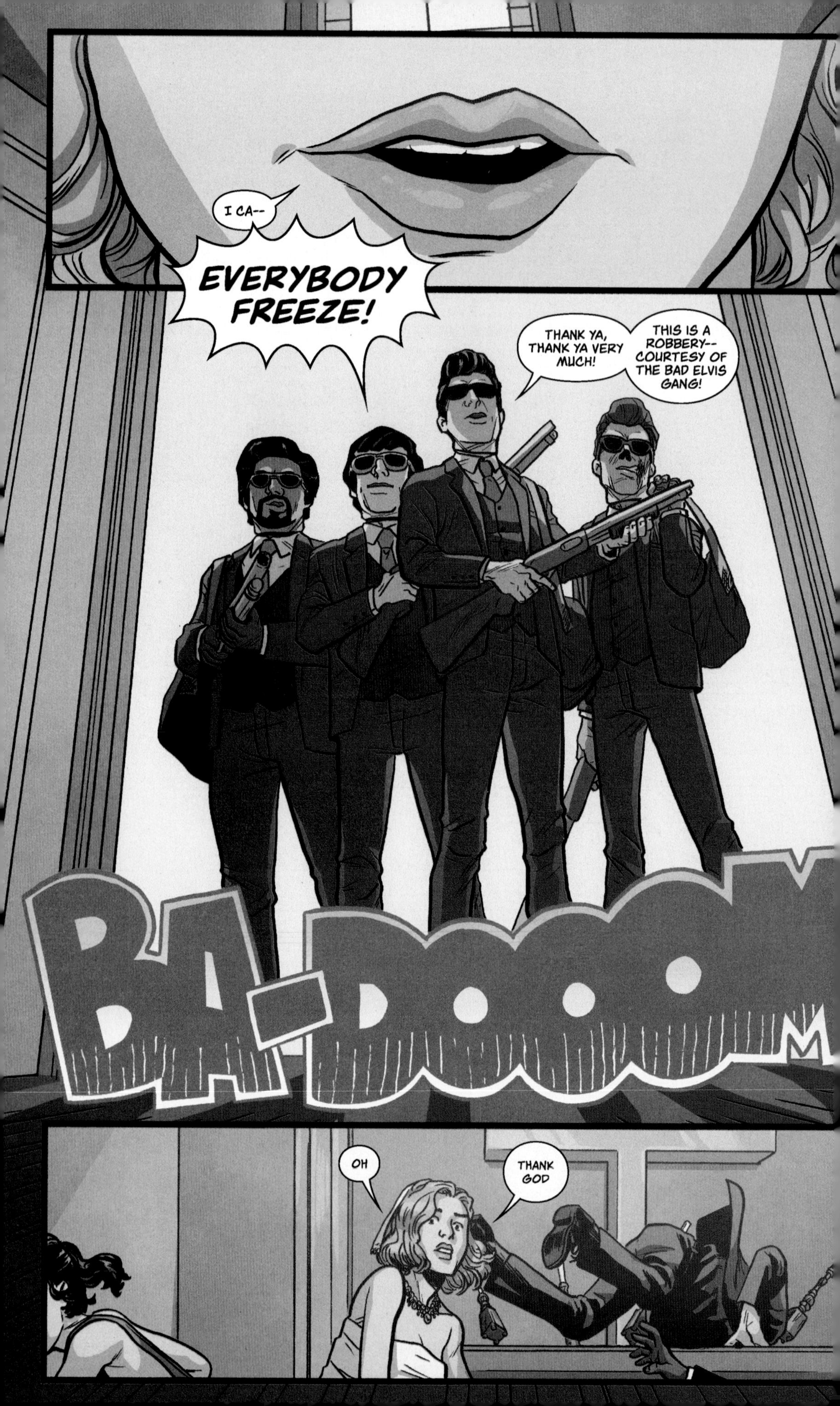

I CA--
EVERYBODY FREEZE!
THANK YA, THANK YA VERY MUCH!
THIS IS A ROBBERY-- COURTESY OF THE BAD ELVIS GANG!
BA-DOOOM
OH
THANK GOD

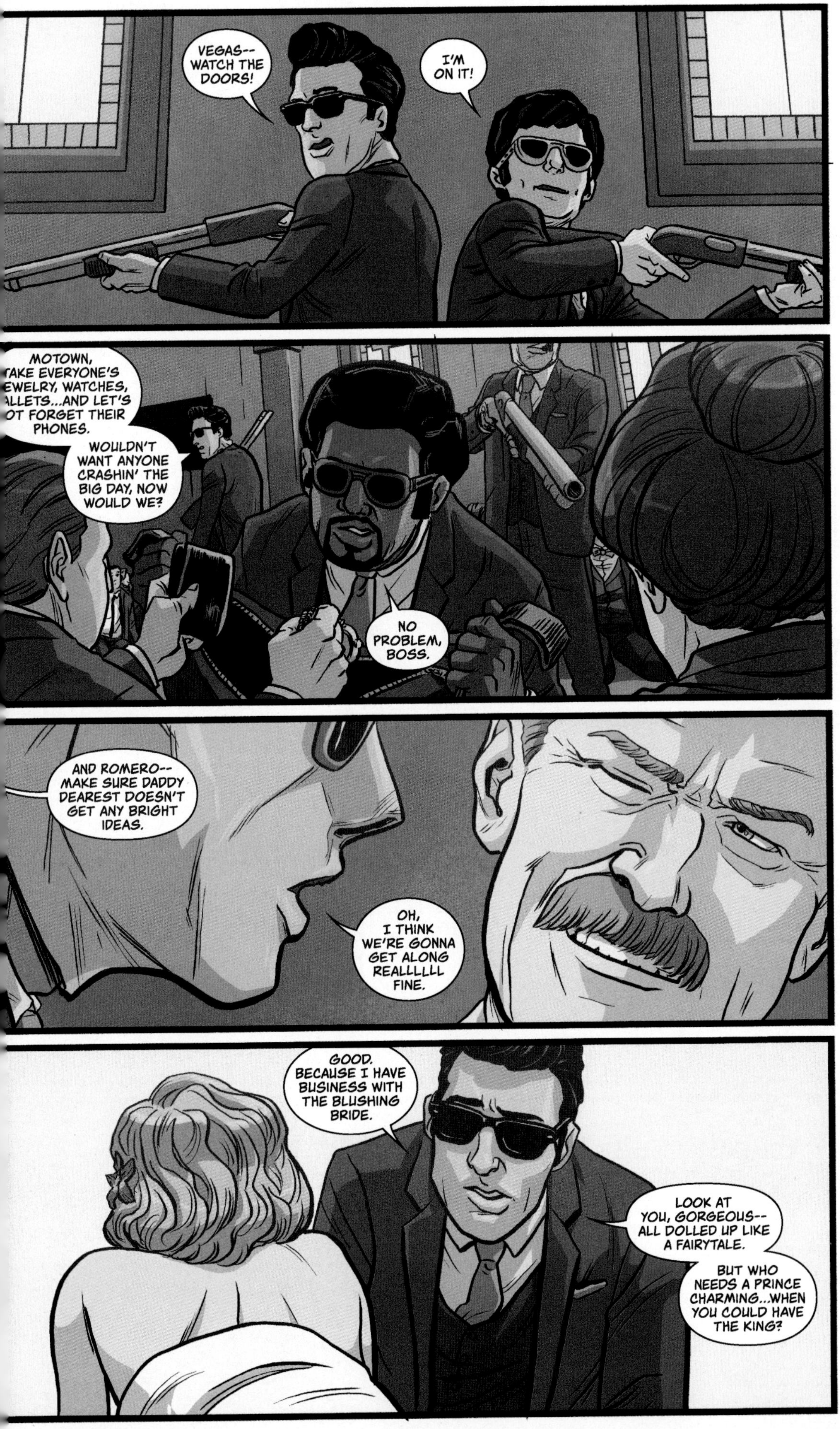
VEGAS--
WATCH THE
DOORS!
I'M
ON IT!
MOTOWN,
TAKE EVERYONE'S
JEWELRY, WATCHES,
WALLETS...AND LET'S
NOT FORGET THEIR
PHONES.
WOULDN'T
WANT ANYONE
CRASHIN' THE
BIG DAY, NOW
WOULD WE?
NO
PROBLEM,
BOSS.
AND ROMERO--
MAKE SURE DADDY
DEAREST DOESN'T
GET ANY BRIGHT
IDEAS.
OH,
I THINK
WE'RE GONNA
GET ALONG
REALLLLLL
FINE.
GOOD.
BECAUSE I HAVE
BUSINESS WITH
THE BLUSHING
BRIDE.
LOOK AT
YOU, GORGEOUS--
ALL DOLLED UP LIKE
A FAIRYTALE.
BUT WHO
NEEDS A PRINCE
CHARMING...WHEN
YOU COULD HAVE
THE KING?

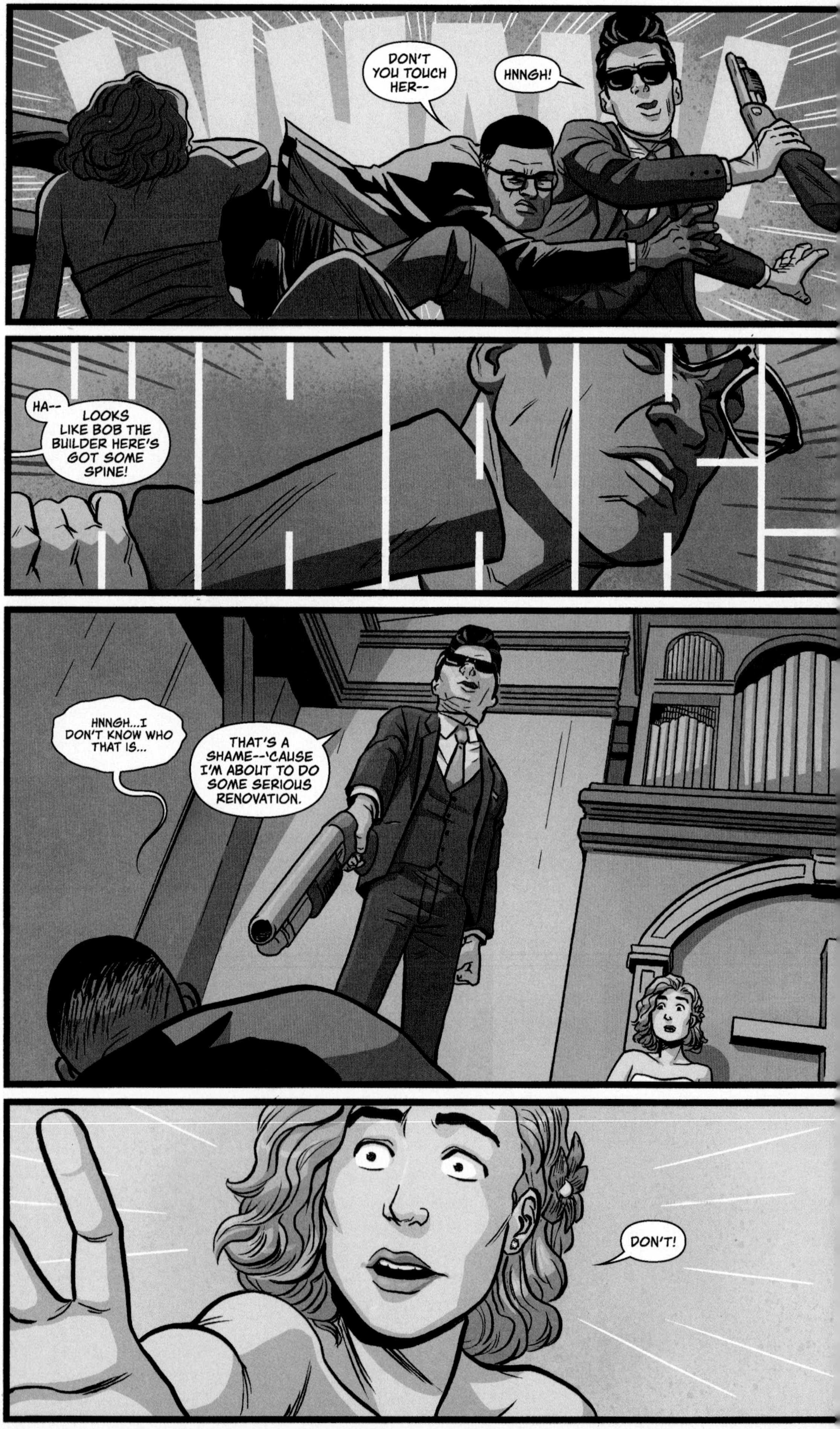
DON'T YOU TOUCH HER--
HNNGH!
HA--
LOOKS LIKE BOB THE BUILDER HERE'S GOT SOME SPINE!
HNNGH...I DON'T KNOW WHO THAT IS...
THAT'S A SHAME--'CAUSE I'M ABOUT TO DO SOME SERIOUS RENOVATION.
DON'T!

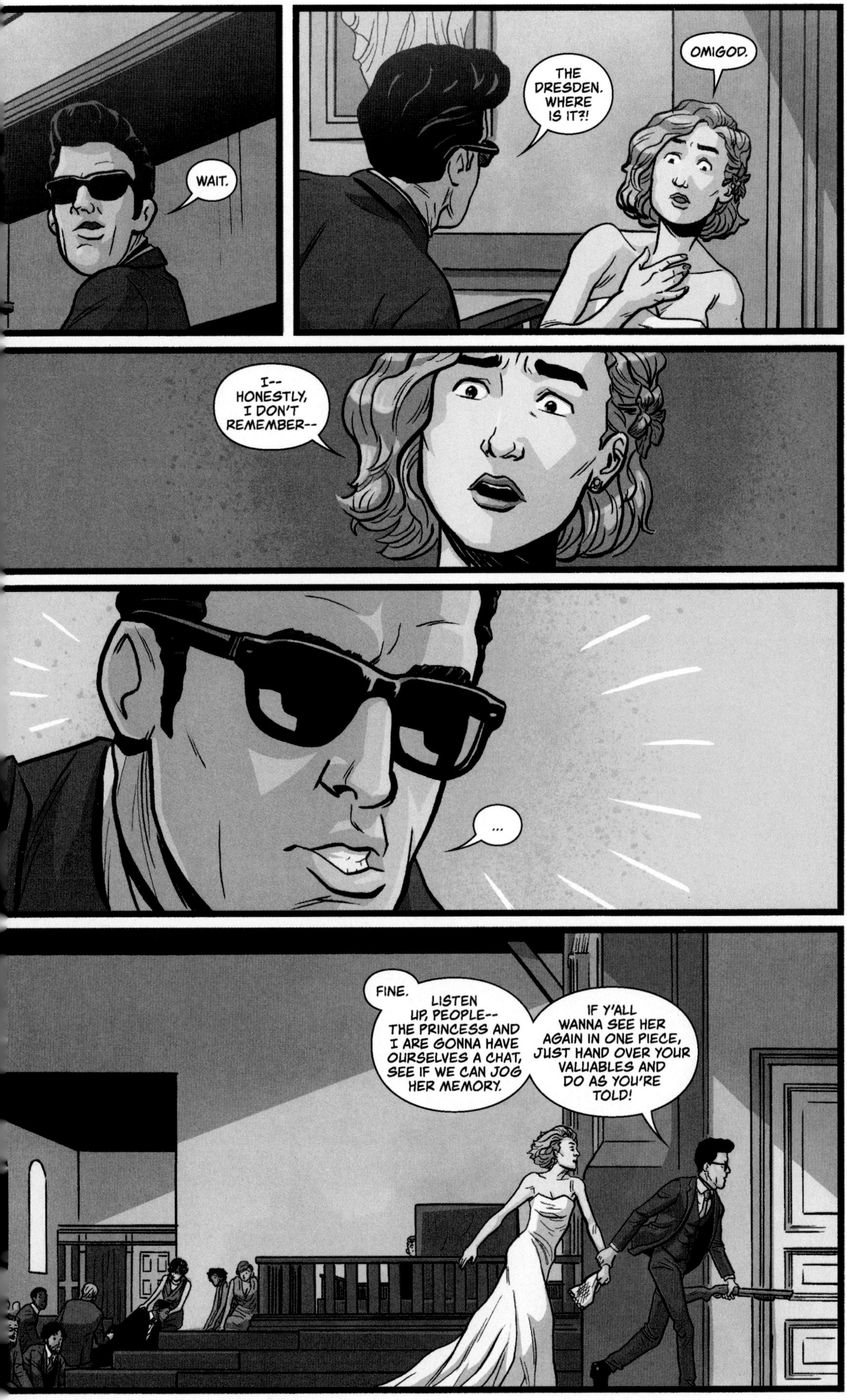
WAIT.
THE DRESDEN. WHERE IS IT?!
OMIGOD.
I-- HONESTLY, I DON'T REMEMBER--
...
FINE.
LISTEN UP, PEOPLE-- THE PRINCESS AND I ARE GONNA HAVE OURSELVES A CHAT, SEE IF WE CAN JOG HER MEMORY.
IF Y'ALL WANNA SEE HER AGAIN IN ONE PIECE, JUST HAND OVER YOUR VALUABLES AND DO AS YOU'RE TOLD!

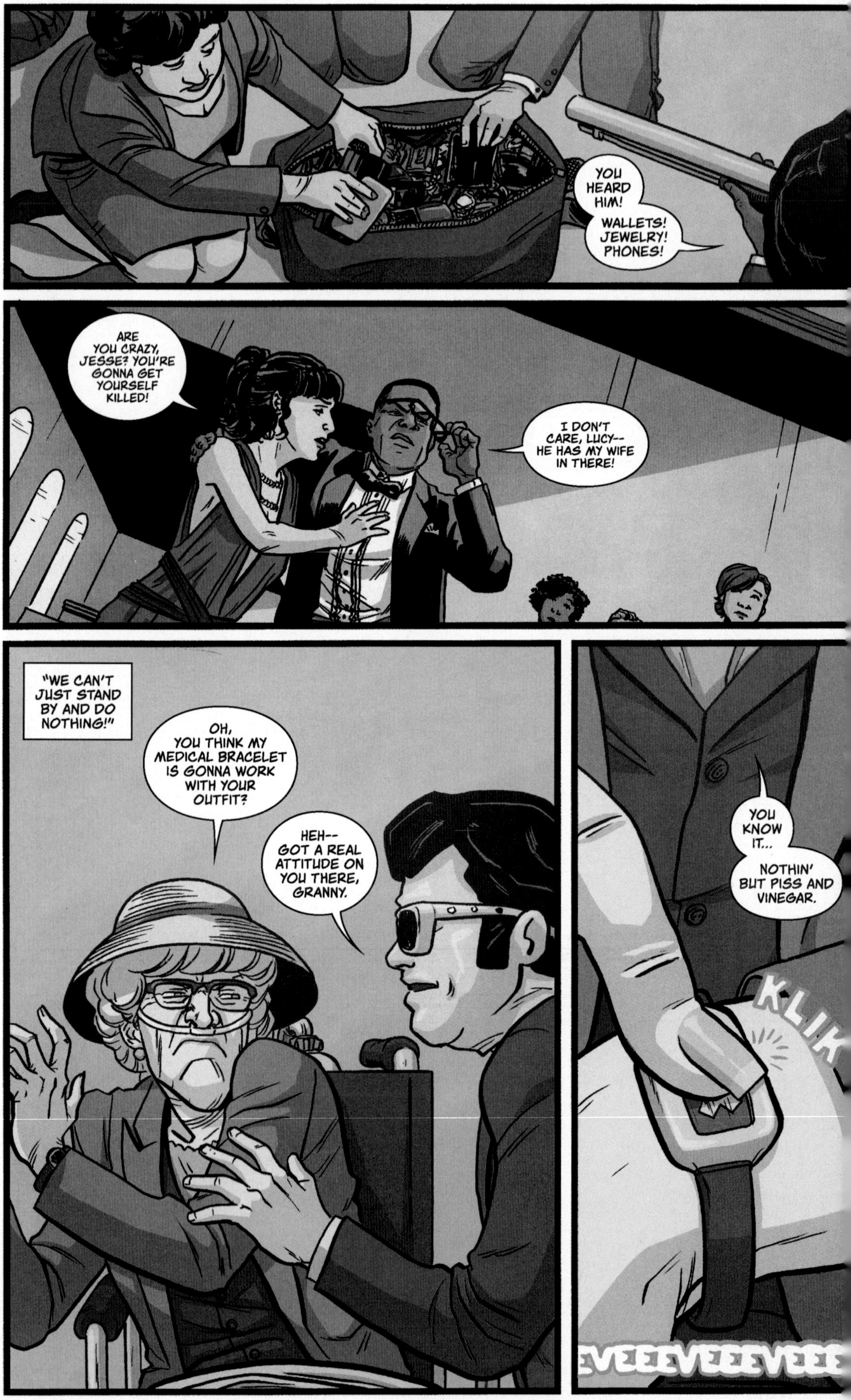

YOU HEARD HIM!
WALLETS! JEWELRY! PHONES!
ARE YOU CRAZY, JESSE? YOU'RE GONNA GET YOURSELF KILLED!
I DON'T CARE, LUCY-- HE HAS MY WIFE IN THERE!
"WE CAN'T JUST STAND BY AND DO NOTHING!"
OH, YOU THINK MY MEDICAL BRACELET IS GONNA WORK WITH YOUR OUTFIT?
HEH-- GOT A REAL ATTITUDE ON YOU THERE, GRANNY.
YOU KNOW IT...
NOTHIN' BUT PISS AND VINEGAR.
KLIK
EEEEEEEEEEEEEEEE

RING RING

ROCKFORD COUNTY DISPATCH.

WHADDYA GOT?

AH, IT'S NOTHIN', WALT-- JUST ONE OF THEM ELECTRONIC MEDICAL BRACELETS. "I'VE FALLEN AND I CAN'T GET UP."

ROCKFORD COUNTRY

GOT GPS, BUT NO RESPONSE ON THE PHONES, THOUGH.

PROBABLY A FALSE ALARM-- I'LL JUST SEND AN AMBULANCE TO ST. JUDE'S TO SWING BY.

BAD ELVIS GANG STILL AT LARGE
Sixth Local Bank Robbed This Year

The Rockford Gazette

HEIRESS TO WED AT ST. JUDE'S
$250M Necklace On Loan For Gala

...WHERE'D YOU SAY THAT CALL WAS COMING FROM?

BAD ELVIS GANG STILL AT LARGE
Sixth Local Bank Robbed This Year

The Rockford Gazette

HEIRESS TO WED AT ST. JUDE'S

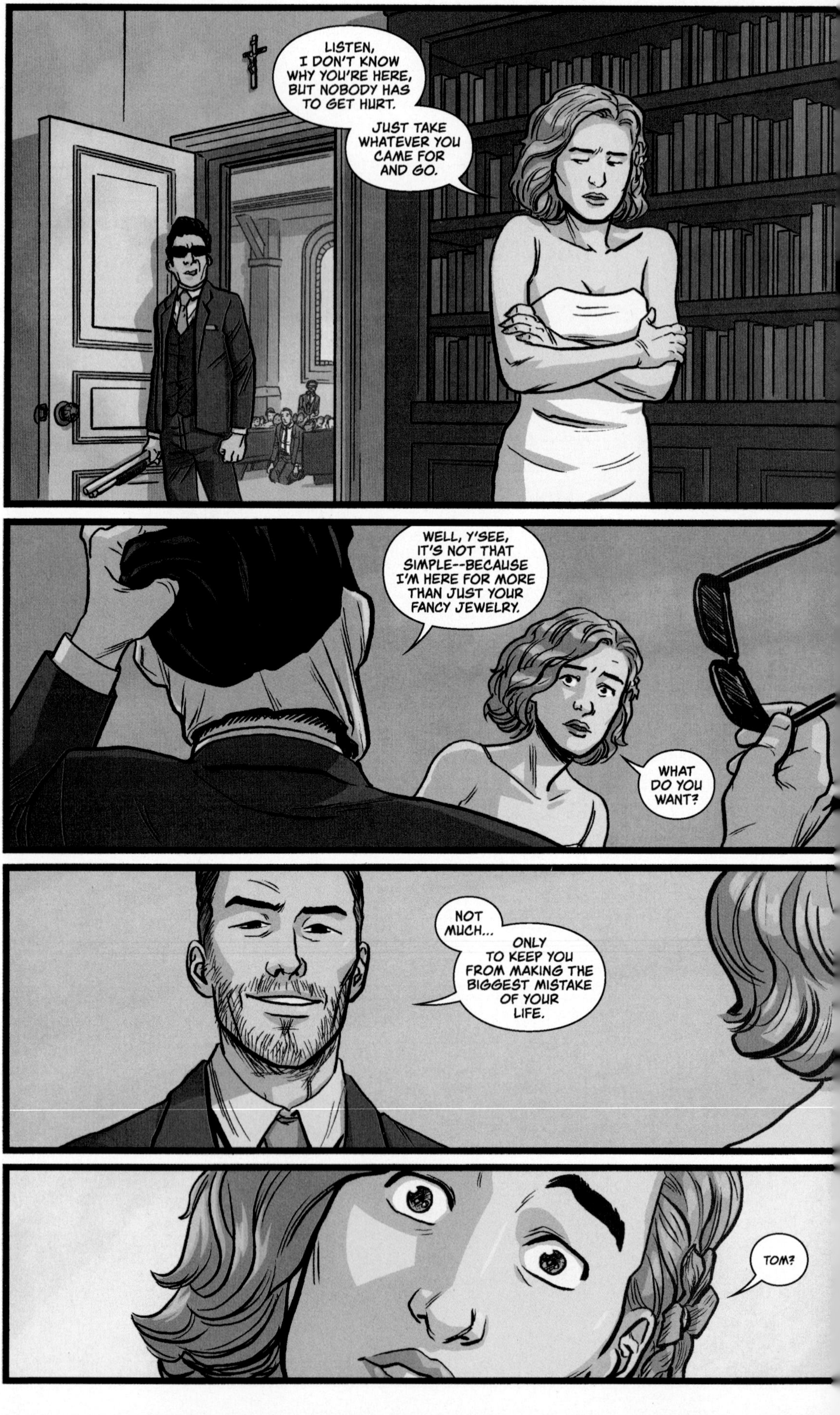
LISTEN, I DON'T KNOW WHY YOU'RE HERE, BUT NOBODY HAS TO GET HURT.
JUST TAKE WHATEVER YOU CAME FOR AND GO.
WELL, Y'SEE, IT'S NOT THAT SIMPLE--BECAUSE I'M HERE FOR MORE THAN JUST YOUR FANCY JEWELRY.
WHAT DO YOU WANT?
NOT MUCH...
ONLY TO KEEP YOU FROM MAKING THE BIGGEST MISTAKE OF YOUR LIFE.
TOM?

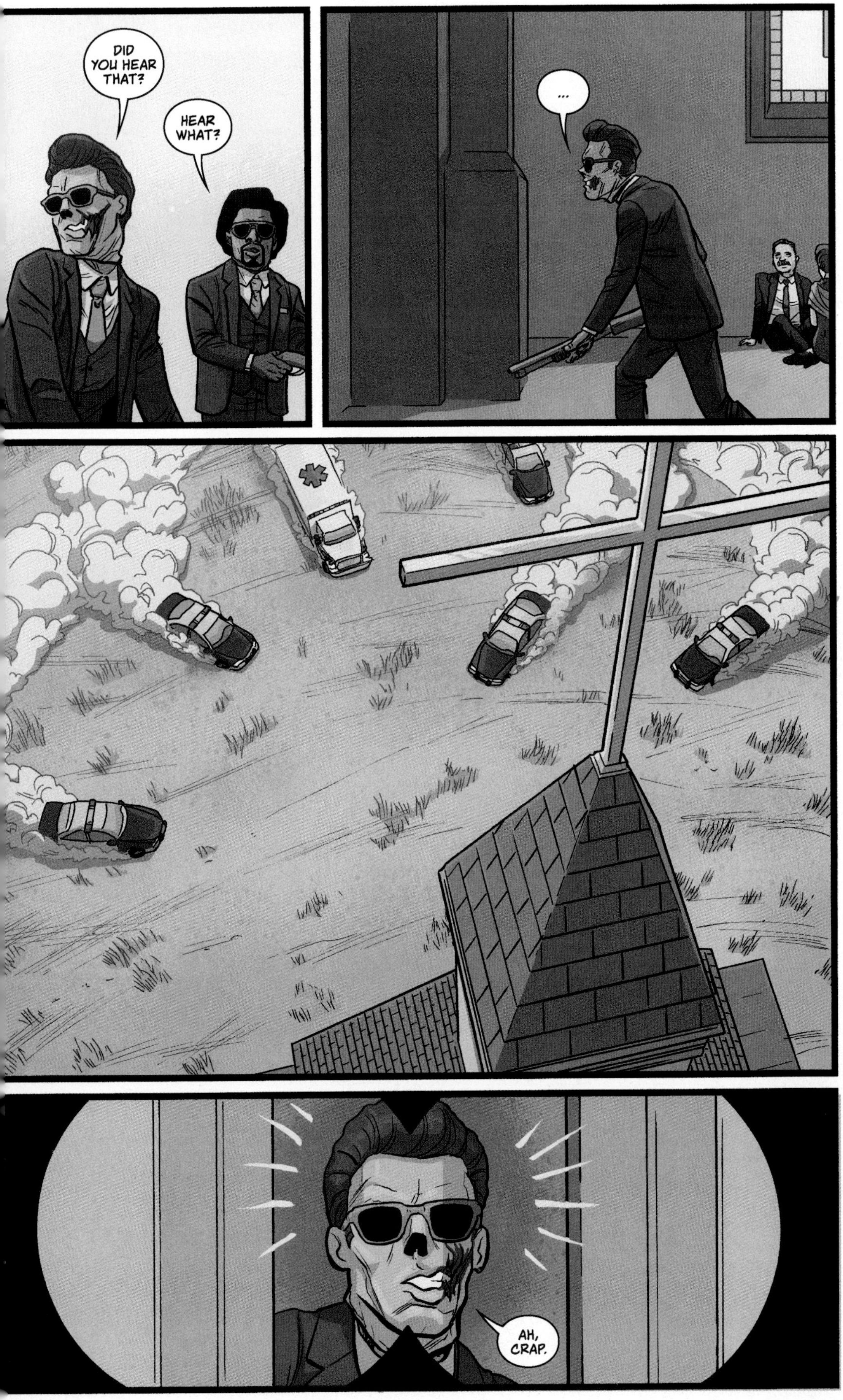
DID YOU HEAR THAT?
HEAR WHAT?
...
AH, CRAP.

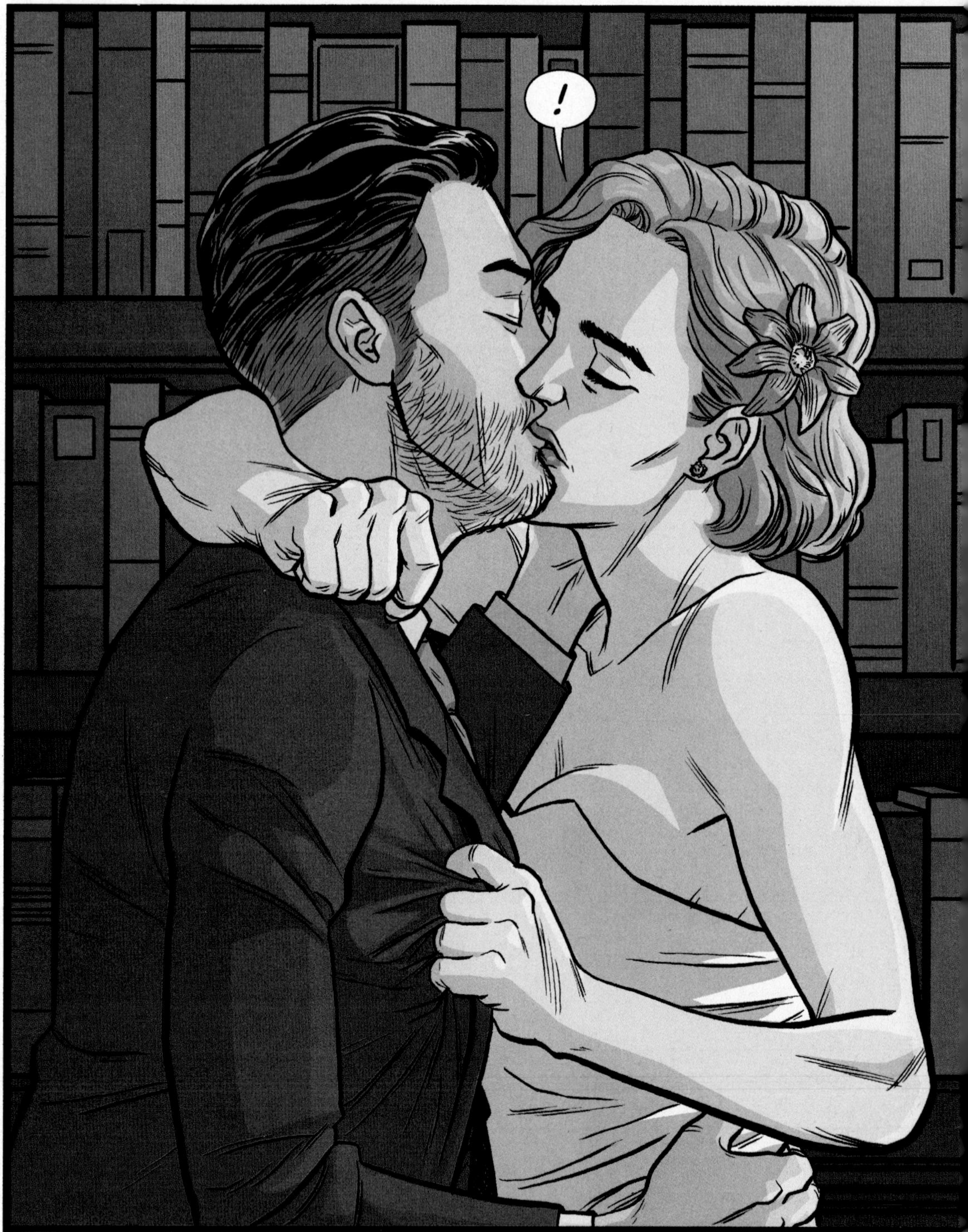
!

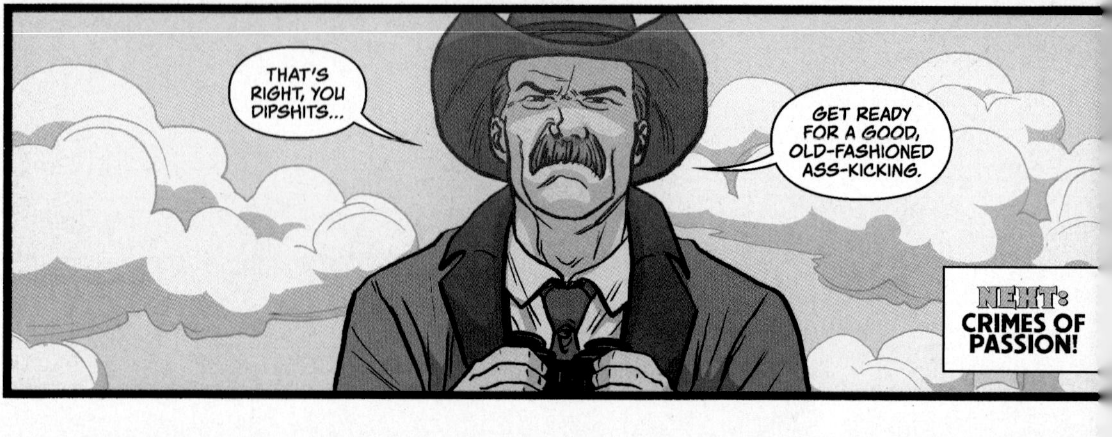
THAT'S RIGHT, YOU DIPSHITS...
GET READY FOR A GOOD, OLD-FASHIONED ASS-KICKING.
NEXT: CRIMES OF PASSION!

CHAPTER TWO

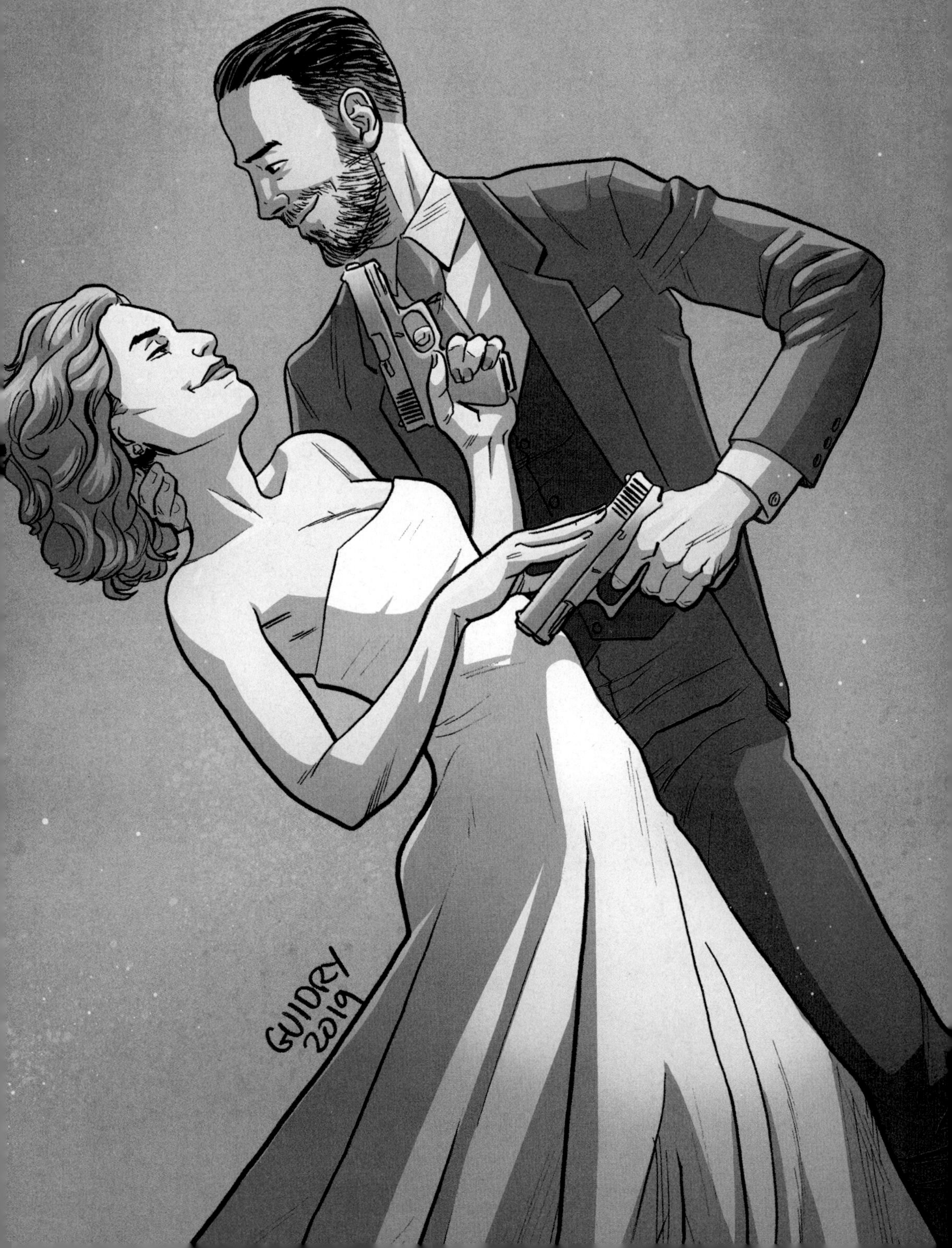
GUIDRY
2019

Going to the CHAPEL

2

Written by
DAVID PEPOSE

Art by
GAVIN GUIDRY

Colors by
ELIZABETH KRAMER

Lettering by
ARIANA MAHER

Covers by
SWEENEY BOO, MAAN HOUSE AND GAVIN GUIDRY

Chapel Of Love
Words and Music by Phil Spector, Ellie Greenwich and Jeff Barry
Copyright (c) 1964 UNIVERSAL - SONGS OF POLYGRAM INTERNATIONAL, INC., TRIO MUSIC
COMPANY and MOTHER BERTHA MUSIC, INC.
Copyright Renewed
All Rights for TRIO MUSIC COMPANY Administered by BMG RIGHTS MANAGEMENT (US) LLC
All Rights for MOTHER BERTHA MUSIC, INC. Controlled and Administered by EMI APRIL MUSIC INC.
All Rights Reserved Used by Permission
Reprinted by Permission of Hal Leonard LLC

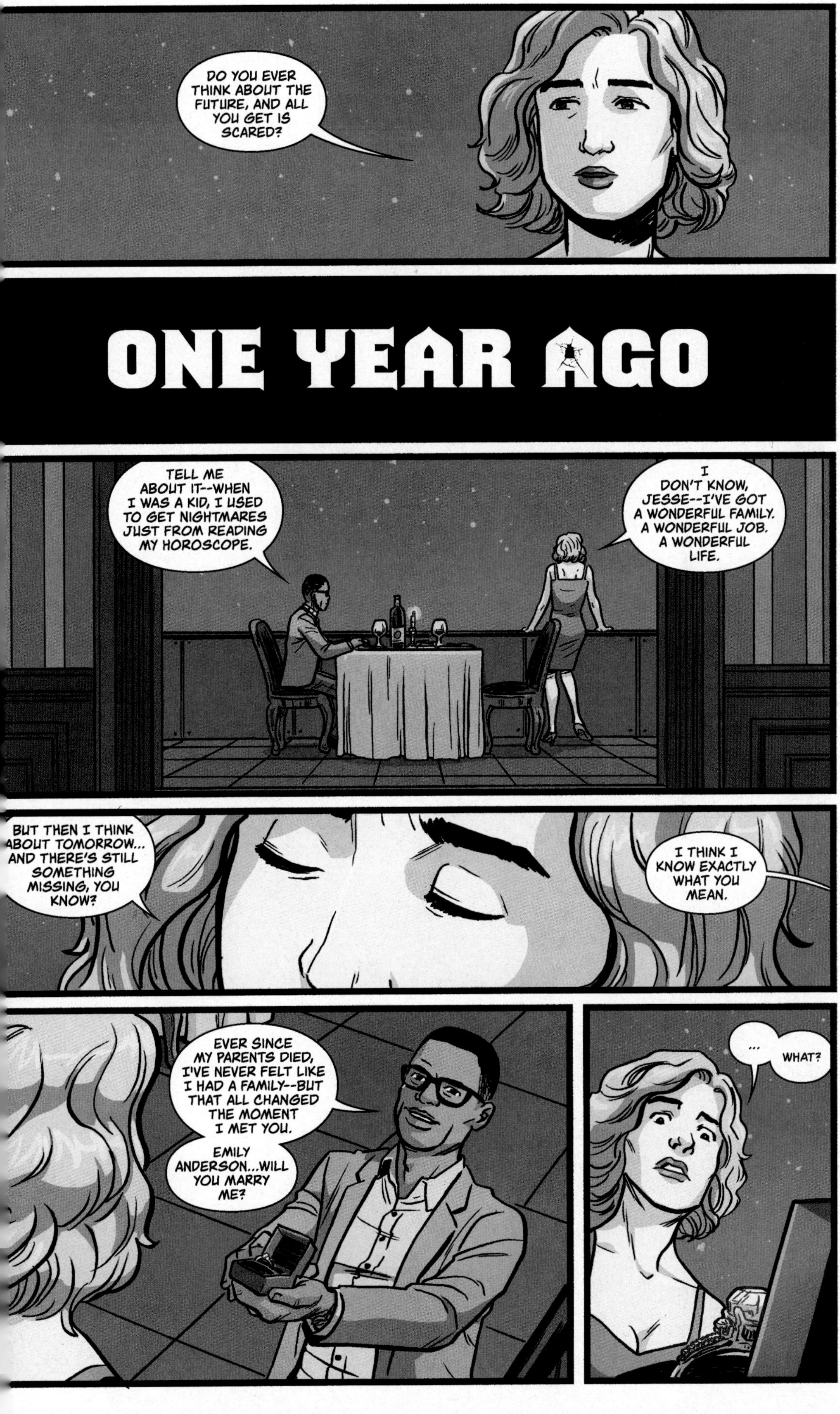
DO YOU EVER THINK ABOUT THE FUTURE, AND ALL YOU GET IS SCARED?
ONE YEAR AGO
TELL ME ABOUT IT--WHEN I WAS A KID, I USED TO GET NIGHTMARES JUST FROM READING MY HOROSCOPE.
I DON'T KNOW, JESSE--I'VE GOT A WONDERFUL FAMILY. A WONDERFUL JOB. A WONDERFUL LIFE.
BUT THEN I THINK ABOUT TOMORROW... AND THERE'S STILL SOMETHING MISSING, YOU KNOW?
I THINK I KNOW EXACTLY WHAT YOU MEAN.
EVER SINCE MY PARENTS DIED, I'VE NEVER FELT LIKE I HAD A FAMILY--BUT THAT ALL CHANGED THE MOMENT I MET YOU.
EMILY ANDERSON...WILL YOU MARRY ME?
...
WHAT?

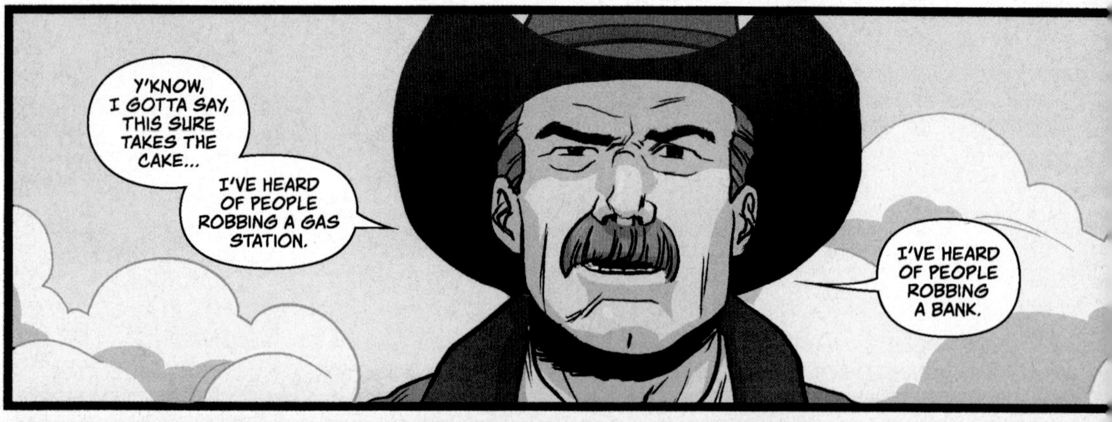

Y'KNOW, I GOTTA SAY, THIS SURE TAKES THE CAKE...
I'VE HEARD OF PEOPLE ROBBING A GAS STATION.
I'VE HEARD OF PEOPLE ROBBING A BANK.

NOW

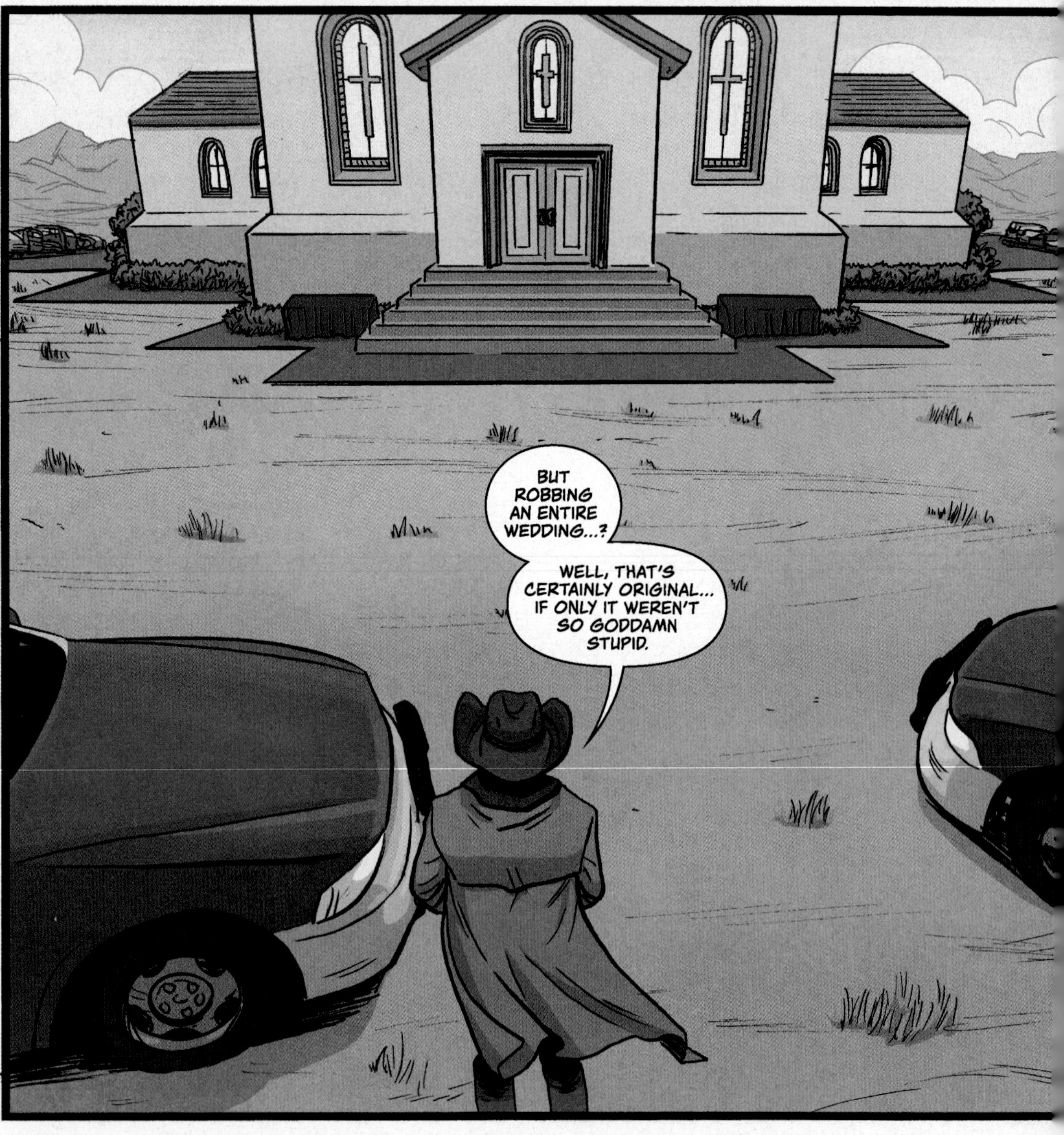

BUT ROBBING AN ENTIRE WEDDING...?
WELL, THAT'S CERTAINLY ORIGINAL... IF ONLY IT WEREN'T SO GODDAMN STUPID.

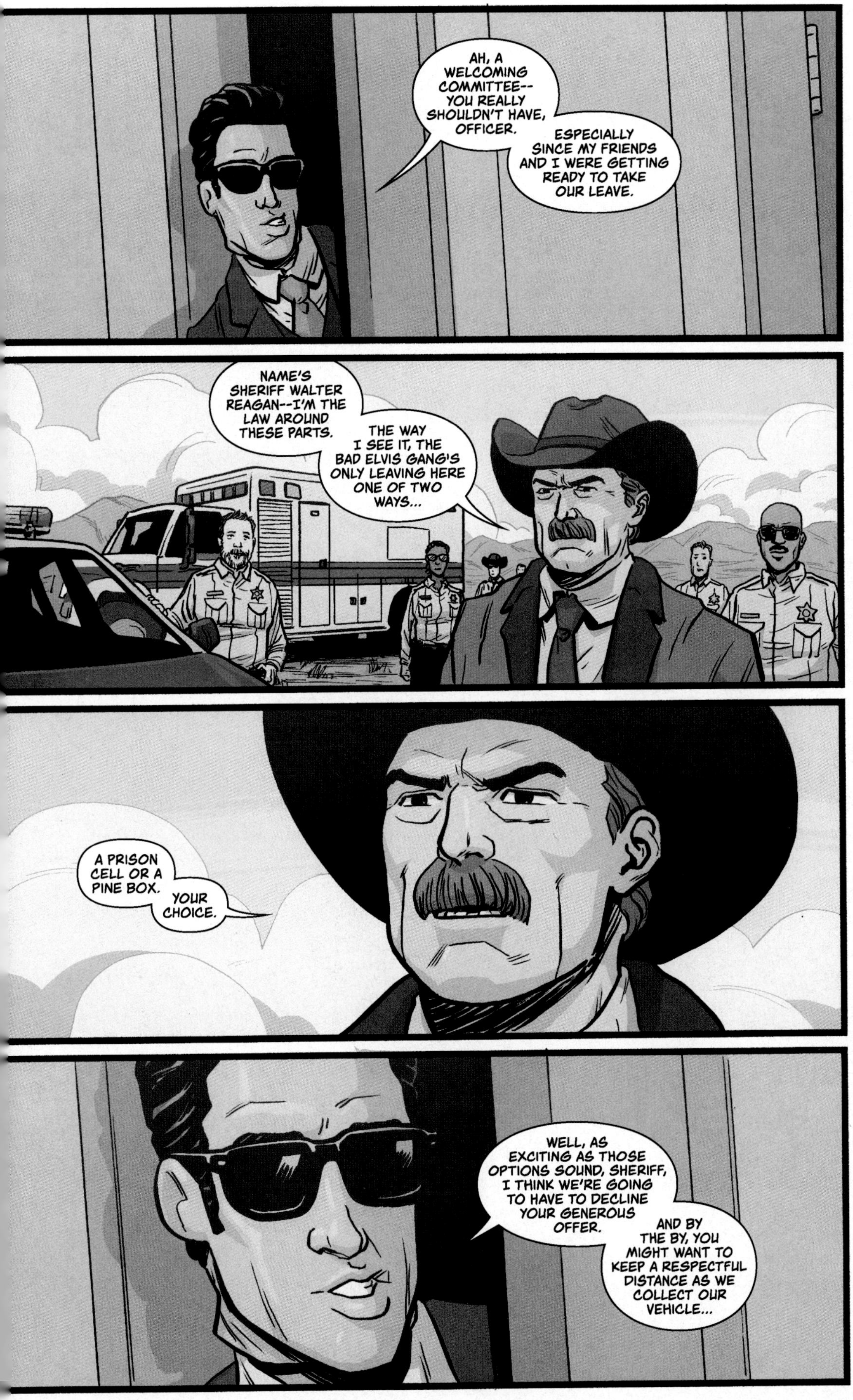
AH, A WELCOMING COMMITTEE-- YOU REALLY SHOULDN'T HAVE, OFFICER.
ESPECIALLY SINCE MY FRIENDS AND I WERE GETTING READY TO TAKE OUR LEAVE.
NAME'S SHERIFF WALTER REAGAN--I'M THE LAW AROUND THESE PARTS.
THE WAY I SEE IT, THE BAD ELVIS GANG'S ONLY LEAVING HERE ONE OF TWO WAYS...
A PRISON CELL OR A PINE BOX.
YOUR CHOICE.
WELL, AS EXCITING AS THOSE OPTIONS SOUND, SHERIFF, I THINK WE'RE GOING TO HAVE TO DECLINE YOUR GENEROUS OFFER.
AND BY THE BY, YOU MIGHT WANT TO KEEP A RESPECTFUL DISTANCE AS WE COLLECT OUR VEHICLE...

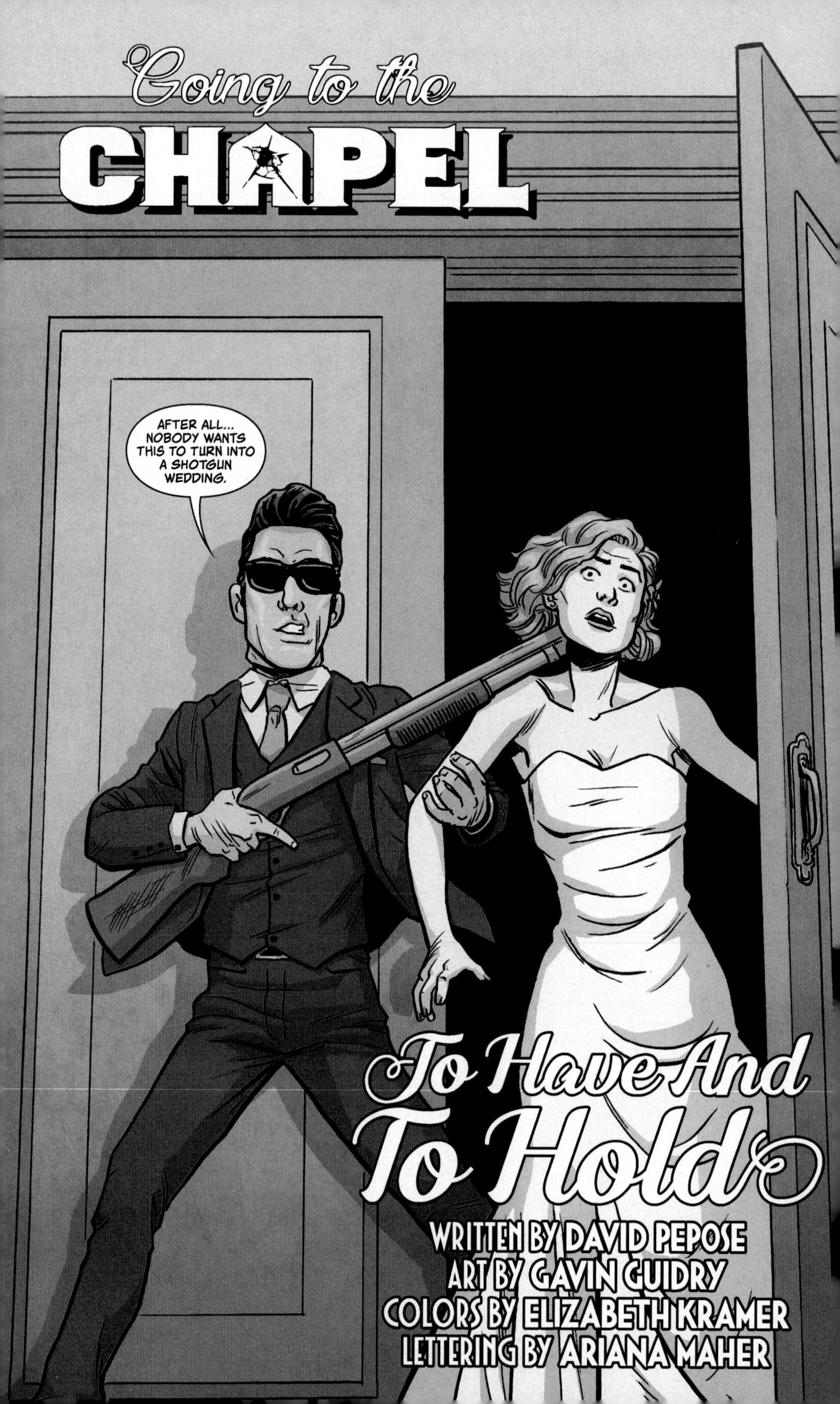
Going to the
CHAPEL
AFTER ALL... NOBODY WANTS THIS TO TURN INTO A SHOTGUN WEDDING.
To Have And To Hold
WRITTEN BY DAVID PEPOSE
ART BY GAVIN GUIDRY
COLORS BY ELIZABETH KRAMER
LETTERING BY ARIANA MAHER

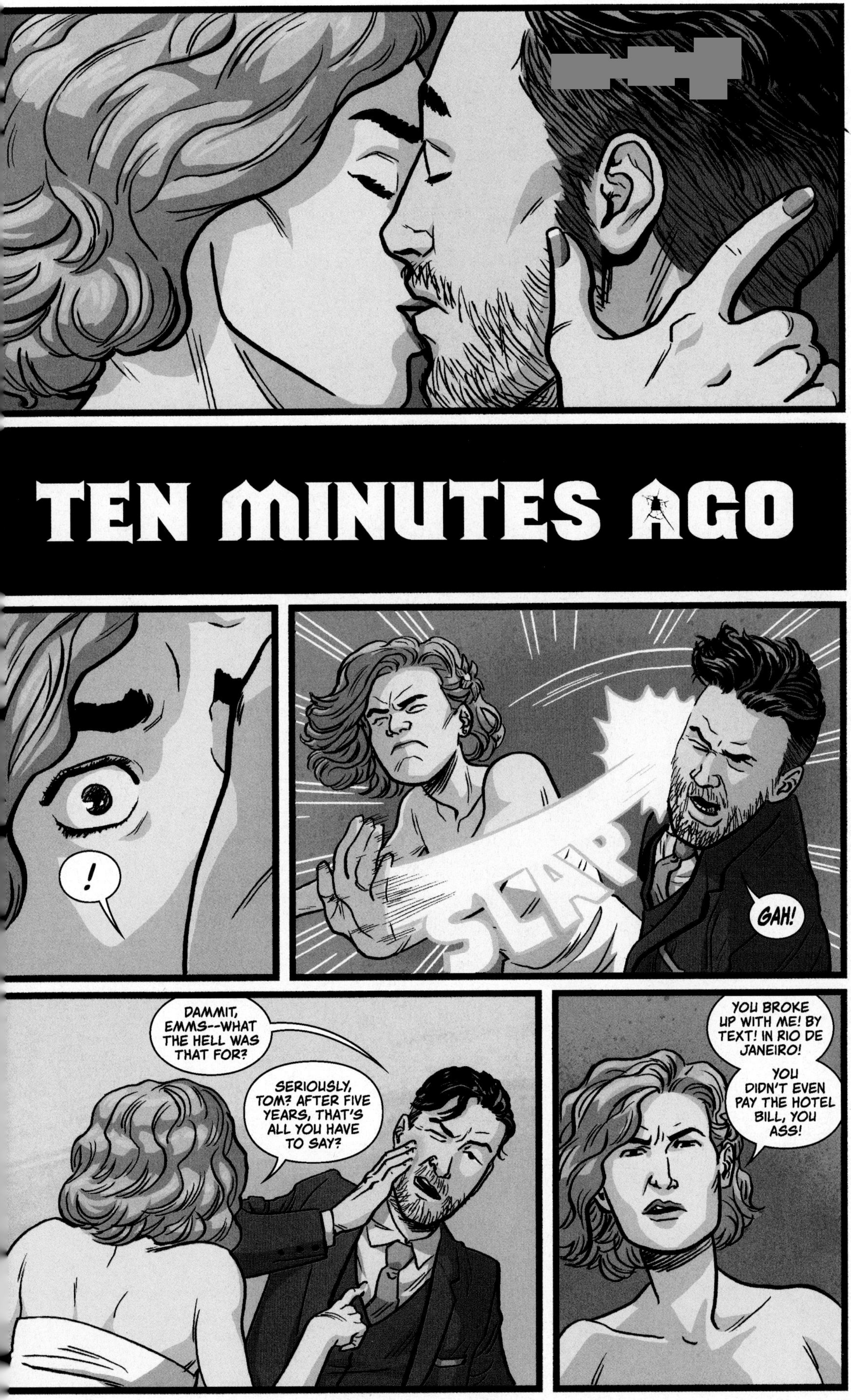
TEN MINUTES AGO
!
SLAP
GAH!
DAMMIT, EMMS--WHAT THE HELL WAS THAT FOR?
SERIOUSLY, TOM? AFTER FIVE YEARS, THAT'S ALL YOU HAVE TO SAY?
YOU BROKE UP WITH ME! BY TEXT! IN RIO DE JANEIRO!
YOU DIDN'T EVEN PAY THE HOTEL BILL, YOU ASS!

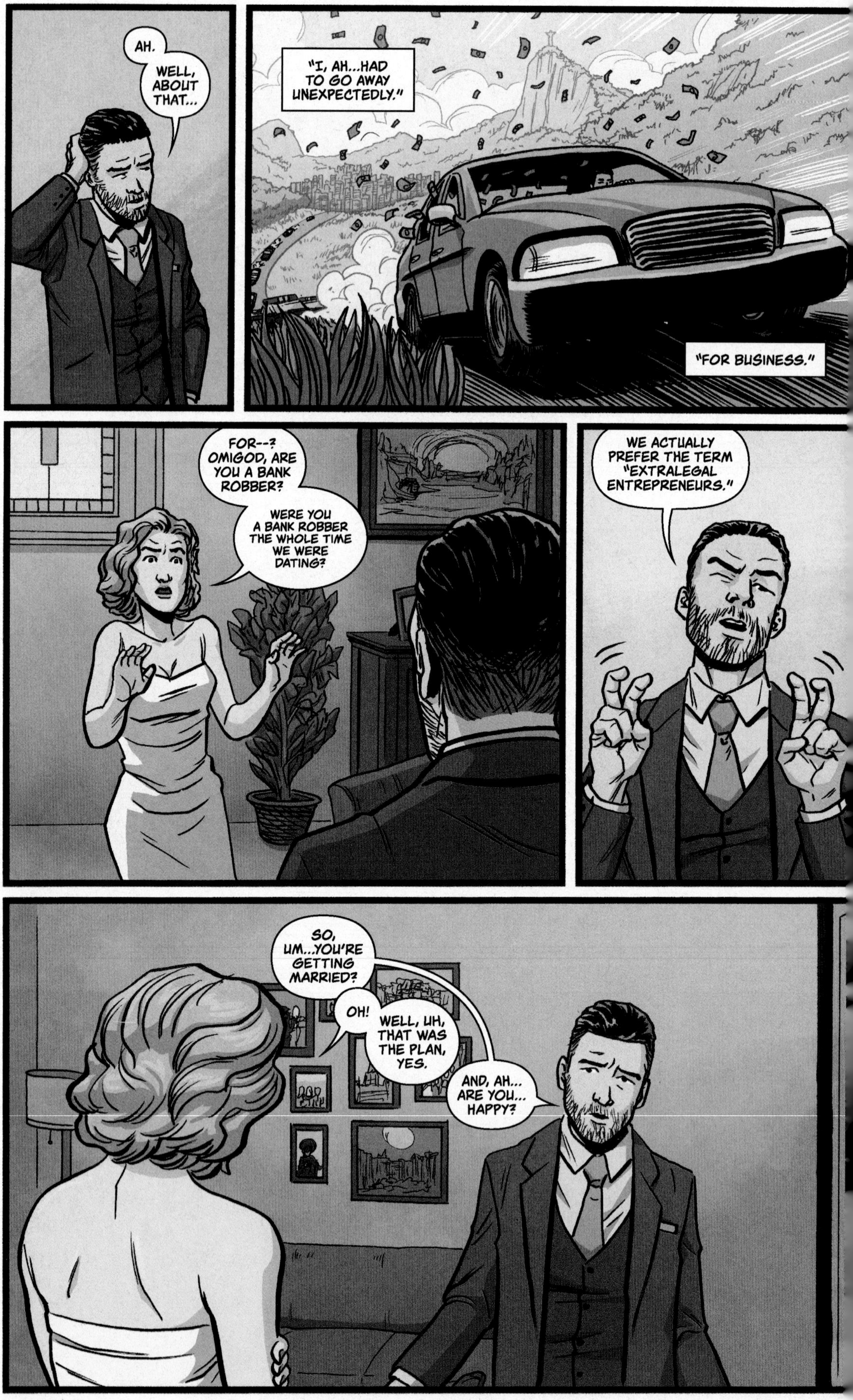
AH.
WELL, ABOUT THAT...
"I, AH...HAD TO GO AWAY UNEXPECTEDLY."
"FOR BUSINESS."
FOR--? OMIGOD, ARE YOU A BANK ROBBER?
WERE YOU A BANK ROBBER THE WHOLE TIME WE WERE DATING?
WE ACTUALLY PREFER THE TERM "EXTRALEGAL ENTREPRENEURS."
SO, UM...YOU'RE GETTING MARRIED?
OH!
WELL, UH, THAT WAS THE PLAN, YES.
AND, AH... ARE YOU... HAPPY?

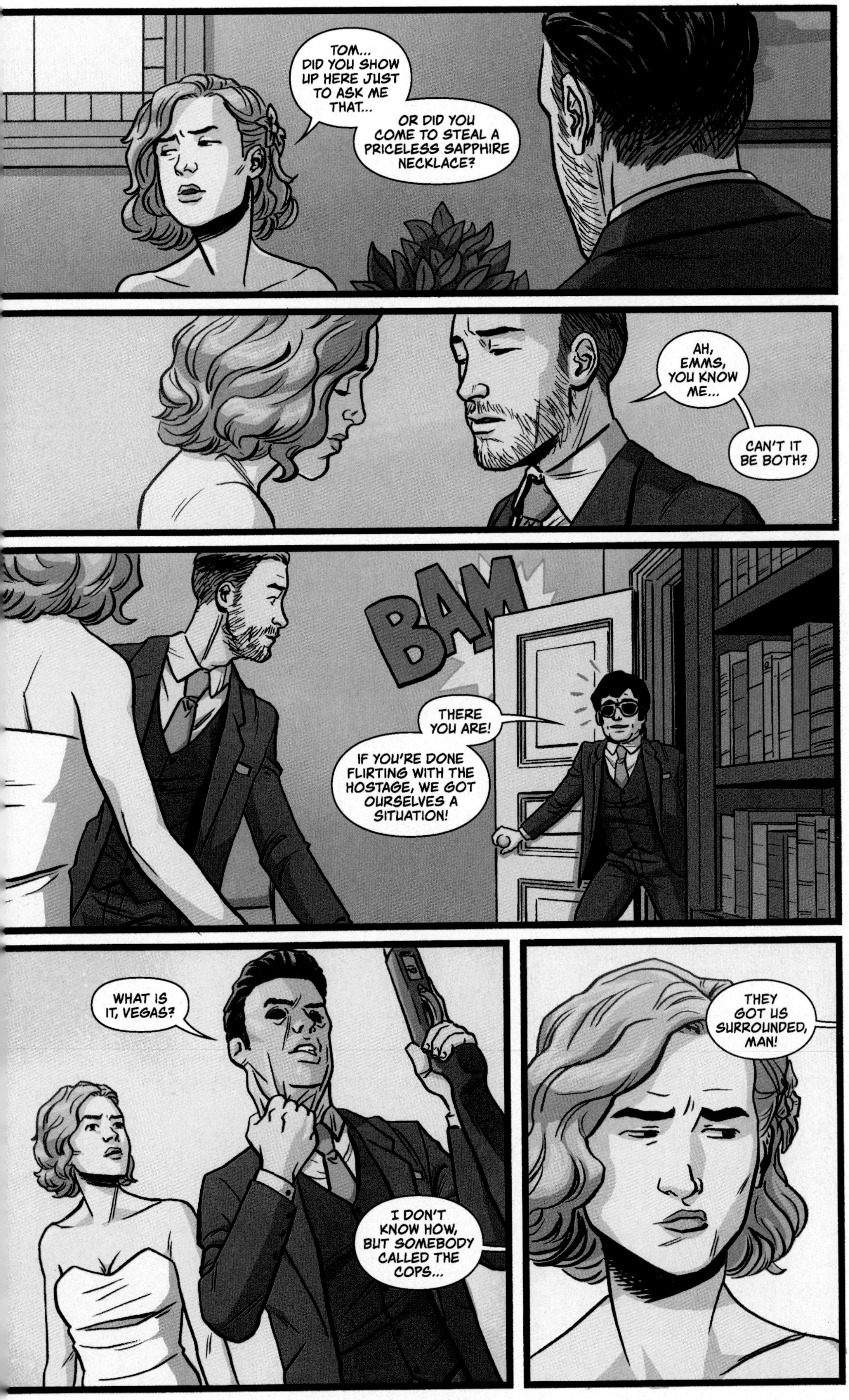
TOM... DID YOU SHOW UP HERE JUST TO ASK ME THAT...
OR DID YOU COME TO STEAL A PRICELESS SAPPHIRE NECKLACE?
AH, EMMS, YOU KNOW ME...
CAN'T IT BE BOTH?
BAM
THERE YOU ARE!
IF YOU'RE DONE FLIRTING WITH THE HOSTAGE, WE GOT OURSELVES A SITUATION!
WHAT IS IT, VEGAS?
I DON'T KNOW HOW, BUT SOMEBODY CALLED THE COPS...
THEY GOT US SURROUNDED, MAN!

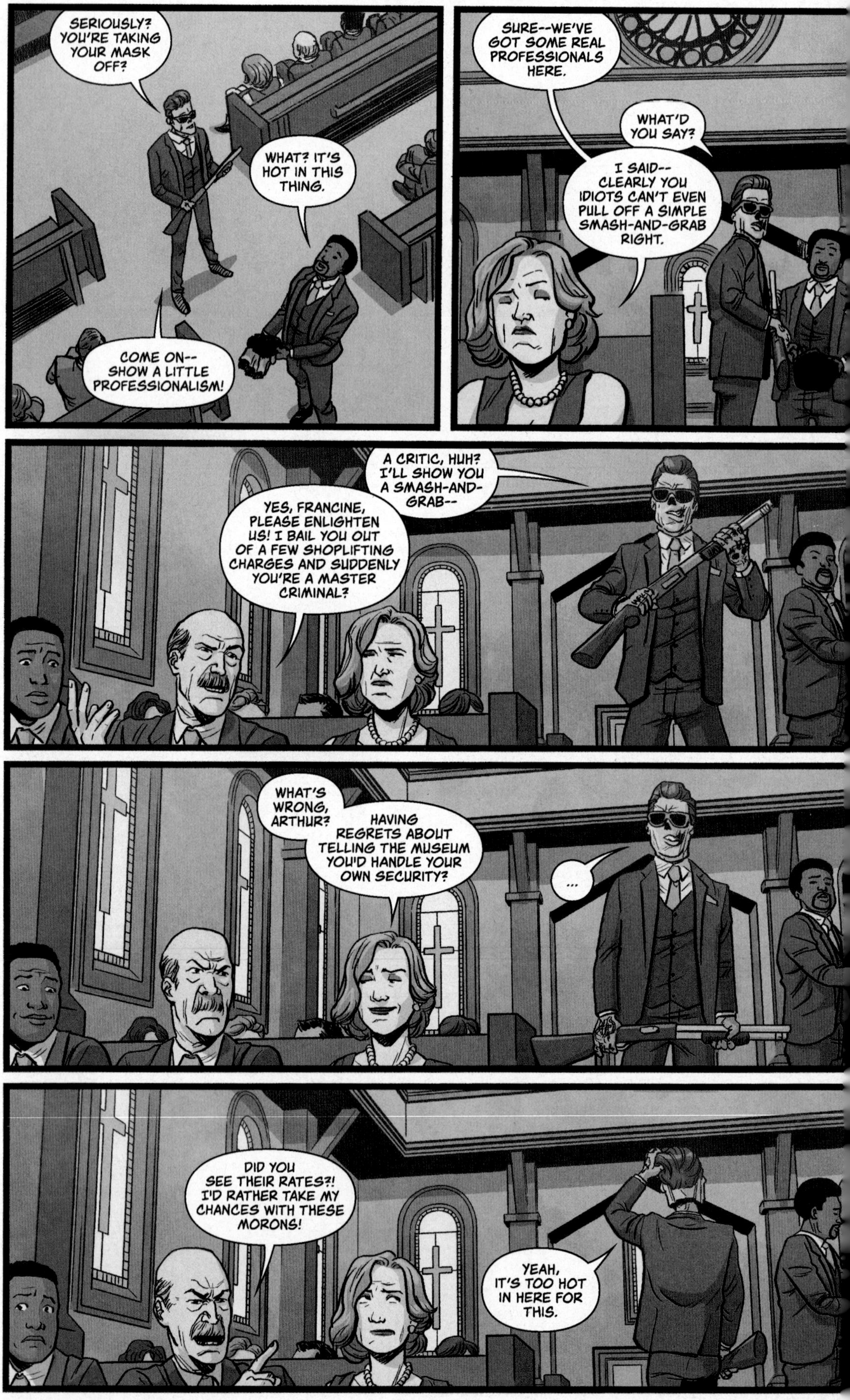
SERIOUSLY? YOU'RE TAKING YOUR MASK OFF?
WHAT? IT'S HOT IN THIS THING.
COME ON-- SHOW A LITTLE PROFESSIONALISM!
SURE--WE'VE GOT SOME REAL PROFESSIONALS HERE.
WHAT'D YOU SAY?
I SAID-- CLEARLY YOU IDIOTS CAN'T EVEN PULL OFF A SIMPLE SMASH-AND-GRAB RIGHT.
A CRITIC, HUH? I'LL SHOW YOU A SMASH-AND-GRAB--
YES, FRANCINE, PLEASE ENLIGHTEN US! I BAIL YOU OUT OF A FEW SHOPLIFTING CHARGES AND SUDDENLY YOU'RE A MASTER CRIMINAL?
WHAT'S WRONG, ARTHUR?
HAVING REGRETS ABOUT TELLING THE MUSEUM YOU'D HANDLE YOUR OWN SECURITY?
...
DID YOU SEE THEIR RATES?! I'D RATHER TAKE MY CHANCES WITH THESE MORONS!
YEAH, IT'S TOO HOT IN HERE FOR THIS.

SO WHAT'S YOUR PLAN--YOU GONNA SKETCH THE BAD GUYS TO DEATH?

I MEAN, I APPRECIATE THE VALUE OF FINE ARTS AND ALL, JESSE, BUT...

I'M AN ARCHITECT, B.J.-- AND THIS CHAPEL IS HUNDREDS OF YEARS OLD.

THERE'S GOT TO BE POINTS OF EGRESS SOME-WHERE...

AND THAT'S HOW I'M GOING TO GET EMILY OUT.

WOW. BIG DIE HARD MOOD.

YOU THINK IF I TRIED THAT ON THAT FINE MAID OF HONOR, SHE'D GIVE ME HER NUMBER?

I'M LITERALLY SITTING RIGHT HERE, YOU JACKASS.

B.J.'S CHARMING PERSONALITY ASIDE, HE'S GOT A POINT.

IF WE COULD FIND A WAY TO CONTACT THE POLICE, TELL THEM WHAT WE KNOW...MAYBE THEY'D BE ABLE TO GET A JUMP ON THESE GUYS.

YEAH, BUT HOW ARE WE GOING TO DO THAT WITH NO PHONES?

OKAY, EVERYBODY SMILE--AND REMEMBER, #MOORE EMILYMOORE PROBLEMS!

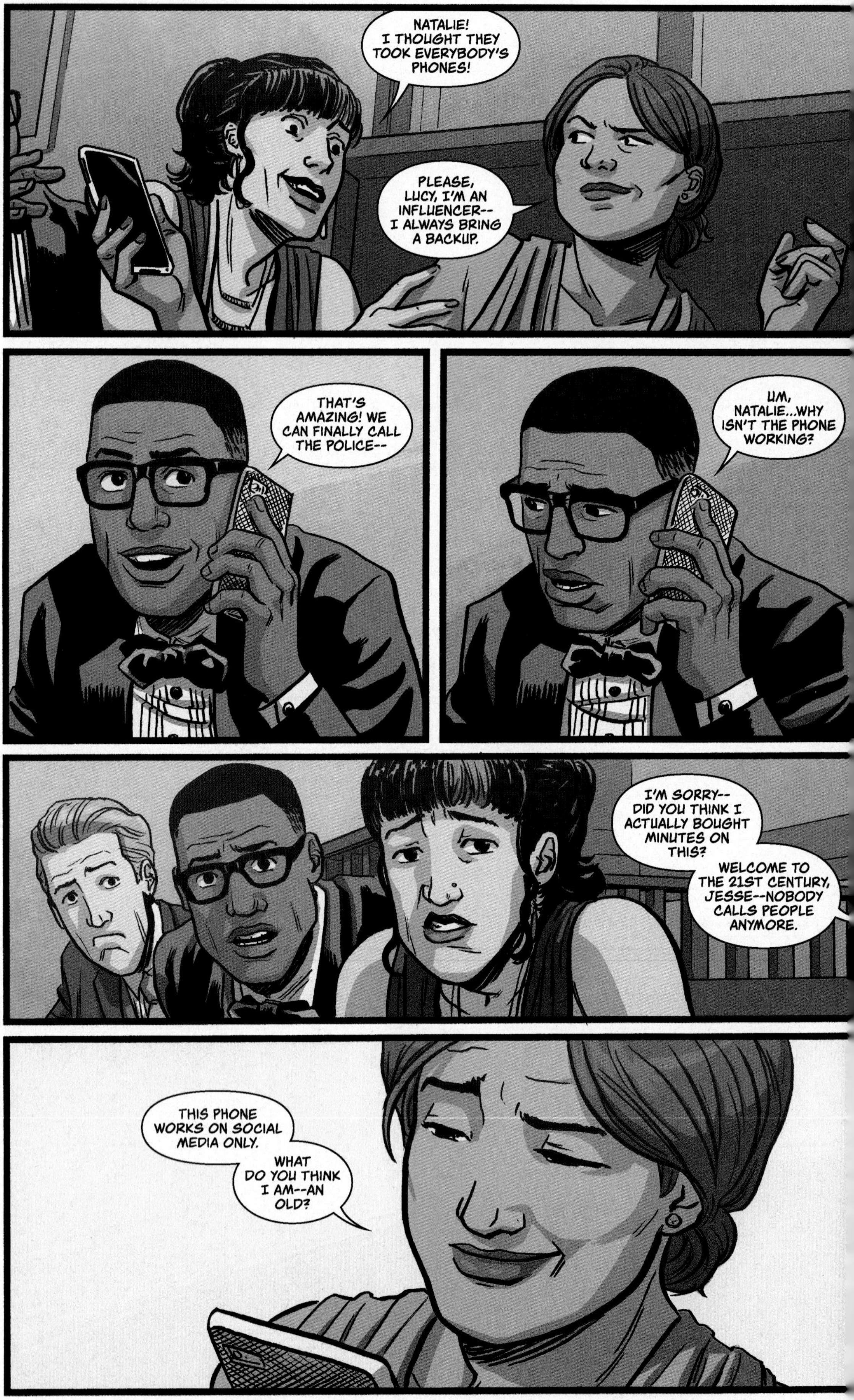
NATALIE! I THOUGHT THEY TOOK EVERYBODY'S PHONES!
PLEASE, LUCY, I'M AN INFLUENCER-- I ALWAYS BRING A BACKUP.
THAT'S AMAZING! WE CAN FINALLY CALL THE POLICE--
UM, NATALIE...WHY ISN'T THE PHONE WORKING?
I'M SORRY-- DID YOU THINK I ACTUALLY BOUGHT MINUTES ON THIS?
WELCOME TO THE 21ST CENTURY, JESSE--NOBODY CALLS PEOPLE ANYMORE.
THIS PHONE WORKS ON SOCIAL MEDIA ONLY.
WHAT DO YOU THINK I AM--AN OLD?

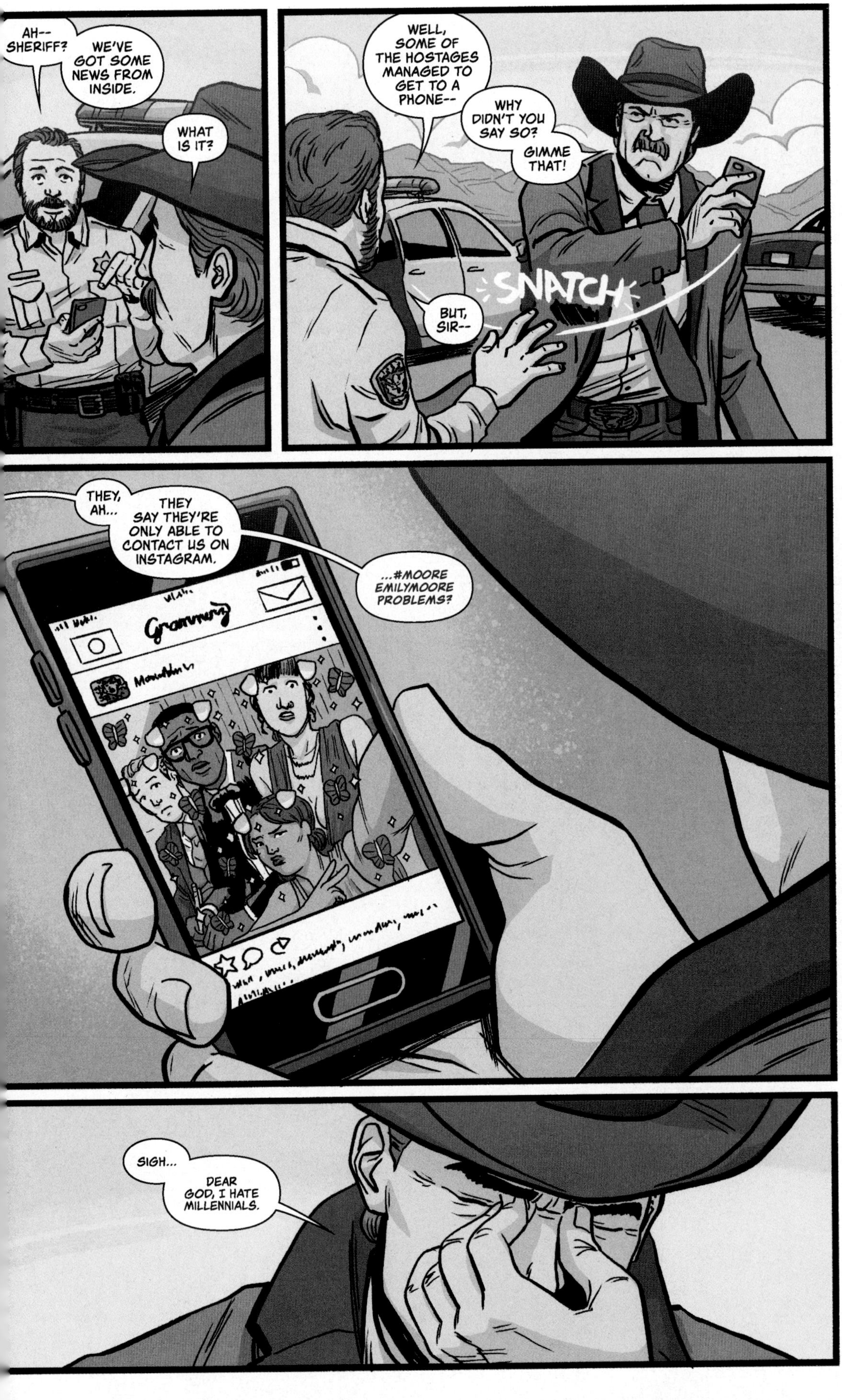
AH-- SHERIFF?
WE'VE GOT SOME NEWS FROM INSIDE.
WHAT IS IT?
WELL, SOME OF THE HOSTAGES MANAGED TO GET TO A PHONE--
WHY DIDN'T YOU SAY SO?
GIMME THAT!
SNATCH
BUT, SIR--
THEY, AH...
THEY SAY THEY'RE ONLY ABLE TO CONTACT US ON INSTAGRAM.
...#MOORE EMILYMOORE PROBLEMS?
SIGH...
DEAR GOD, I HATE MILLENNIALS.

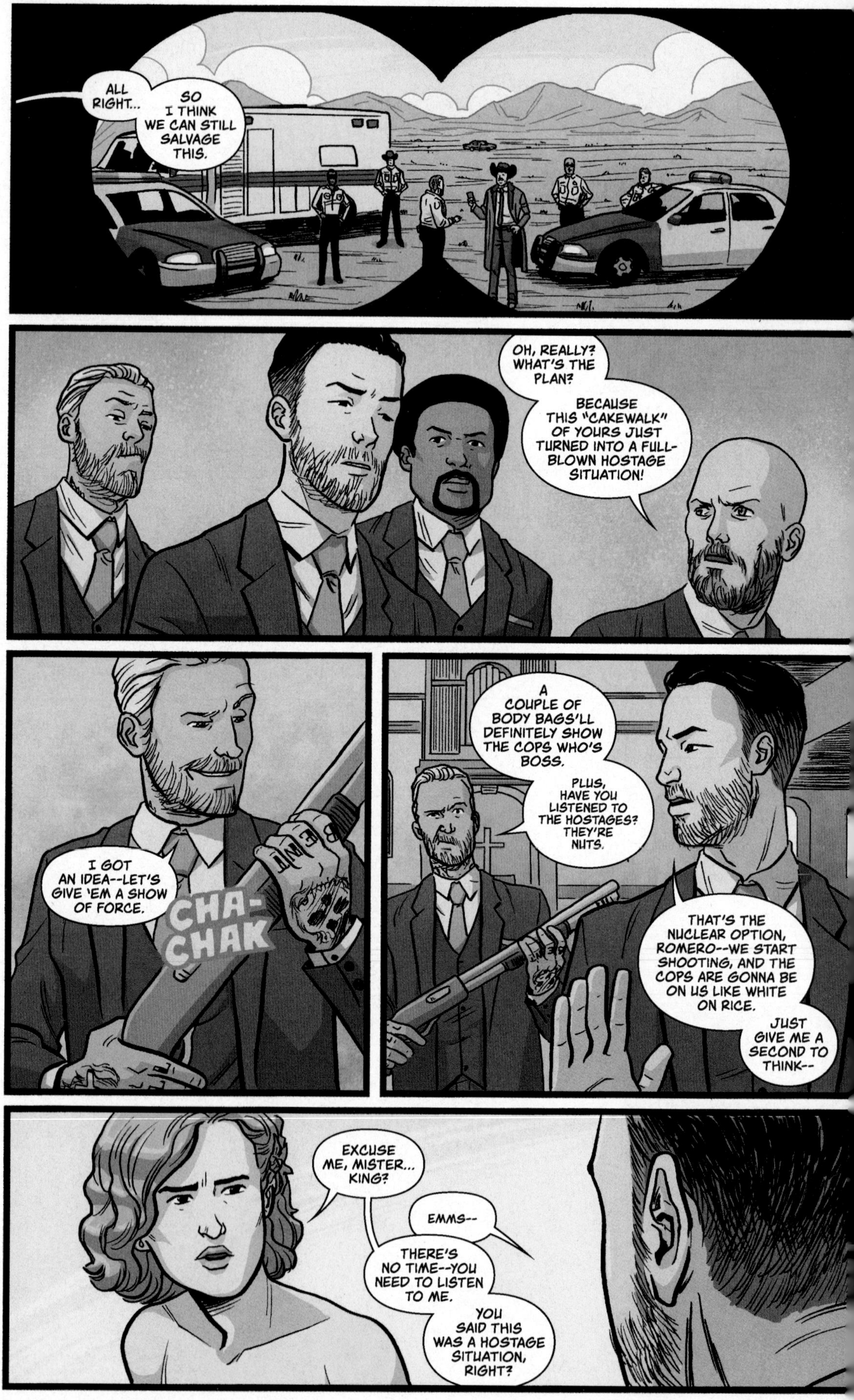
ALL RIGHT...
SO I THINK WE CAN STILL SALVAGE THIS.
OH, REALLY? WHAT'S THE PLAN?
BECAUSE THIS "CAKEWALK" OF YOURS JUST TURNED INTO A FULL-BLOWN HOSTAGE SITUATION!
I GOT AN IDEA--LET'S GIVE 'EM A SHOW OF FORCE.
CHA-CHAK
A COUPLE OF BODY BAGS'LL DEFINITELY SHOW THE COPS WHO'S BOSS.
PLUS, HAVE YOU LISTENED TO THE HOSTAGES? THEY'RE NUTS.
THAT'S THE NUCLEAR OPTION, ROMERO--WE START SHOOTING, AND THE COPS ARE GONNA BE ON US LIKE WHITE ON RICE.
JUST GIVE ME A SECOND TO THINK--
EXCUSE ME, MISTER... KING?
EMMS--
THERE'S NO TIME--YOU NEED TO LISTEN TO ME.
YOU SAID THIS WAS A HOSTAGE SITUATION, RIGHT?

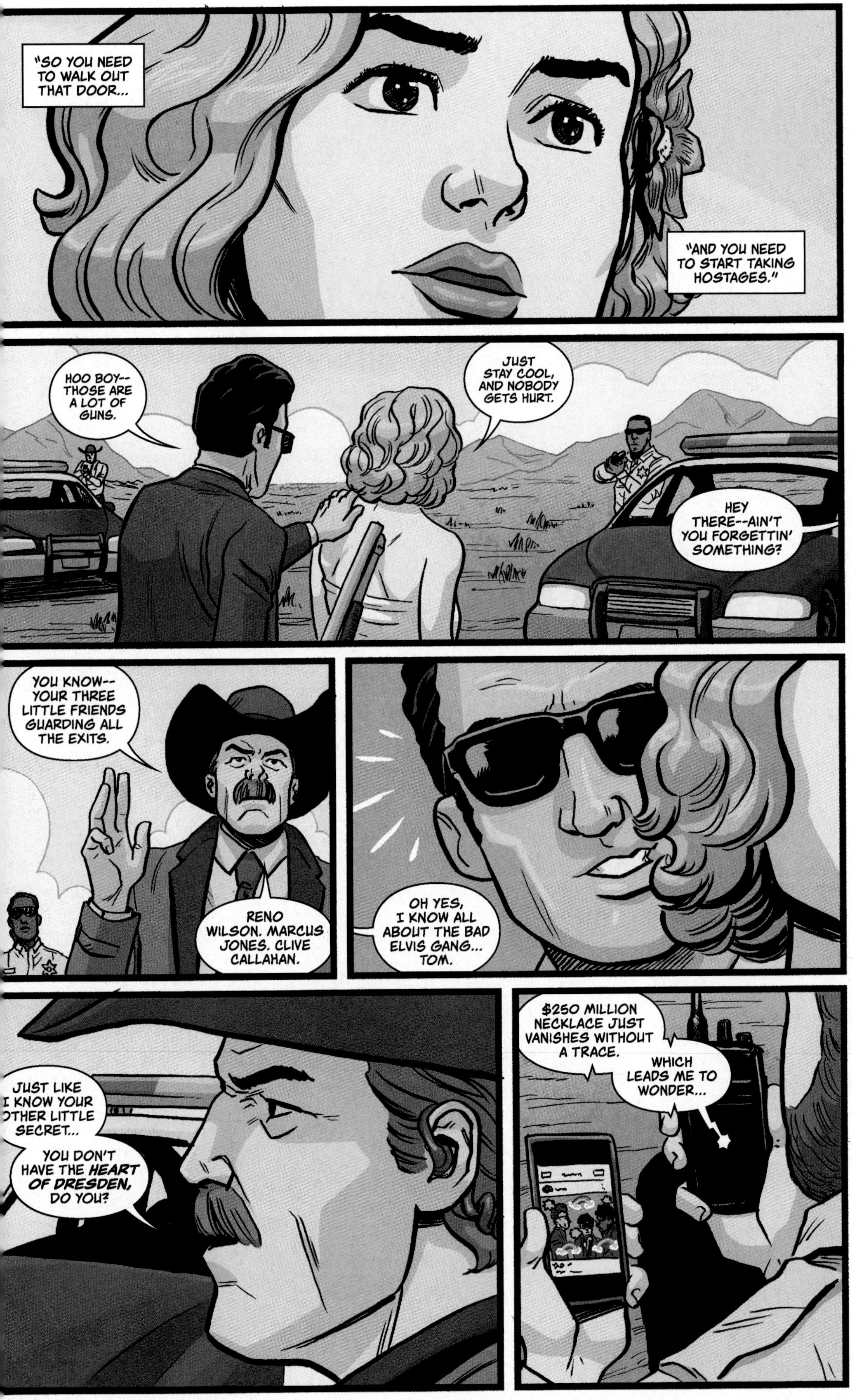

"SO YOU NEED TO WALK OUT THAT DOOR...
"AND YOU NEED TO START TAKING HOSTAGES."
HOO BOY-- THOSE ARE A LOT OF GUNS.
JUST STAY COOL, AND NOBODY GETS HURT.
HEY THERE--AIN'T YOU FORGETTIN' SOMETHING?
YOU KNOW-- YOUR THREE LITTLE FRIENDS GUARDING ALL THE EXITS.
RENO WILSON. MARCUS JONES. CLIVE CALLAHAN.
OH YES, I KNOW ALL ABOUT THE BAD ELVIS GANG... TOM.
JUST LIKE I KNOW YOUR OTHER LITTLE SECRET...
YOU DON'T HAVE THE ***HEART OF DRESDEN,*** DO YOU?
$250 MILLION NECKLACE JUST VANISHES WITHOUT A TRACE.
WHICH LEADS ME TO WONDER...

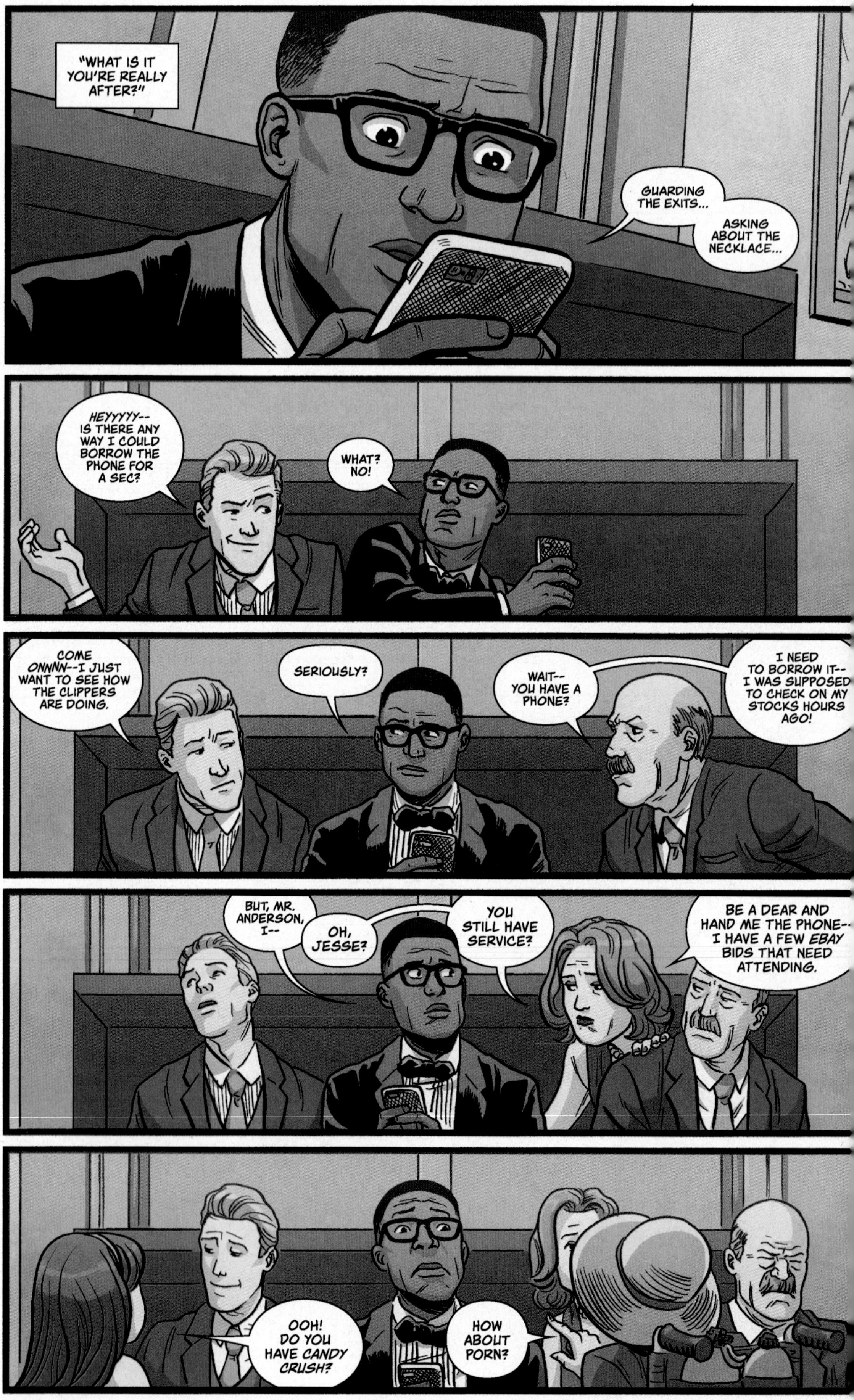
"WHAT IS IT YOU'RE REALLY AFTER?"
GUARDING THE EXITS...
ASKING ABOUT THE NECKLACE...
HEYYYYY-- IS THERE ANY WAY I COULD BORROW THE PHONE FOR A SEC?
WHAT? NO!
COME *ONNNN*--I JUST WANT TO SEE HOW THE CLIPPERS ARE DOING.
SERIOUSLY?
WAIT-- YOU HAVE A PHONE?
I NEED TO BORROW IT-- I WAS SUPPOSED TO CHECK ON MY STOCKS HOURS AGO!
BUT, MR. ANDERSON, I--
OH, JESSE?
YOU STILL HAVE SERVICE?
BE A DEAR AND HAND ME THE PHONE-- I HAVE A FEW *EBAY* BIDS THAT NEED ATTENDING.
OOH! DO YOU HAVE *CANDY CRUSH*?
HOW ABOUT PORN?

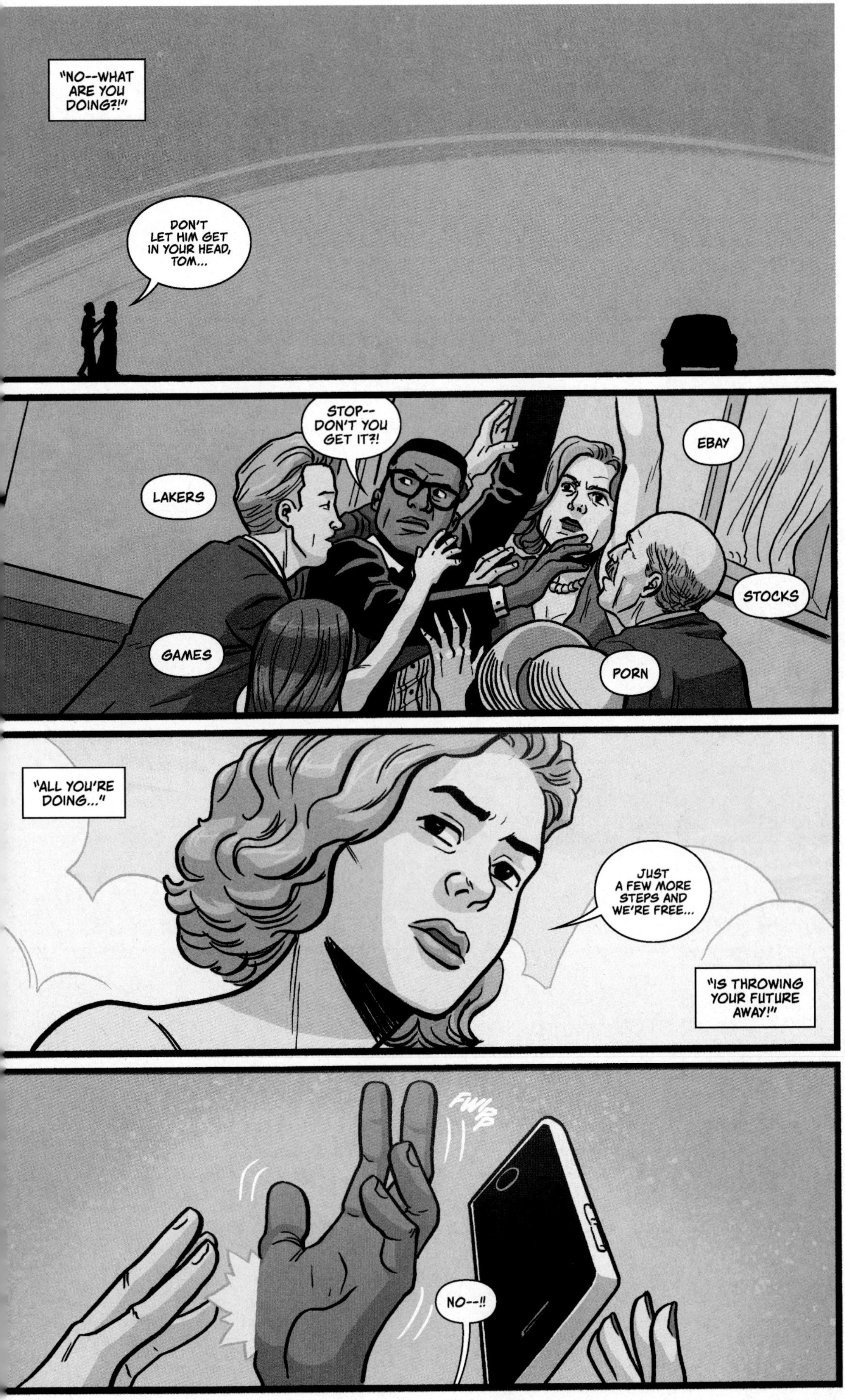

"NO--WHAT ARE YOU DOING?!"
DON'T LET HIM GET IN YOUR HEAD, TOM...
STOP-- DON'T YOU GET IT?!
EBAY
LAKERS
STOCKS
GAMES
PORN
"ALL YOU'RE DOING..."
JUST A FEW MORE STEPS AND WE'RE FREE...
"IS THROWING YOUR FUTURE AWAY!"
FWIP
NO--!!

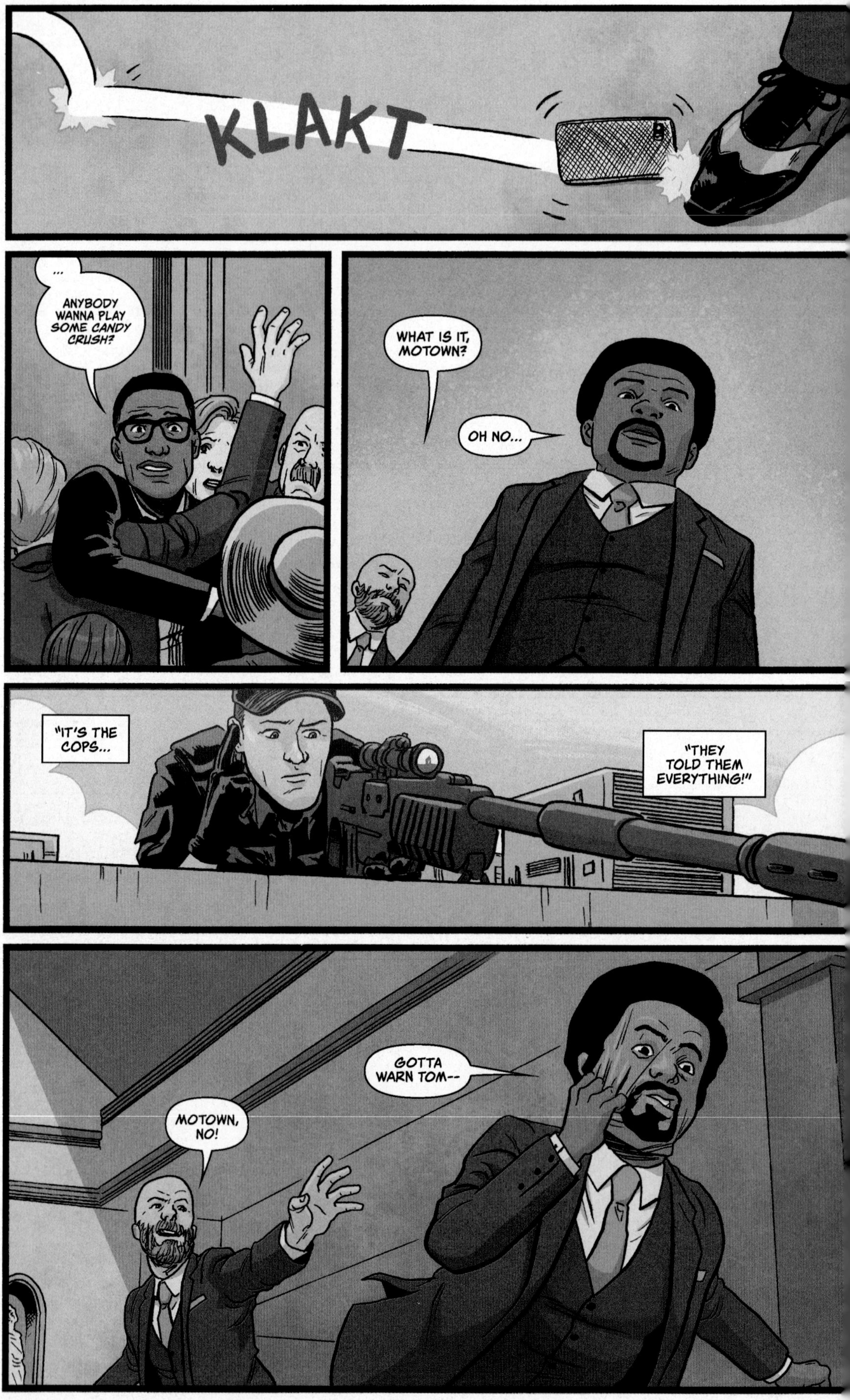
KLAKT
...
ANYBODY WANNA PLAY SOME CANDY CRUSH?
WHAT IS IT, MOTOWN?
OH NO...
"IT'S THE COPS...
"THEY TOLD THEM EVERYTHING!"
GOTTA WARN TOM--
MOTOWN, NO!

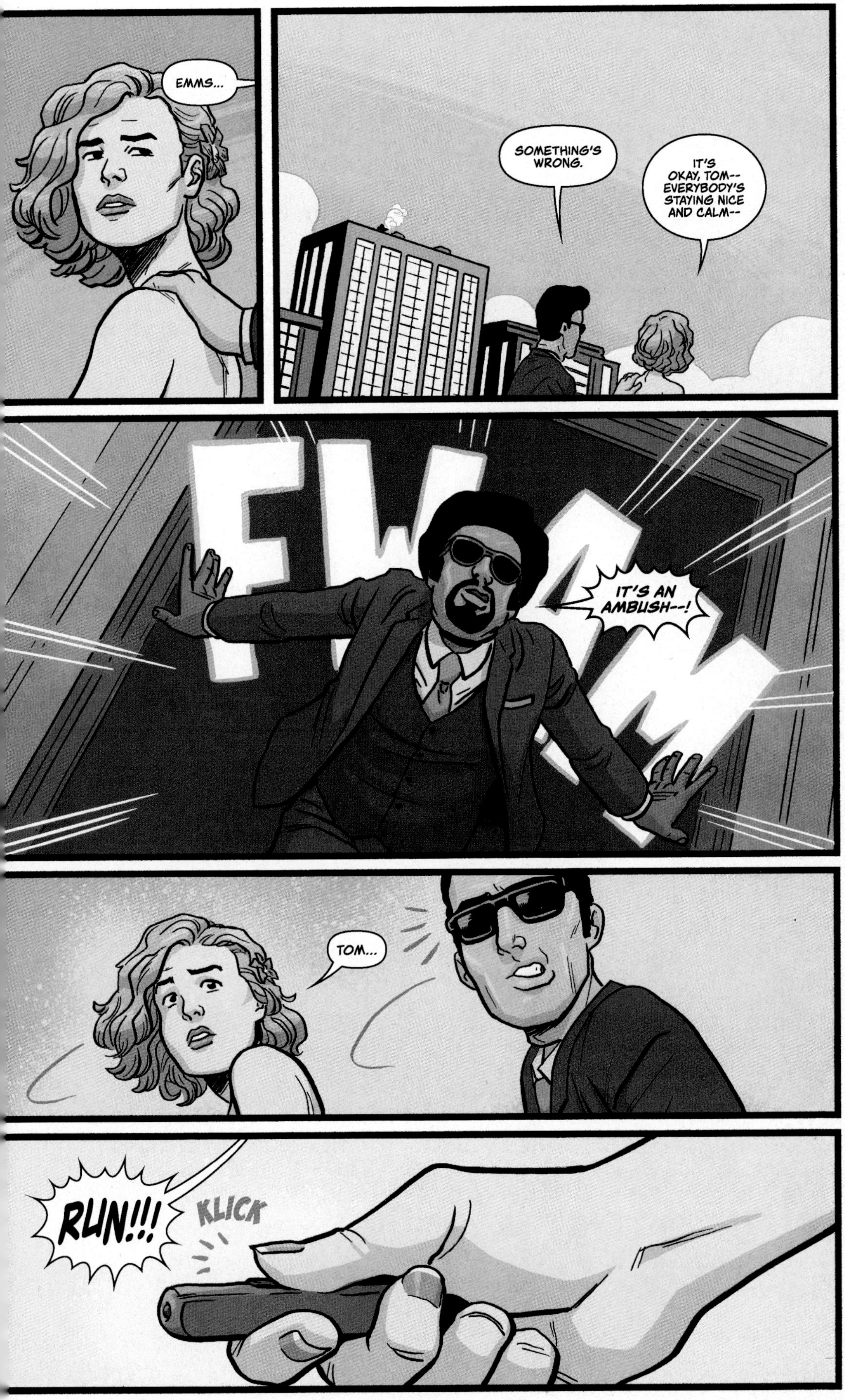
EMMS...
SOMETHING'S WRONG.
IT'S OKAY, TOM-- EVERYBODY'S STAYING NICE AND CALM--
FWAM
IT'S AN AMBUSH--!
TOM...
RUN!!!
KLICK

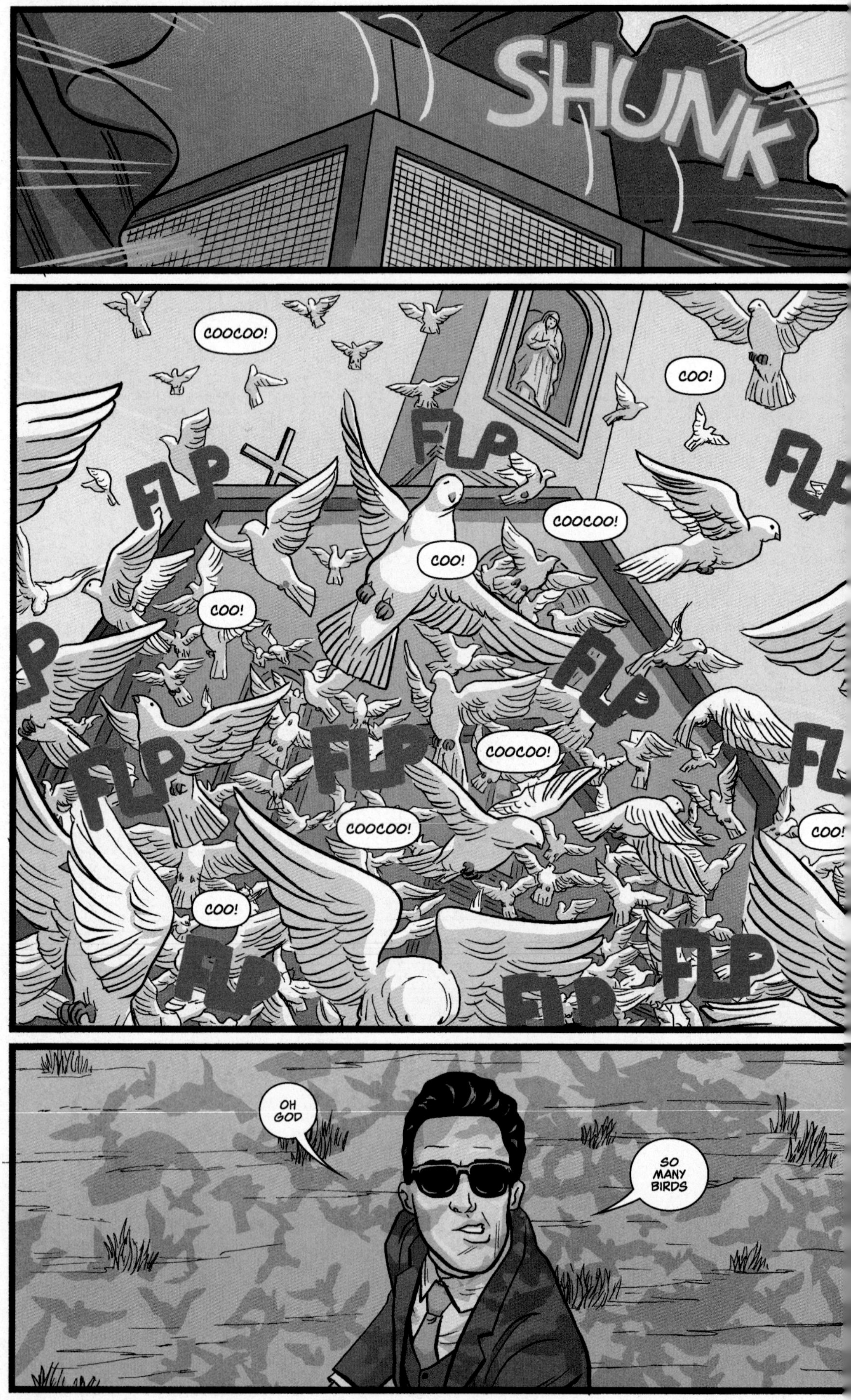
SHUNK
COOCOO!
COO!
FLP
FLP
FLP
COOCOO!
COO!
COO!
FLP
FLP
FLP
FLP
COOCOO!
FLP
COOCOO!
COO!
COO!
FLP
FLP
OH GOD
SO MANY BIRDS

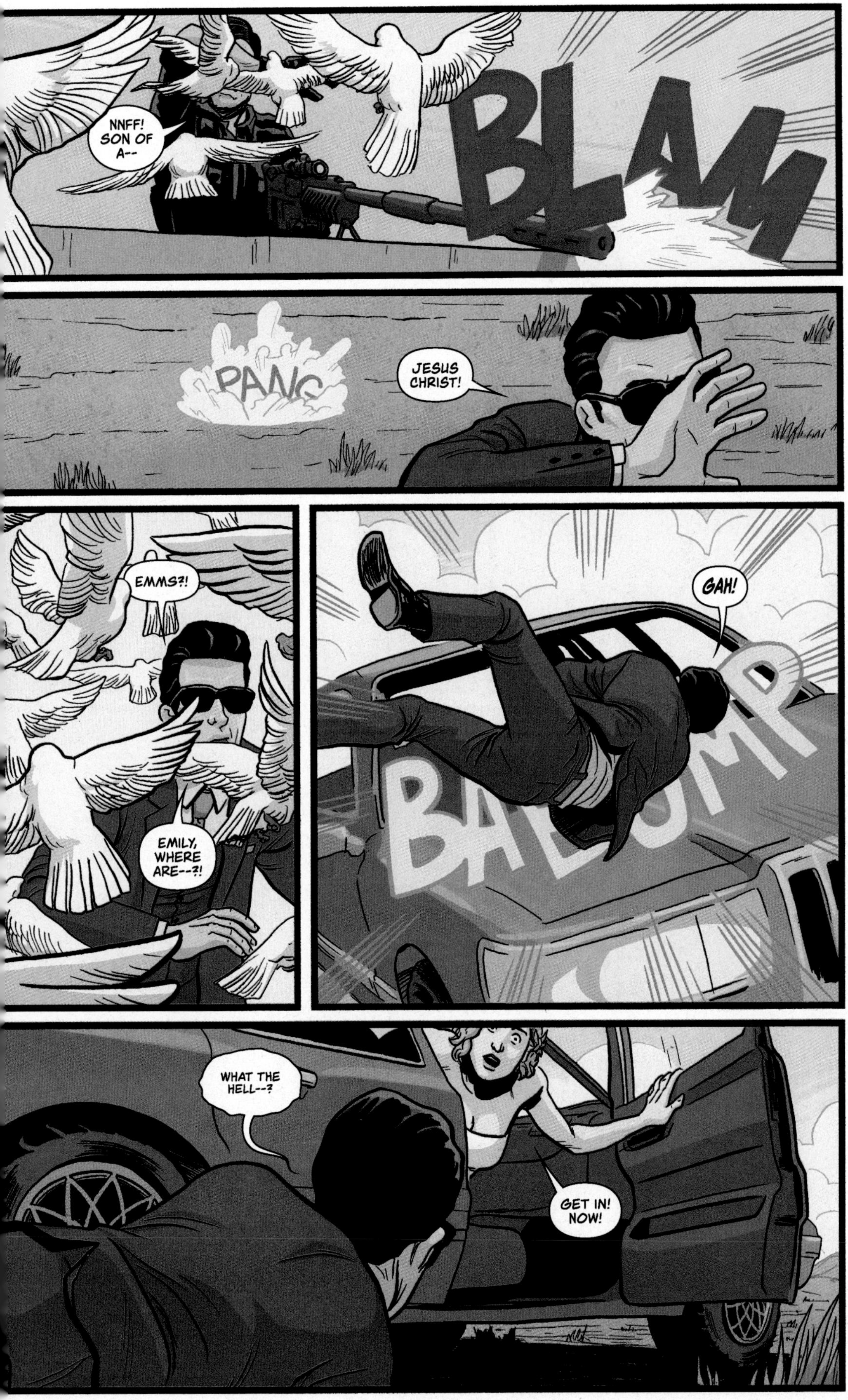
NNFF! SON OF A--
BLAM
PANG
JESUS CHRIST!
EMMS?!
EMILY, WHERE ARE--?!
GAH!
BADOMP
WHAT THE HELL--?
GET IN! NOW!

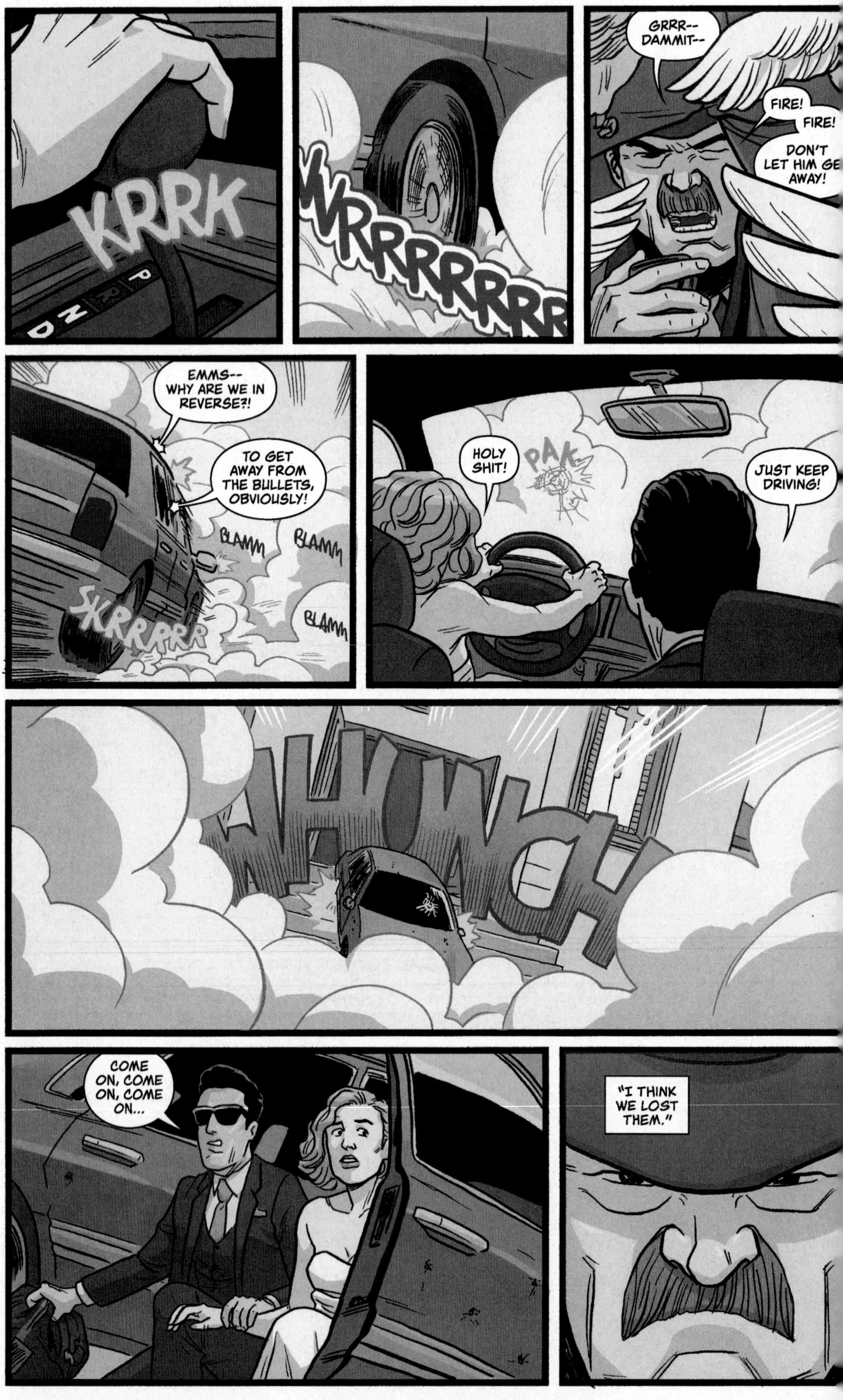
KRRK
VRRRRRRRRR
GRRR--
DAMMIT--
FIRE!
FIRE!
DON'T LET HIM GE
AWAY!
EMMS--
WHY ARE WE IN REVERSE?!
TO GET AWAY FROM THE BULLETS, OBVIOUSLY!
BLAMM
BLAMM
BLAMM
SKRRRRR
HOLY SHIT!
PAK
JUST KEEP DRIVING!
WHUNCH
COME ON, COME ON, COME ON...
"I THINK WE LOST THEM."

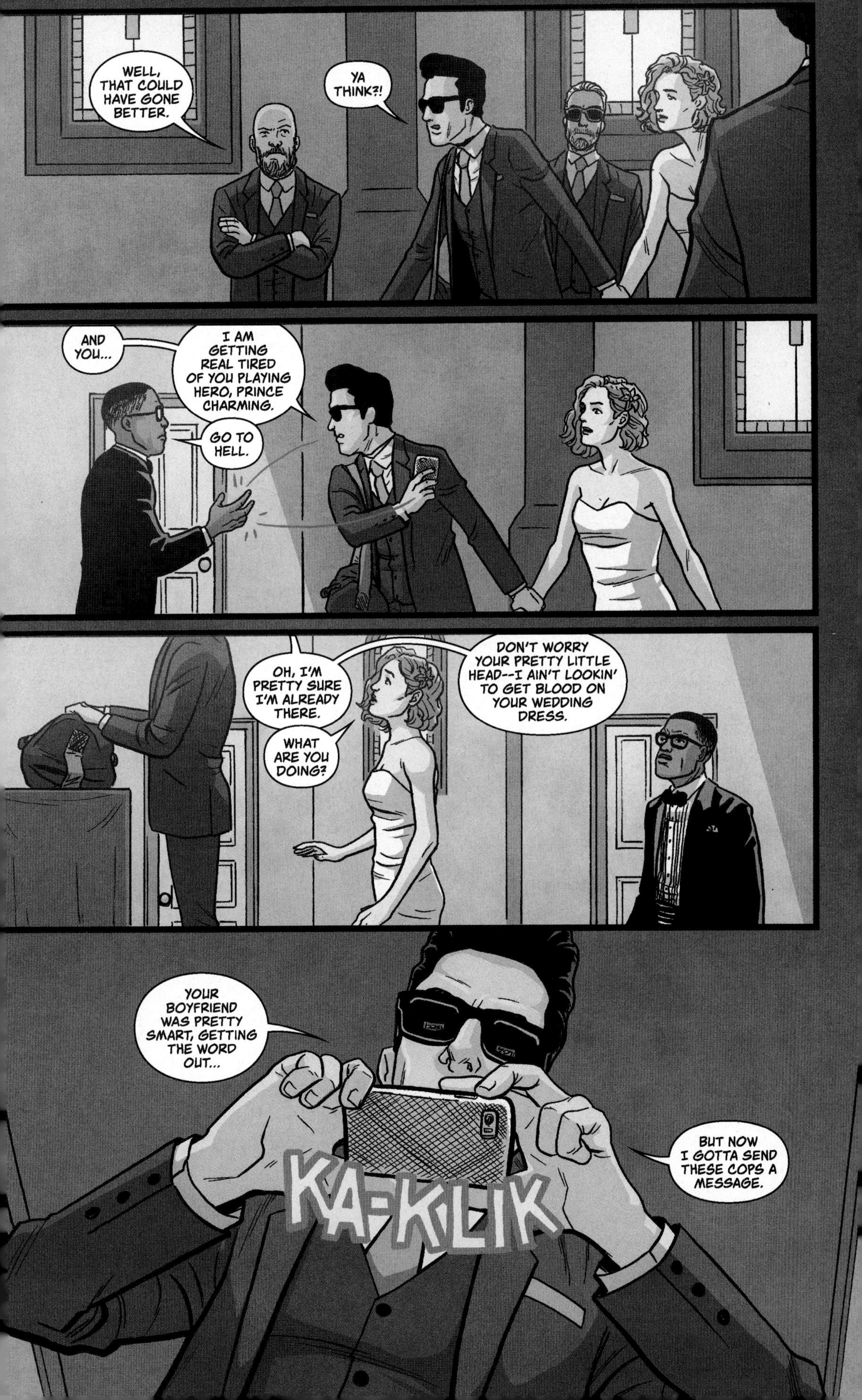
WELL, THAT COULD HAVE GONE BETTER.
YA THINK?!
AND YOU...
I AM GETTING REAL TIRED OF YOU PLAYING HERO, PRINCE CHARMING.
GO TO HELL.
OH, I'M PRETTY SURE I'M ALREADY THERE.
WHAT ARE YOU DOING?
DON'T WORRY YOUR PRETTY LITTLE HEAD--I AIN'T LOOKIN' TO GET BLOOD ON YOUR WEDDING DRESS.
YOUR BOYFRIEND WAS PRETTY SMART, GETTING THE WORD OUT...
KA-KLIK
BUT NOW I GOTTA SEND THESE COPS A MESSAGE.

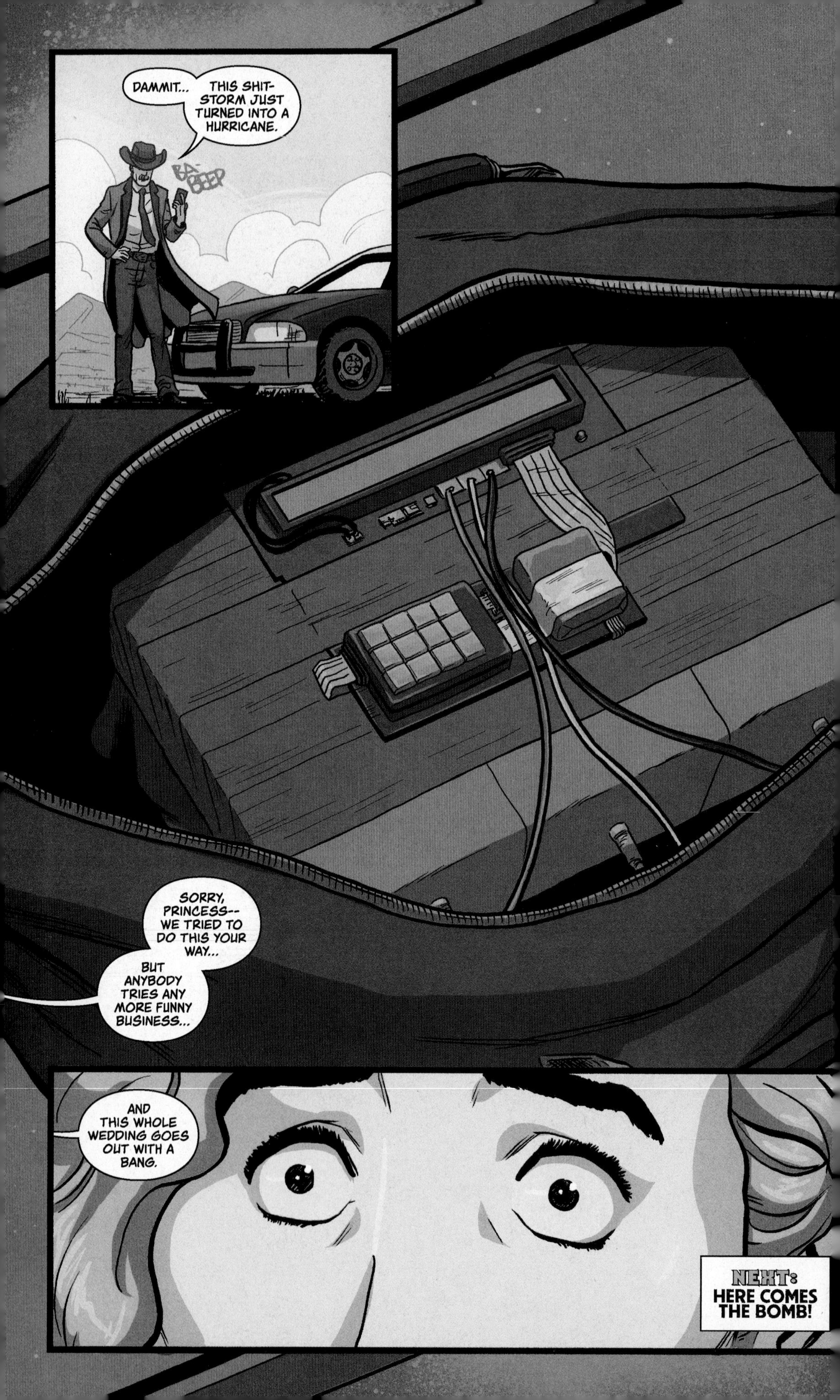
DAMMIT...
THIS SHIT-STORM JUST TURNED INTO A HURRICANE.
BA-BEEP
SORRY, PRINCESS-- WE TRIED TO DO THIS YOUR WAY...
BUT ANYBODY TRIES ANY MORE FUNNY BUSINESS...
AND THIS WHOLE WEDDING GOES OUT WITH A BANG.
NEXT: HERE COMES THE BOMB!

CHAPTER THREE

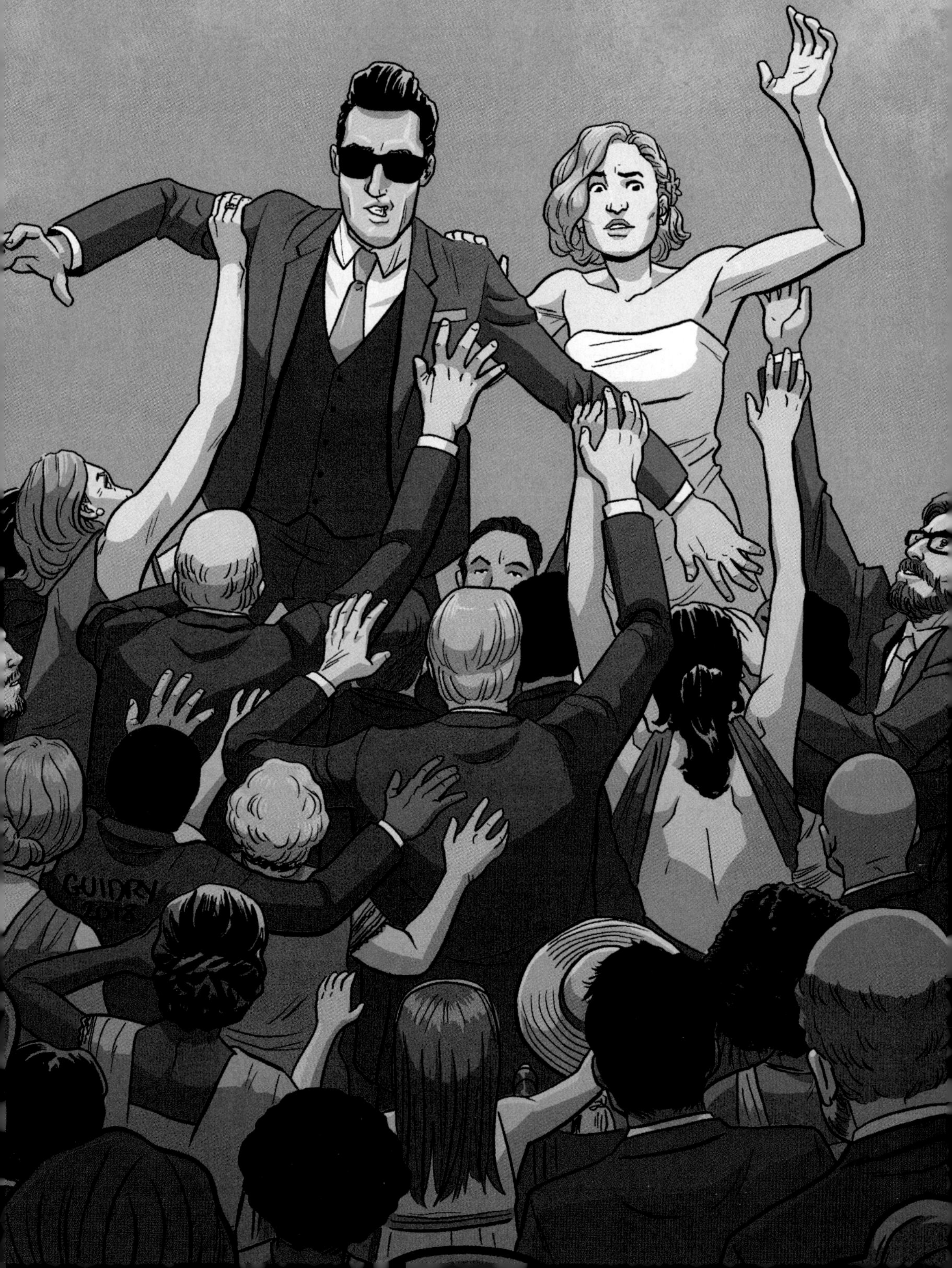

Going to the CHAPEL 3

Written by
DAVID PEPOSE

Art by
GAVIN GUIDRY

Colors by
ELIZABETH KRAMER

Lettering by
ARIANA MAHER

Covers by
EMILY PEARSON, MAAN HOUSE AND GAVIN GUIDRY

Chapel Of Love
Words and Music by Phil Spector, Ellie Greenwich and Jeff Barry
Copyright (c) 1964 UNIVERSAL - SONGS OF POLYGRAM INTERNATIONAL, INC., TRIO MUSIC
COMPANY and MOTHER BERTHA MUSIC, INC.
Copyright Renewed
All Rights for TRIO MUSIC COMPANY Administered by BMG RIGHTS MANAGEMENT (US) LLC
All Rights for MOTHER BERTHA MUSIC, INC. Controlled and Administered by EMI APRIL MUSIC INC.
All Rights Reserved Used by Permission
Reprinted by Permission of Hal Leonard LLC

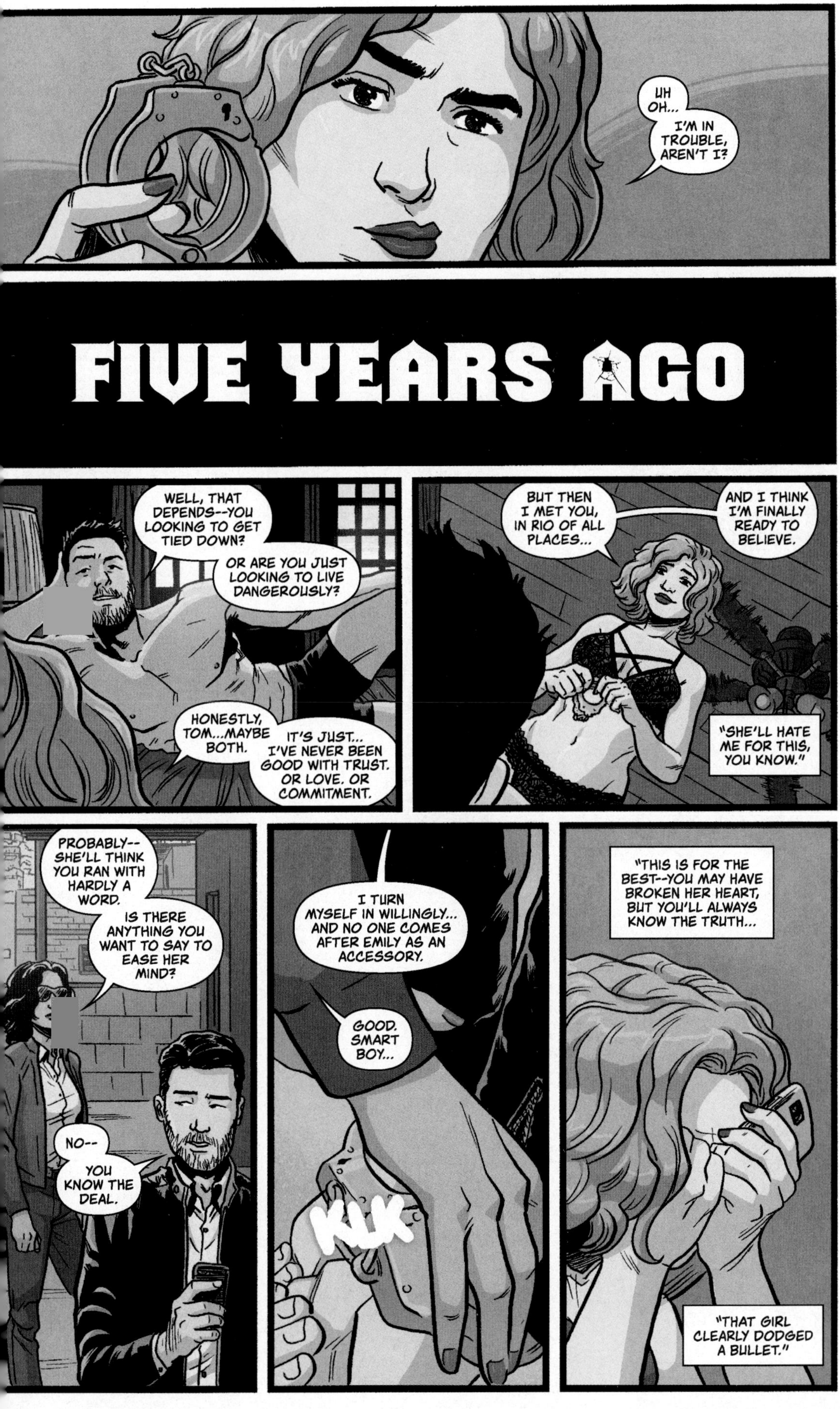

UH OH...
I'M IN TROUBLE, AREN'T I?
FIVE YEARS AGO
WELL, THAT DEPENDS--YOU LOOKING TO GET TIED DOWN?
OR ARE YOU JUST LOOKING TO LIVE DANGEROUSLY?
HONESTLY, TOM...MAYBE BOTH.
IT'S JUST... I'VE NEVER BEEN GOOD WITH TRUST. OR LOVE. OR COMMITMENT.
BUT THEN I MET YOU, IN RIO OF ALL PLACES...
AND I THINK I'M FINALLY READY TO BELIEVE.
"SHE'LL HATE ME FOR THIS, YOU KNOW."
PROBABLY--SHE'LL THINK YOU RAN WITH HARDLY A WORD.
IS THERE ANYTHING YOU WANT TO SAY TO EASE HER MIND?
NO--
YOU KNOW THE DEAL.
I TURN MYSELF IN WILLINGLY... AND NO ONE COMES AFTER EMILY AS AN ACCESSORY.
GOOD. SMART BOY...
KLIK
"THIS IS FOR THE BEST--YOU MAY HAVE BROKEN HER HEART, BUT YOU'LL ALWAYS KNOW THE TRUTH...
"THAT GIRL CLEARLY DODGED A BULLET."

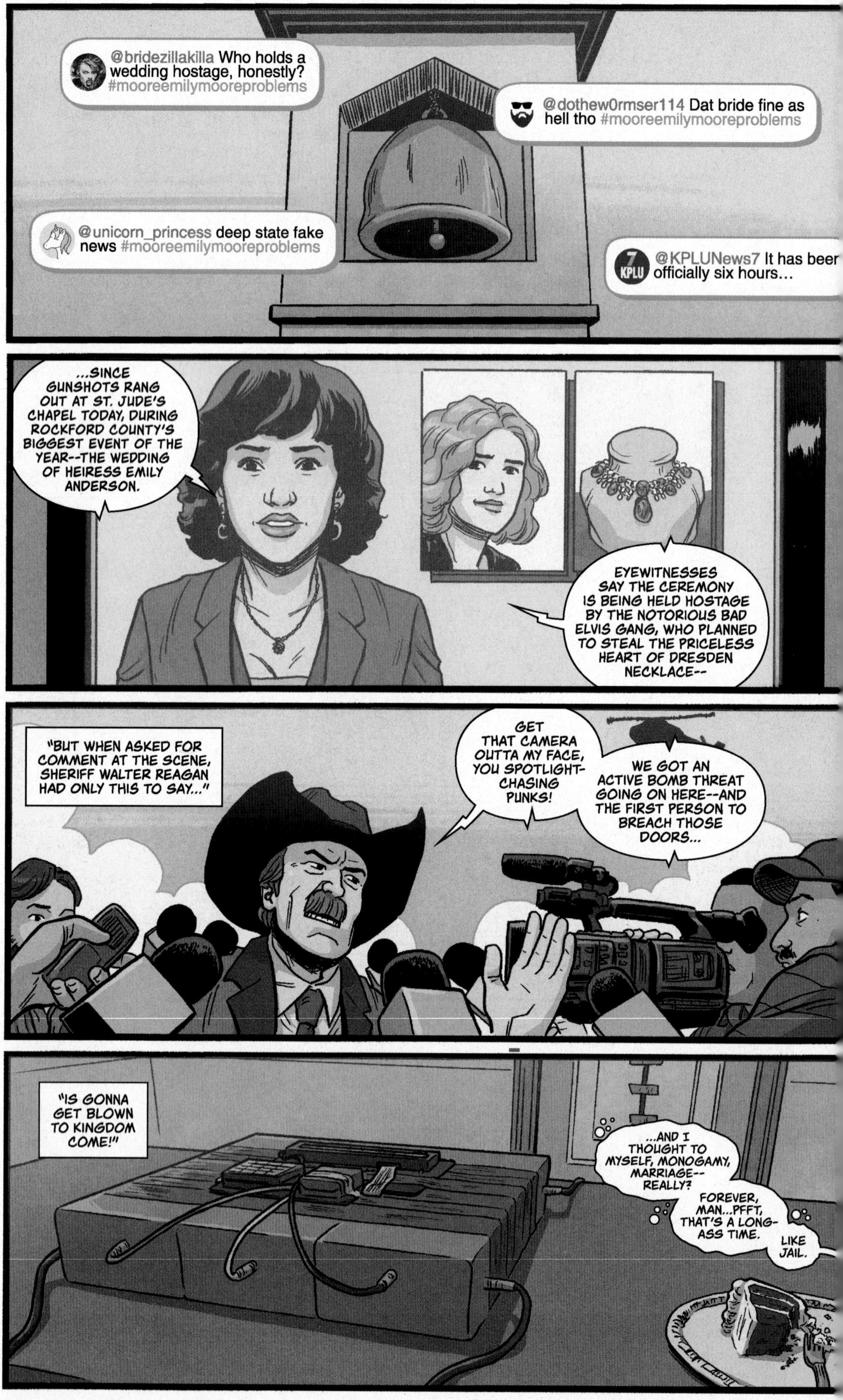
@bridezillakilla Who holds a wedding hostage, honestly? #mooreemilymooreproblems
@dothew0rmser114 Dat bride fine as hell tho #mooreemilymooreproblems
@unicorn_princess deep state fake news #mooreemilymooreproblems
@KPLUNews7 It has beer officially six hours...
...SINCE GUNSHOTS RANG OUT AT ST. JUDE'S CHAPEL TODAY, DURING ROCKFORD COUNTY'S BIGGEST EVENT OF THE YEAR--THE WEDDING OF HEIRESS EMILY ANDERSON.
EYEWITNESSES SAY THE CEREMONY IS BEING HELD HOSTAGE BY THE NOTORIOUS BAD ELVIS GANG, WHO PLANNED TO STEAL THE PRICELESS HEART OF DRESDEN NECKLACE--
"BUT WHEN ASKED FOR COMMENT AT THE SCENE, SHERIFF WALTER REAGAN HAD ONLY THIS TO SAY..."
GET THAT CAMERA OUTTA MY FACE, YOU SPOTLIGHT-CHASING PUNKS!
WE GOT AN ACTIVE BOMB THREAT GOING ON HERE--AND THE FIRST PERSON TO BREACH THOSE DOORS...
"IS GONNA GET BLOWN TO KINGDOM COME!"
...AND I THOUGHT TO MYSELF, MONOGAMY, MARRIAGE--REALLY?
FOREVER, MAN...PFFT, THAT'S A LONG-ASS TIME.
LIKE JAIL.

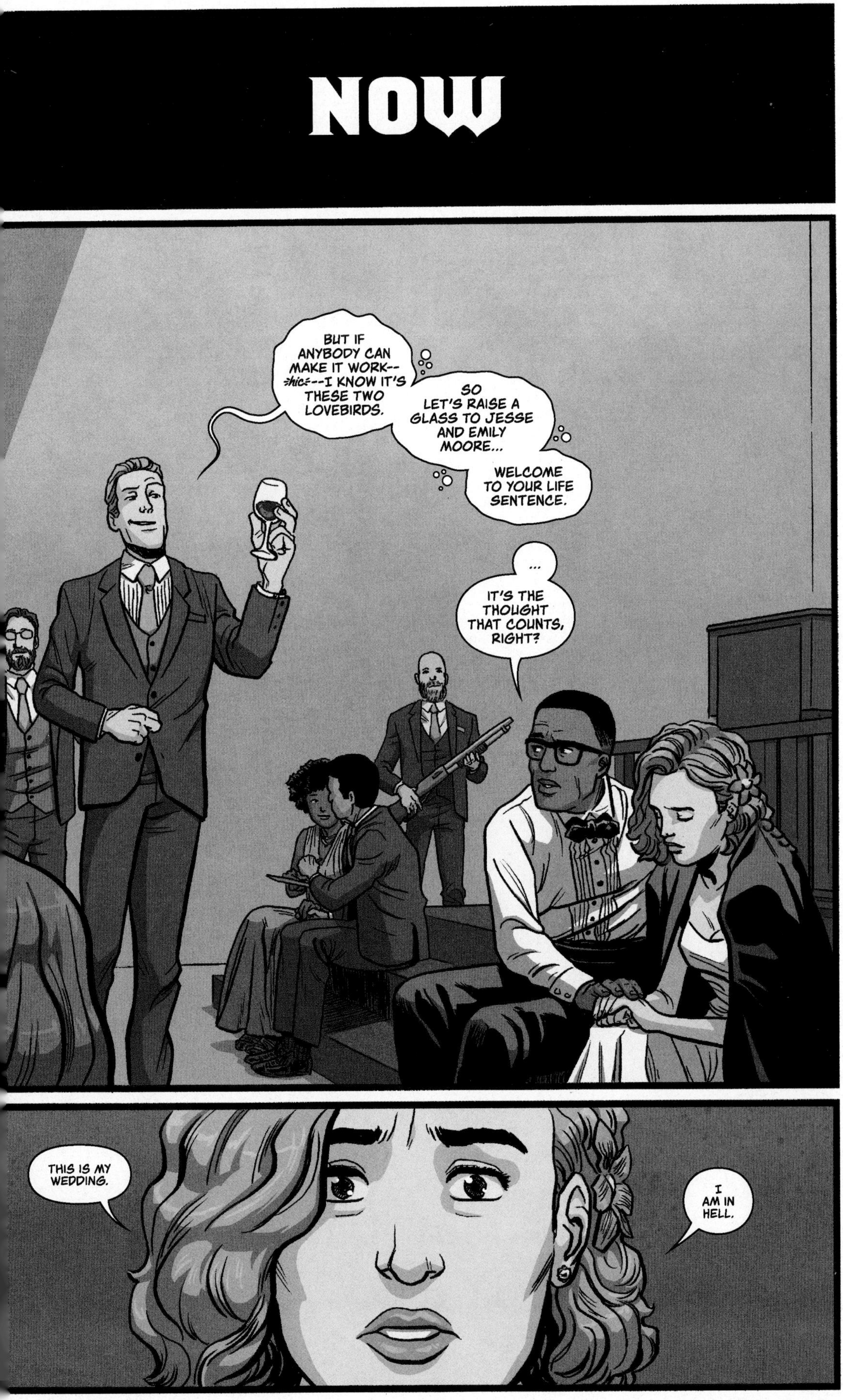
NOW
BUT IF ANYBODY CAN MAKE IT WORK-- hic --I KNOW IT'S THESE TWO LOVEBIRDS.
SO LET'S RAISE A GLASS TO JESSE AND EMILY MOORE...
WELCOME TO YOUR LIFE SENTENCE.
...
IT'S THE THOUGHT THAT COUNTS, RIGHT?
THIS IS MY WEDDING.
I AM IN HELL.

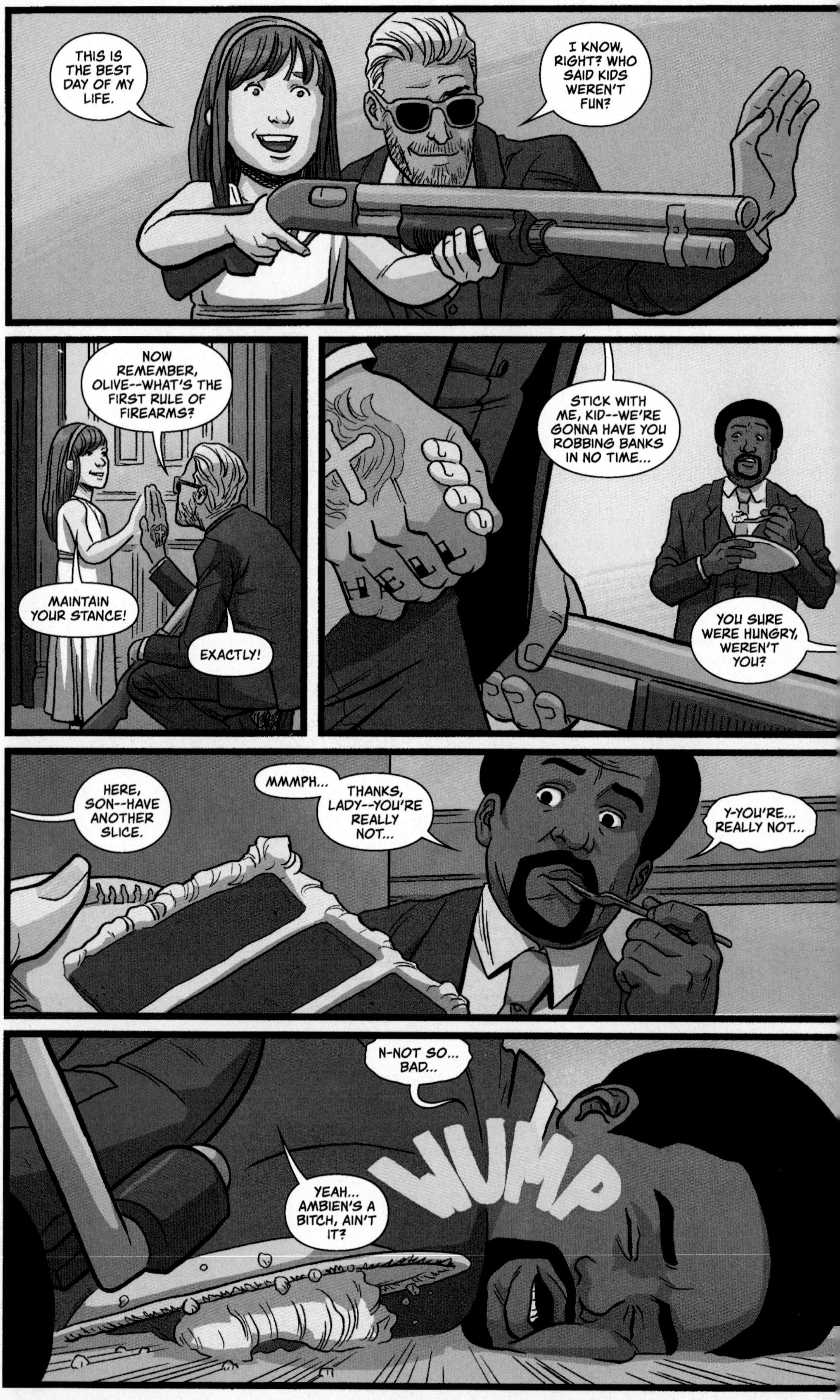
THIS IS THE BEST DAY OF MY LIFE.
I KNOW, RIGHT? WHO SAID KIDS WEREN'T FUN?
NOW REMEMBER, OLIVE--WHAT'S THE FIRST RULE OF FIREARMS?
MAINTAIN YOUR STANCE!
EXACTLY!
STICK WITH ME, KID--WE'RE GONNA HAVE YOU ROBBING BANKS IN NO TIME...
YOU SURE WERE HUNGRY, WEREN'T YOU?
HERE, SON--HAVE ANOTHER SLICE.
MMMPH...
THANKS, LADY--YOU'RE REALLY NOT...
Y-YOU'RE... REALLY NOT...
N-NOT SO... BAD...
WUMP
YEAH... AMBIEN'S A BITCH, AIN'T IT?

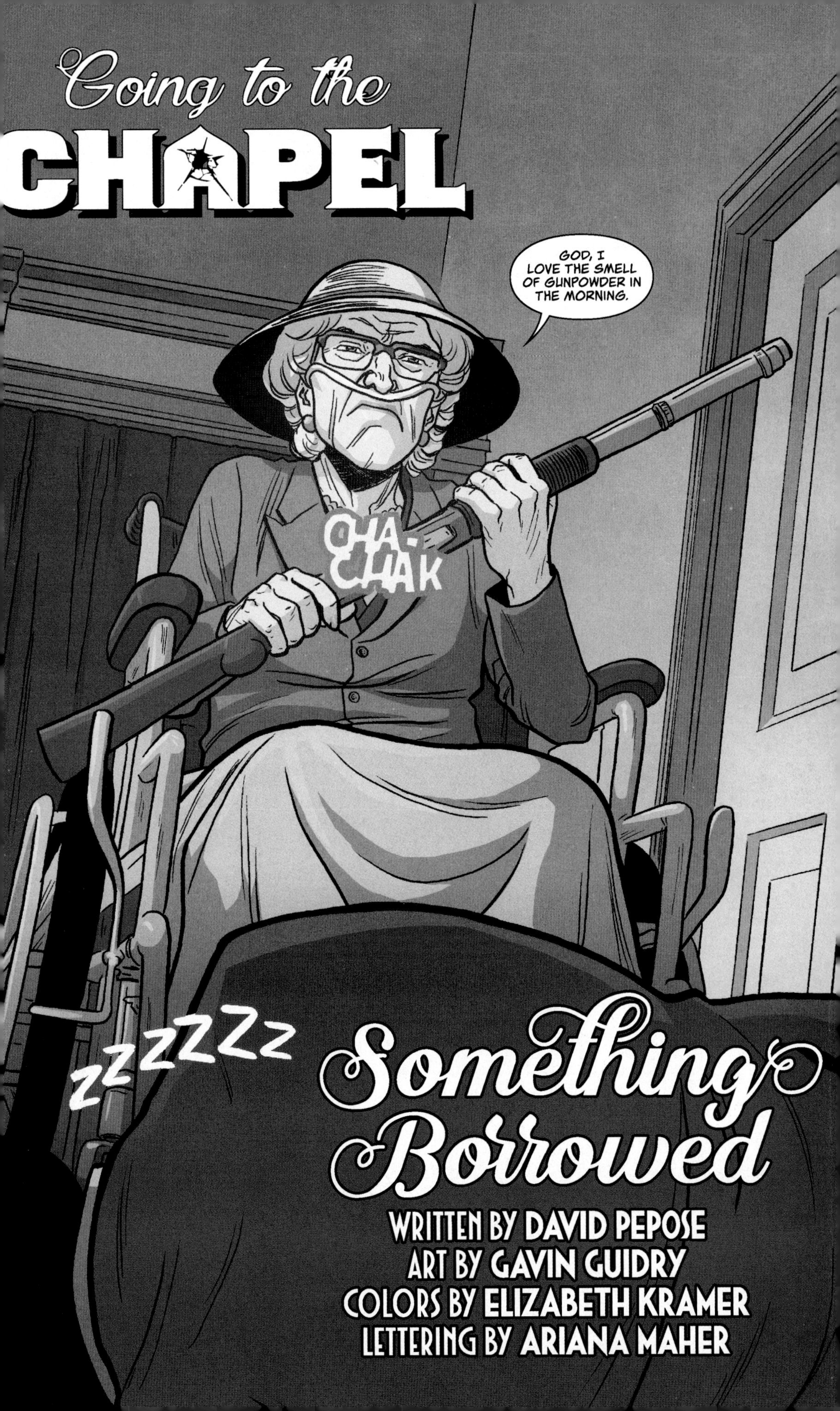
Going to the CHAPEL
GOD, I LOVE THE SMELL OF GUNPOWDER IN THE MORNING.
CHA-CHAK
ZZZZZZ
Something Borrowed
WRITTEN BY DAVID PEPOSE
ART BY GAVIN GUIDRY
COLORS BY ELIZABETH KRAMER
LETTERING BY ARIANA MAHER

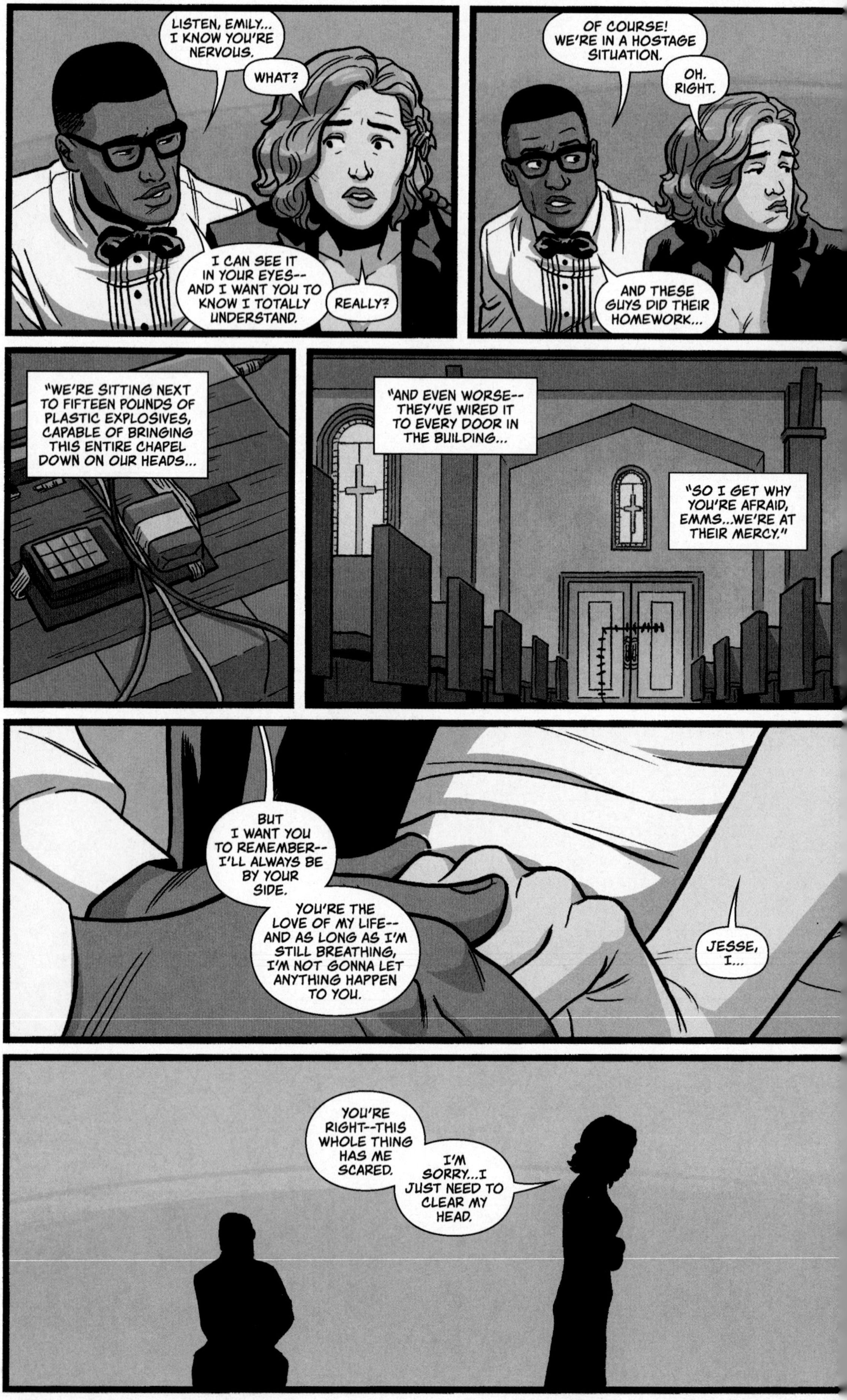
LISTEN, EMILY... I KNOW YOU'RE NERVOUS.
WHAT?
I CAN SEE IT IN YOUR EYES--AND I WANT YOU TO KNOW I TOTALLY UNDERSTAND.
REALLY?
OF COURSE! WE'RE IN A HOSTAGE SITUATION.
OH. RIGHT.
AND THESE GUYS DID THEIR HOMEWORK...
"WE'RE SITTING NEXT TO FIFTEEN POUNDS OF PLASTIC EXPLOSIVES, CAPABLE OF BRINGING THIS ENTIRE CHAPEL DOWN ON OUR HEADS...
"AND EVEN WORSE--THEY'VE WIRED IT TO EVERY DOOR IN THE BUILDING...
"SO I GET WHY YOU'RE AFRAID, EMMS...WE'RE AT THEIR MERCY."
BUT I WANT YOU TO REMEMBER--I'LL ALWAYS BE BY YOUR SIDE.
YOU'RE THE LOVE OF MY LIFE--AND AS LONG AS I'M STILL BREATHING, I'M NOT GONNA LET ANYTHING HAPPEN TO YOU.
JESSE, I...
YOU'RE RIGHT--THIS WHOLE THING HAS ME SCARED.
I'M SORRY...I JUST NEED TO CLEAR MY HEAD.

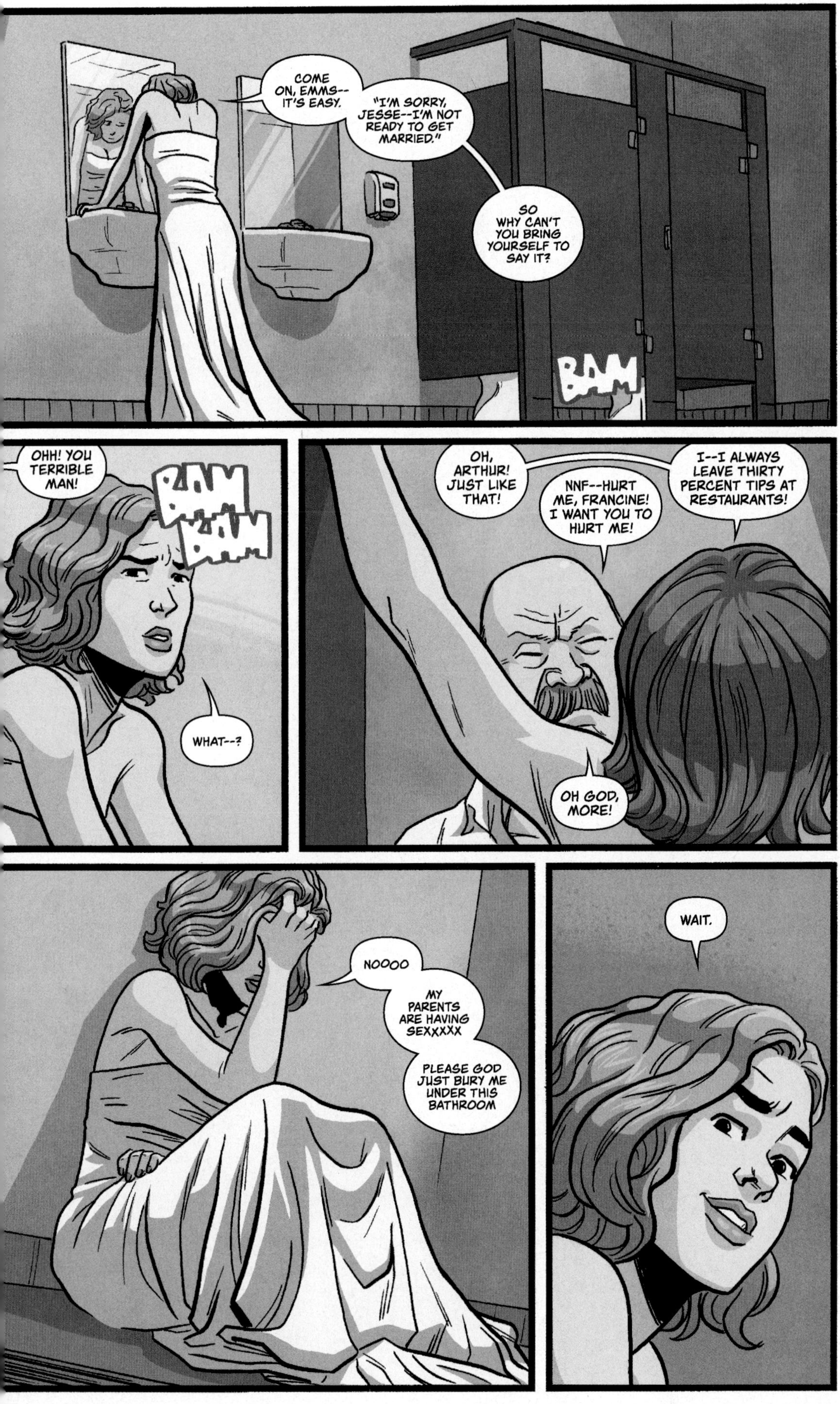
COME ON, EMMS-- IT'S EASY.
"I'M SORRY, JESSE--I'M NOT READY TO GET MARRIED."
SO WHY CAN'T YOU BRING YOURSELF TO SAY IT?
BAM
OHH! YOU TERRIBLE MAN!
BAM BAM BAM
WHAT--?
OH, ARTHUR! JUST LIKE THAT!
I--I ALWAYS LEAVE THIRTY PERCENT TIPS AT RESTAURANTS!
NNF--HURT ME, FRANCINE! I WANT YOU TO HURT ME!
OH GOD, MORE!
NOOOO
MY PARENTS ARE HAVING SEXXXXX
PLEASE GOD JUST BURY ME UNDER THIS BATHROOM
WAIT.

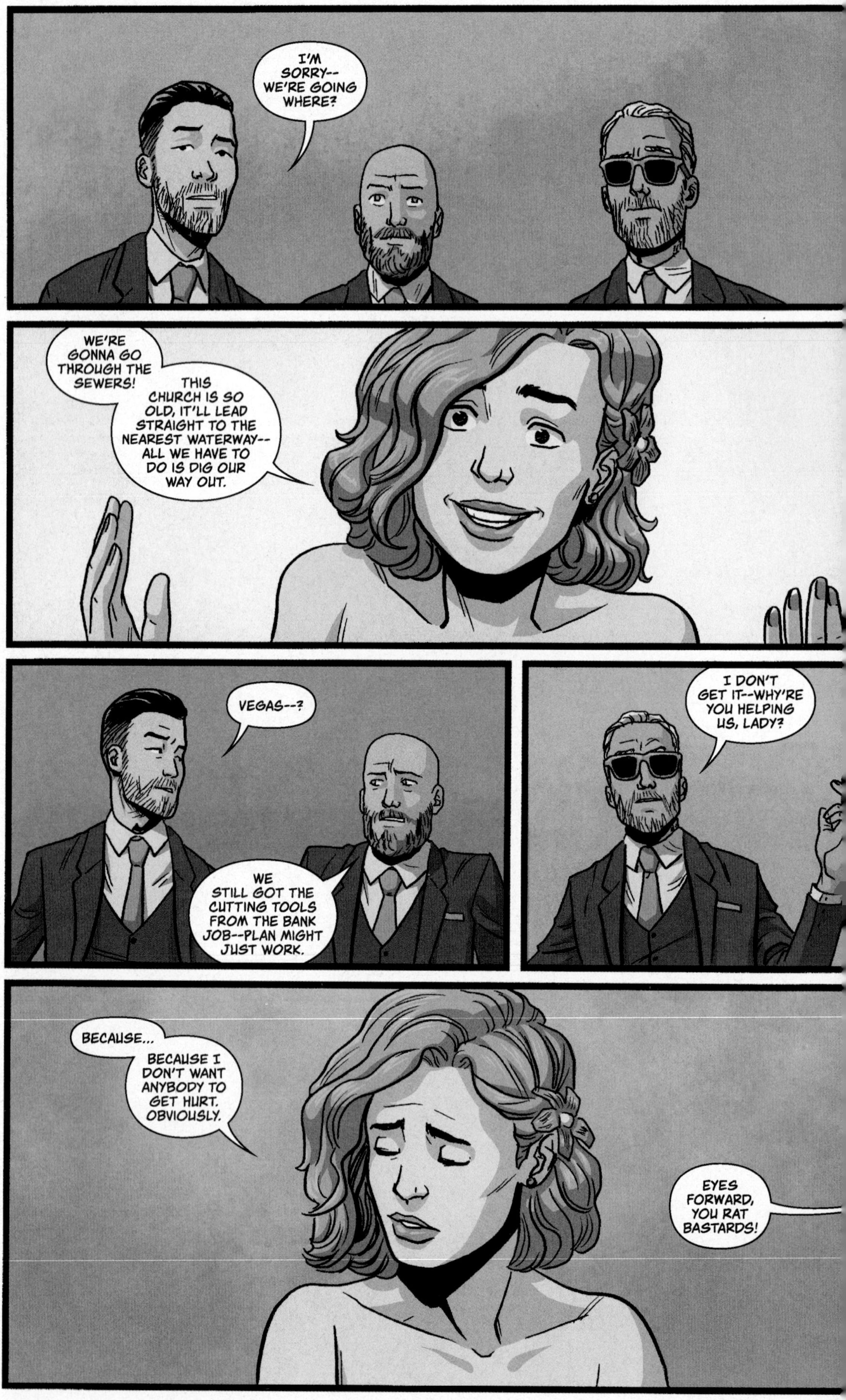
I'M SORRY-- WE'RE GOING WHERE?
WE'RE GONNA GO THROUGH THE SEWERS!
THIS CHURCH IS SO OLD, IT'LL LEAD STRAIGHT TO THE NEAREST WATERWAY-- ALL WE HAVE TO DO IS DIG OUR WAY OUT.
VEGAS--?
WE STILL GOT THE CUTTING TOOLS FROM THE BANK JOB--PLAN MIGHT JUST WORK.
I DON'T GET IT--WHY'RE YOU HELPING US, LADY?
BECAUSE...
BECAUSE I DON'T WANT ANYBODY TO GET HURT. OBVIOUSLY.
EYES FORWARD, YOU RAT BASTARDS!

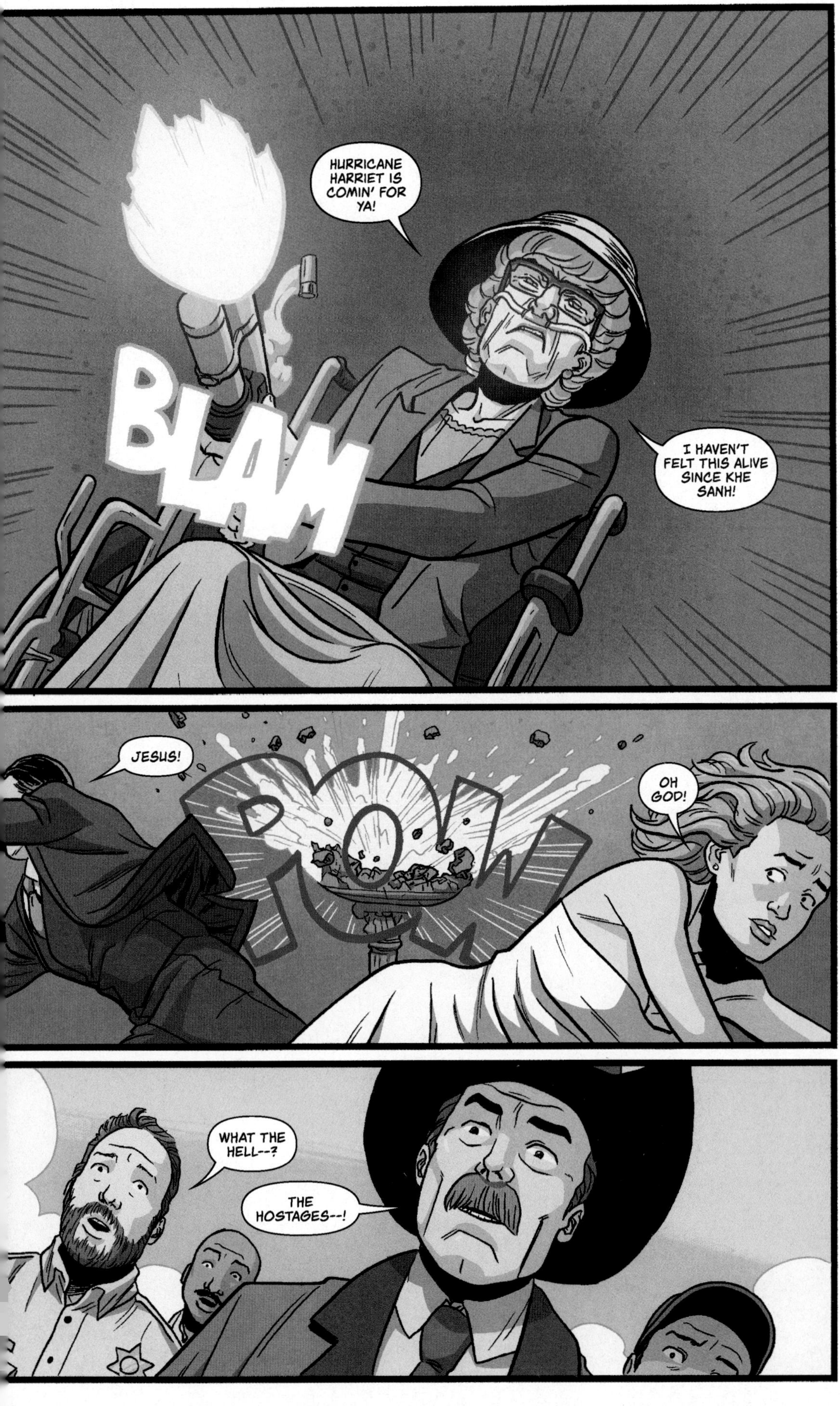
HURRICANE HARRIET IS COMIN' FOR YA!
BLAM
I HAVEN'T FELT THIS ALIVE SINCE KHE SANH!
JESUS!
POW
OH GOD!
WHAT THE HELL--?
THE HOSTAGES--!

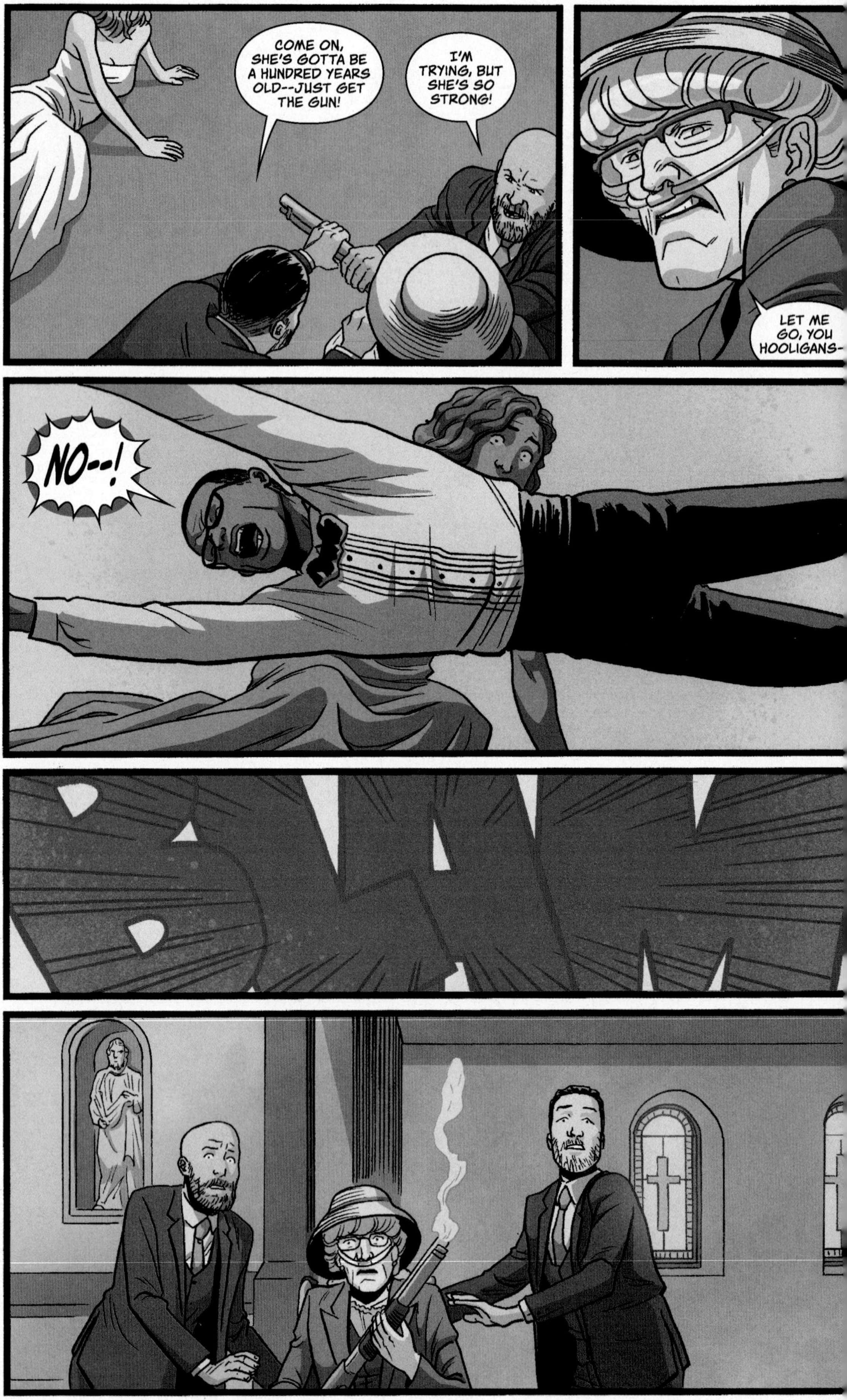
COME ON, SHE'S GOTTA BE A HUNDRED YEARS OLD--JUST GET THE GUN!
I'M TRYING, BUT SHE'S SO STRONG!
LET ME GO, YOU HOOLIGANS-
NO--!

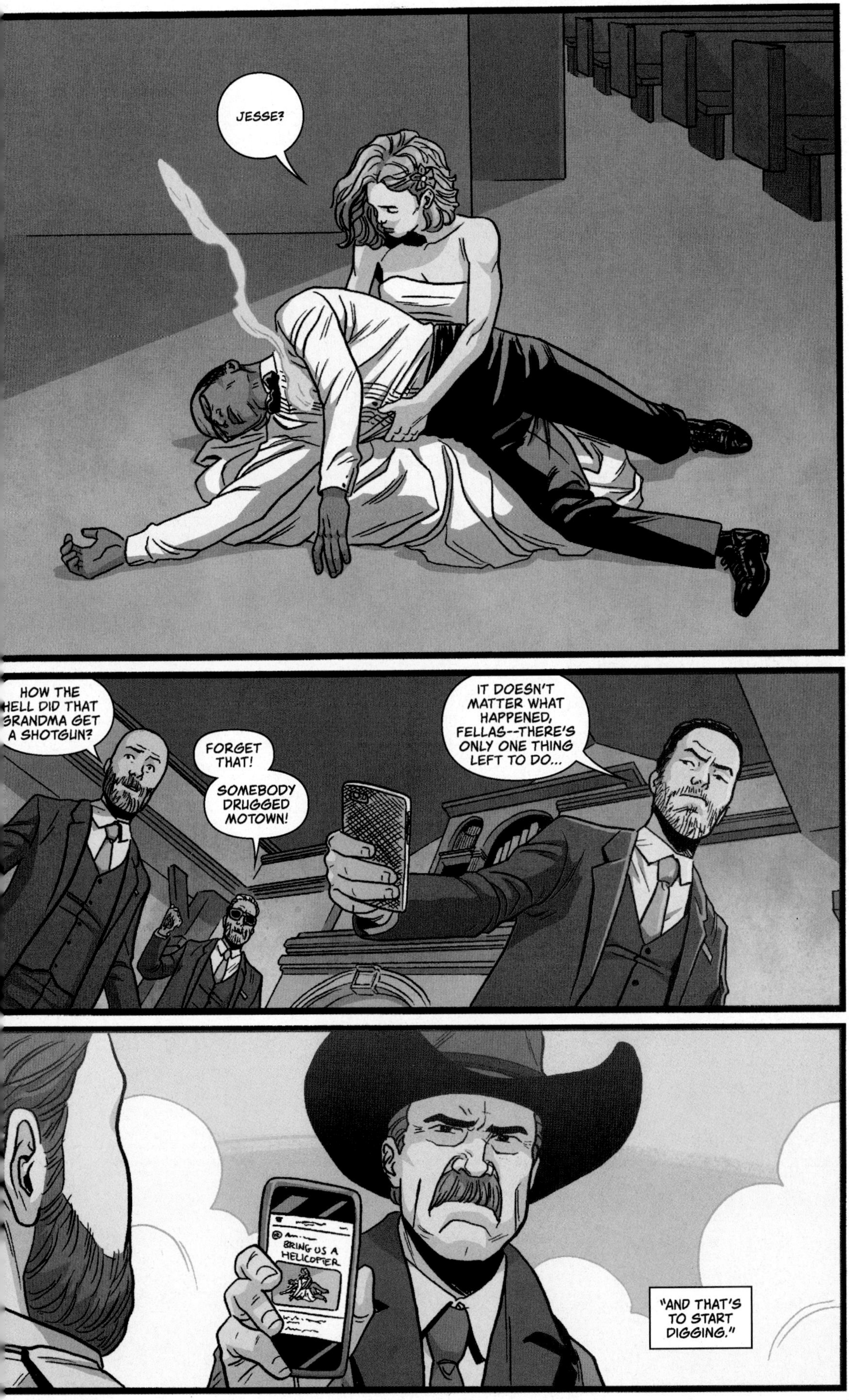
JESSE?
HOW THE HELL DID THAT GRANDMA GET A SHOTGUN?
FORGET THAT!
SOMEBODY DRUGGED MOTOWN!
IT DOESN'T MATTER WHAT HAPPENED, FELLAS--THERE'S ONLY ONE THING LEFT TO DO...
BRING US A HELICOPTER
"AND THAT'S TO START DIGGING."

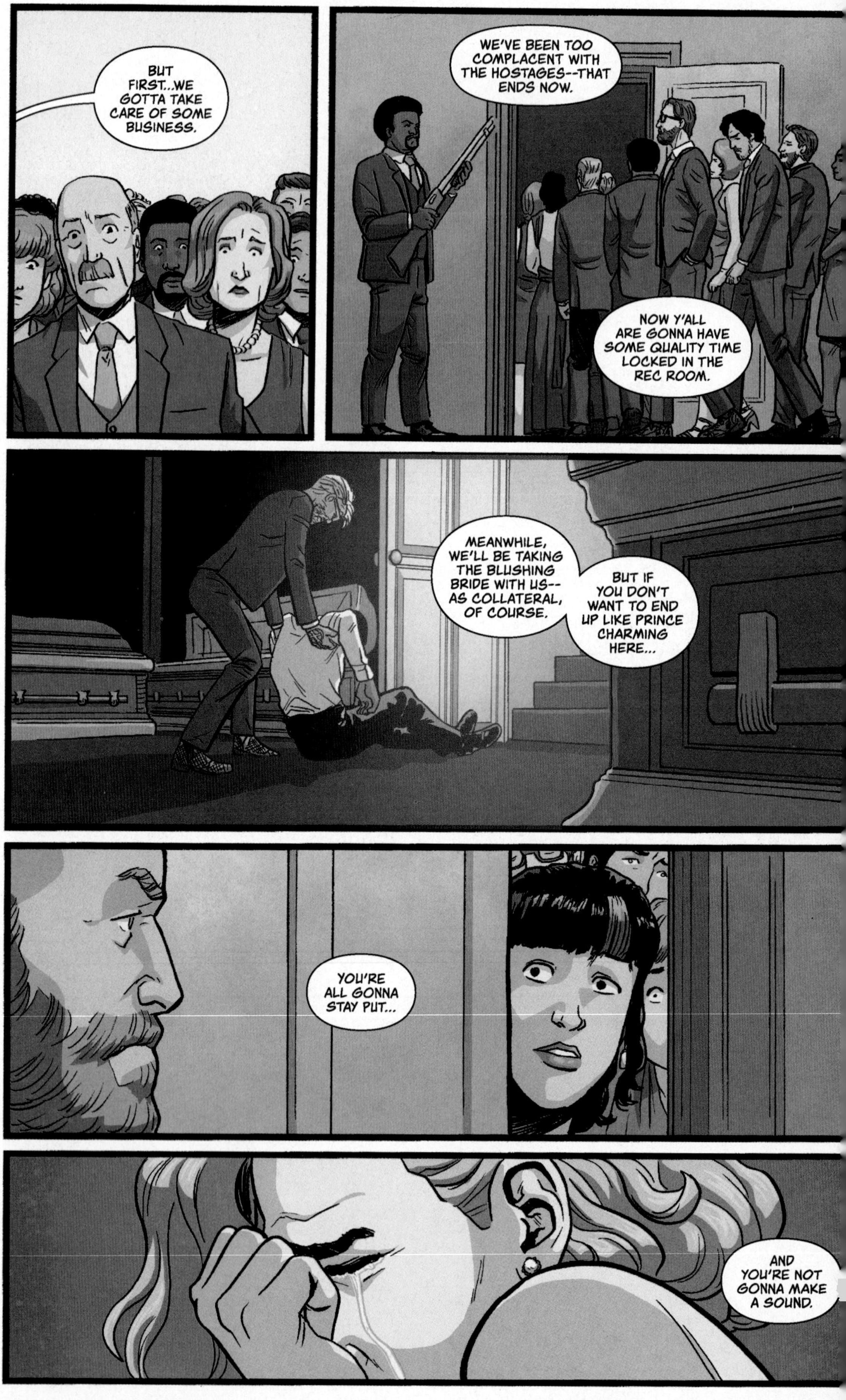

BUT FIRST...WE GOTTA TAKE CARE OF SOME BUSINESS.
WE'VE BEEN TOO COMPLACENT WITH THE HOSTAGES--THAT ENDS NOW.
NOW Y'ALL ARE GONNA HAVE SOME QUALITY TIME LOCKED IN THE REC ROOM.
MEANWHILE, WE'LL BE TAKING THE BLUSHING BRIDE WITH US--AS COLLATERAL, OF COURSE.
BUT IF YOU DON'T WANT TO END UP LIKE PRINCE CHARMING HERE...
YOU'RE ALL GONNA STAY PUT...
AND YOU'RE NOT GONNA MAKE A SOUND.

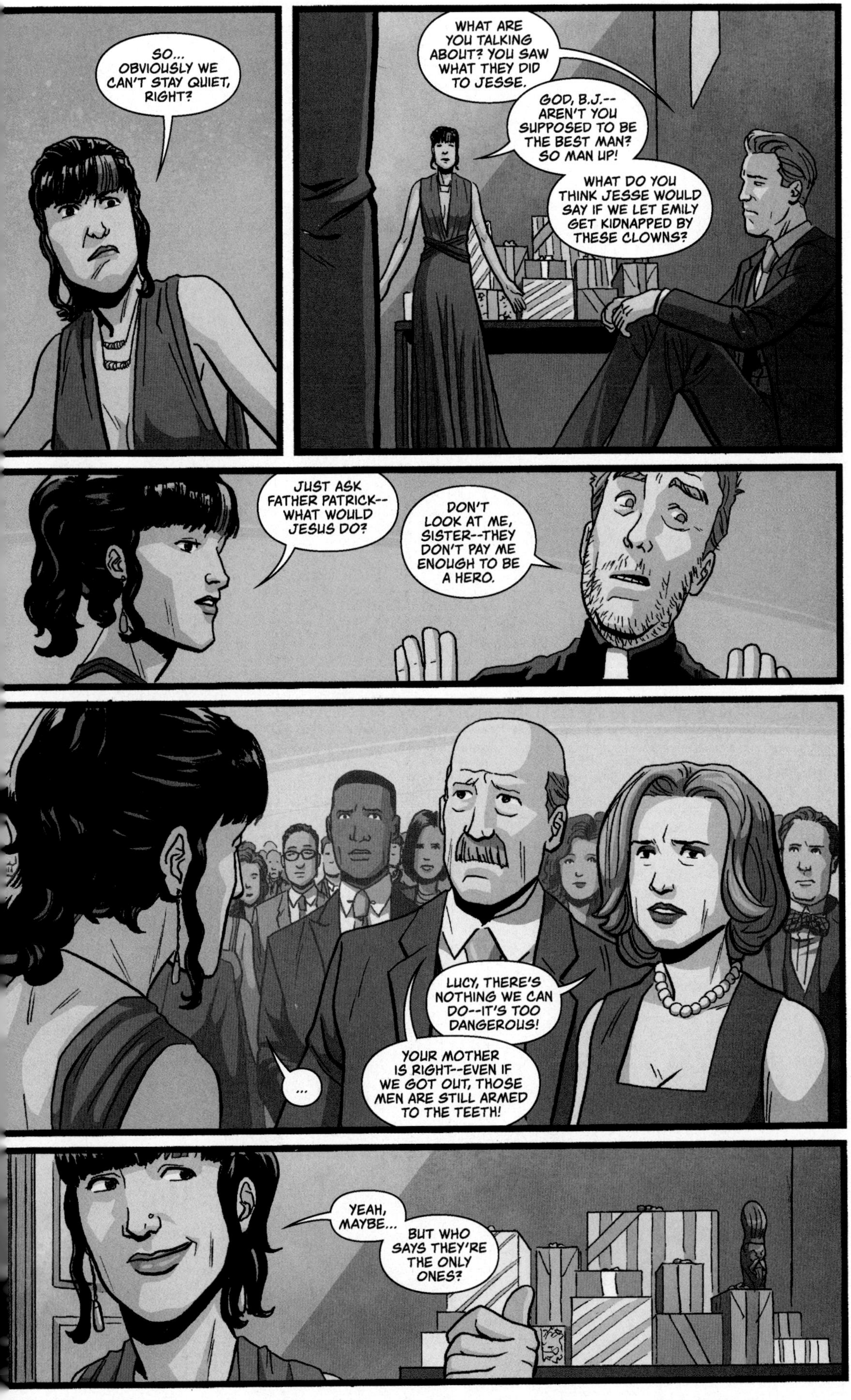
SO... OBVIOUSLY WE CAN'T STAY QUIET, RIGHT?
WHAT ARE YOU TALKING ABOUT? YOU SAW WHAT THEY DID TO JESSE.
GOD, B.J.-- AREN'T YOU SUPPOSED TO BE THE BEST MAN? SO MAN UP!
WHAT DO YOU THINK JESSE WOULD SAY IF WE LET EMILY GET KIDNAPPED BY THESE CLOWNS?
JUST ASK FATHER PATRICK-- WHAT WOULD JESUS DO?
DON'T LOOK AT ME, SISTER--THEY DON'T PAY ME ENOUGH TO BE A HERO.
LUCY, THERE'S NOTHING WE CAN DO--IT'S TOO DANGEROUS!
YOUR MOTHER IS RIGHT--EVEN IF WE GOT OUT, THOSE MEN ARE STILL ARMED TO THE TEETH!
...
YEAH, MAYBE...
BUT WHO SAYS THEY'RE THE ONLY ONES?

EMMS-- WHAT'S WRONG?

TOM... WHAT ARE WE DOING?

WHAT DO YOU--

I MEAN... WE DIG OUT OF HERE AND ESCAPE--THEN WHAT?

WE HIDE FOR THE REST OF OUR LIVES?

OR UNTIL YOU DECIDE TO RUN OFF AGAIN?

RUN--?

I DIDN'T RUN-- I TURNED MYSELF IN! TO KEEP YOU SAFE FROM THE COPS!

SO DON'T TALK TO ME ABOUT RUNNING-- I'M NOT THE ONE BAILING ON THEIR OWN WEDDING!

I--DID YOU HEAR THAT?

DON'T WORRY, EMMS-- THE CAVALRY'S HERE!

YIPPEE-KI-YAY, MOTHERLOVERS!

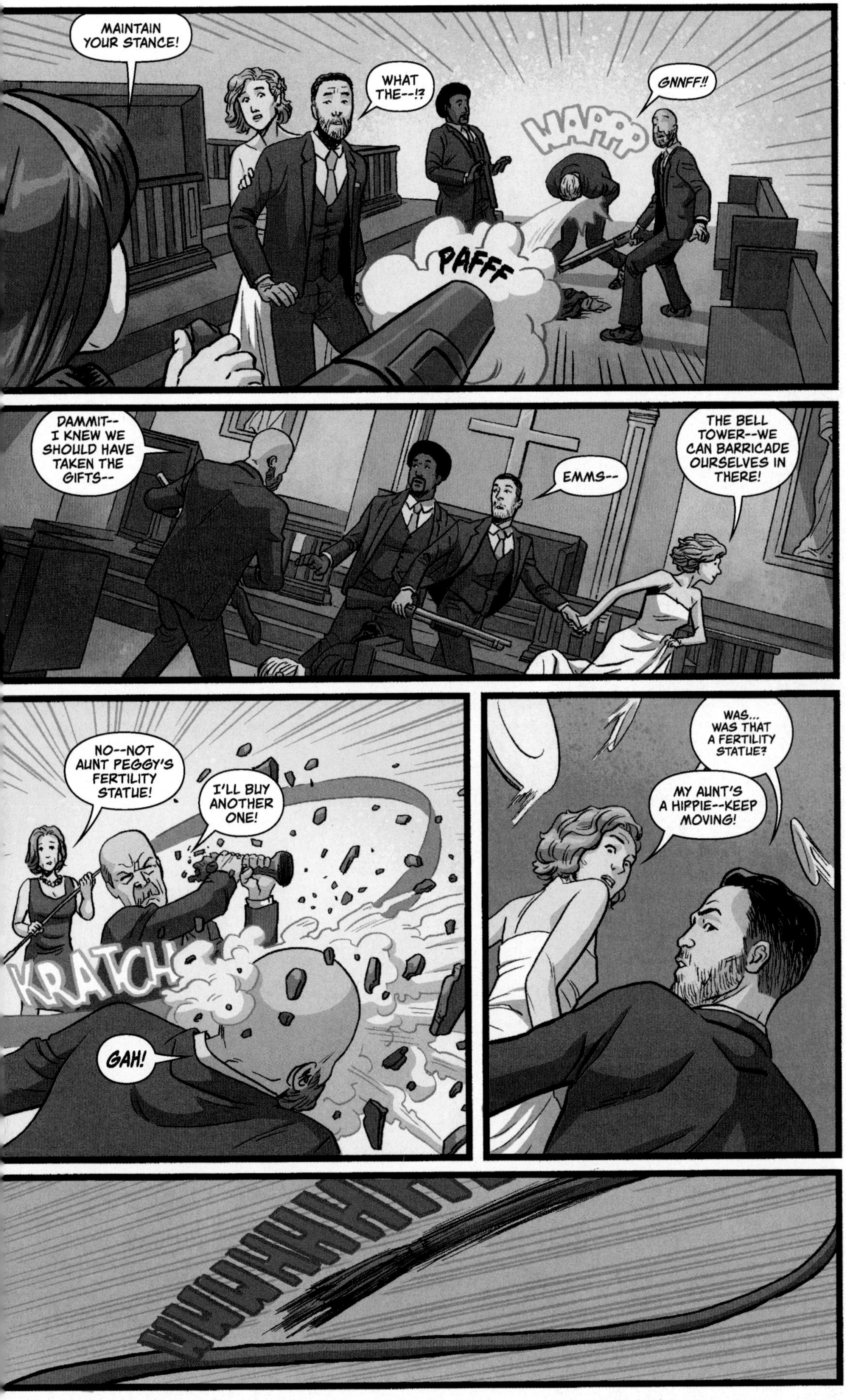

MAINTAIN YOUR STANCE!
WHAT THE--!?
GNNFF!!
WAPPP
PAFFF
DAMMIT-- I KNEW WE SHOULD HAVE TAKEN THE GIFTS--
EMMS--
THE BELL TOWER--WE CAN BARRICADE OURSELVES IN THERE!
NO--NOT AUNT PEGGY'S FERTILITY STATUE!
I'LL BUY ANOTHER ONE!
KRATCH
GAH!
WAS... WAS THAT A FERTILITY STATUE?
MY AUNT'S A HIPPIE--KEEP MOVING!

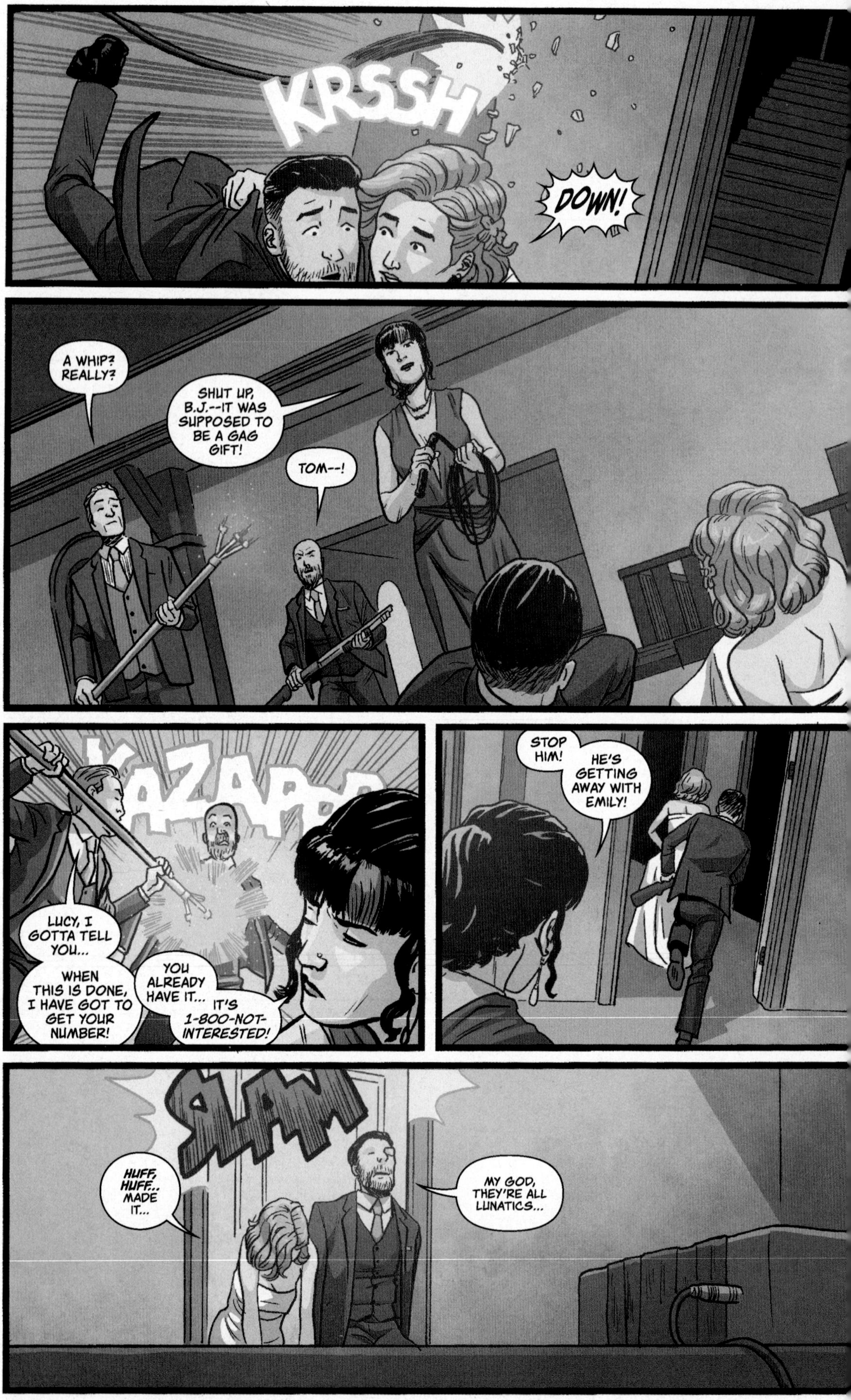
KRSSH
DOWN!
A WHIP? REALLY?
SHUT UP, B.J.--IT WAS SUPPOSED TO BE A GAG GIFT!
TOM--!
LUCY, I GOTTA TELL YOU...
WHEN THIS IS DONE, I HAVE GOT TO GET YOUR NUMBER!
YOU ALREADY HAVE IT...
IT'S 1-800-NOT-INTERESTED!
STOP HIM!
HE'S GETTING AWAY WITH EMILY!
SLAM
HUFF, HUFF... MADE IT...
MY GOD, THEY'RE ALL LUNATICS...

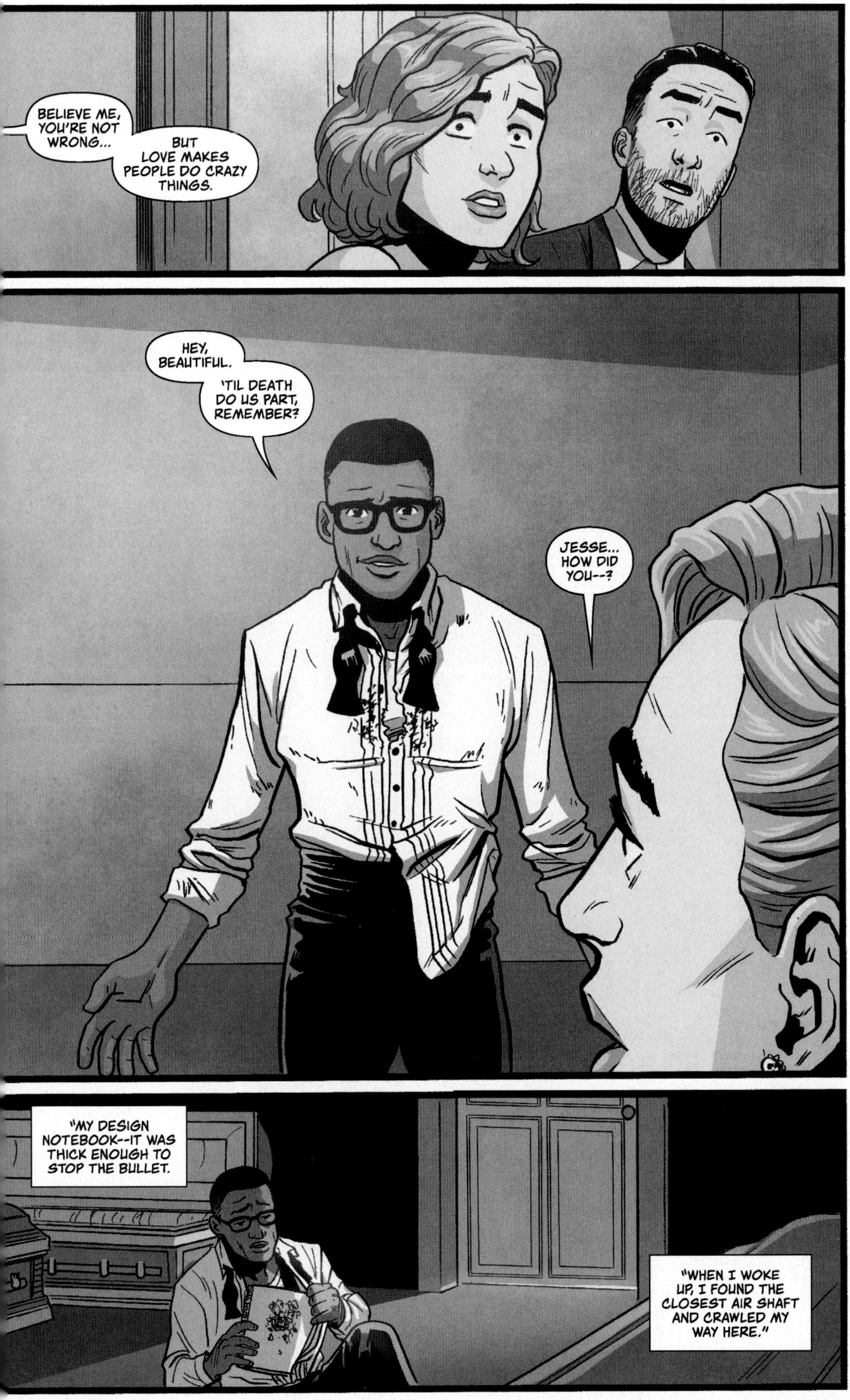

BELIEVE ME, YOU'RE NOT WRONG...
BUT LOVE MAKES PEOPLE DO CRAZY THINGS.
HEY, BEAUTIFUL.
'TIL DEATH DO US PART, REMEMBER?
JESSE... HOW DID YOU--?
"MY DESIGN NOTEBOOK--IT WAS THICK ENOUGH TO STOP THE BULLET.
"WHEN I WOKE UP, I FOUND THE CLOSEST AIR SHAFT AND CRAWLED MY WAY HERE."

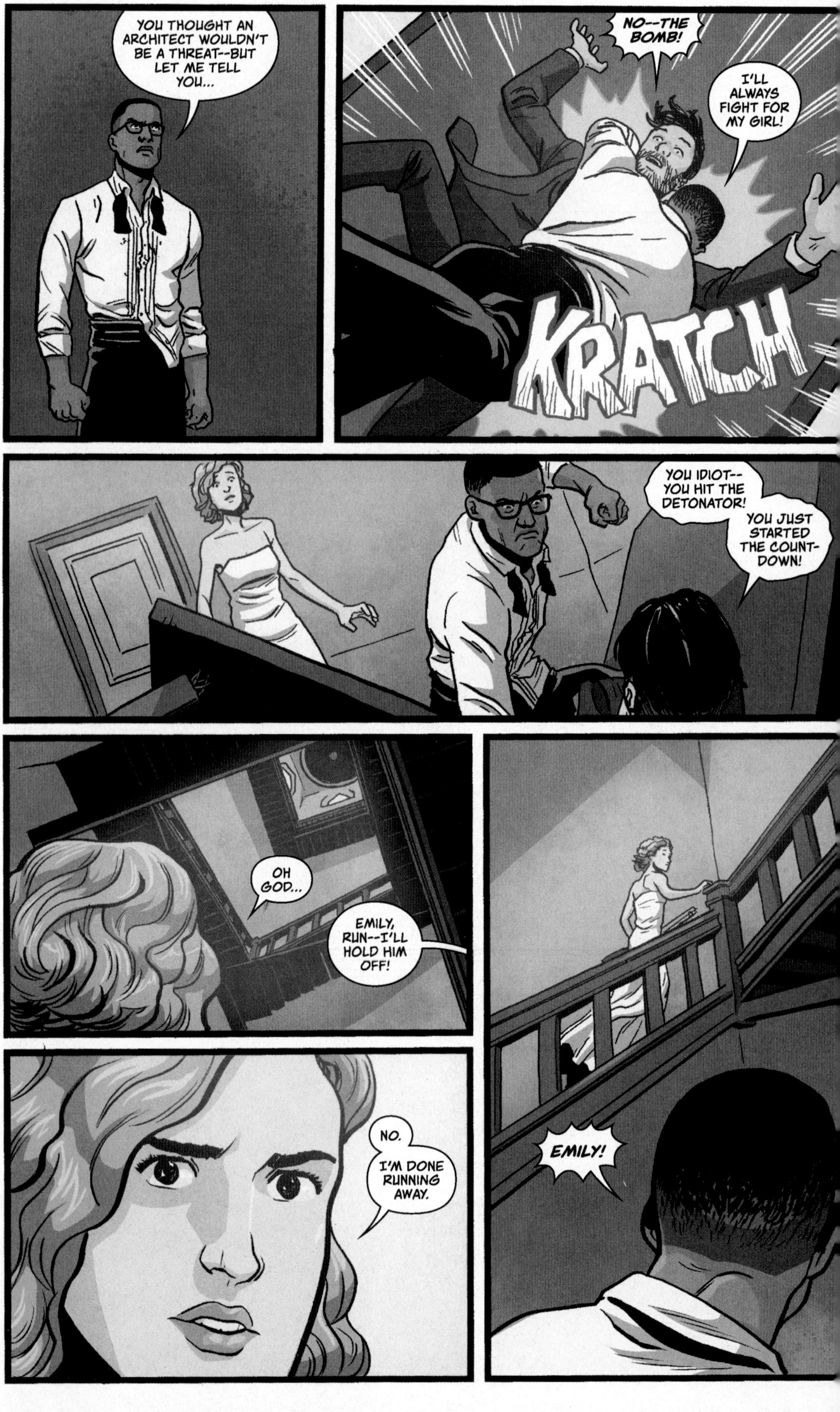

YOU THOUGHT AN ARCHITECT WOULDN'T BE A THREAT--BUT LET ME TELL YOU...
NO--THE BOMB!
I'LL ALWAYS FIGHT FOR MY GIRL!
KRATCH
YOU IDIOT--YOU HIT THE DETONATOR!
YOU JUST STARTED THE COUNT-DOWN!
OH GOD...
EMILY, RUN--I'LL HOLD HIM OFF!
EMILY!
NO.
I'M DONE RUNNING AWAY.

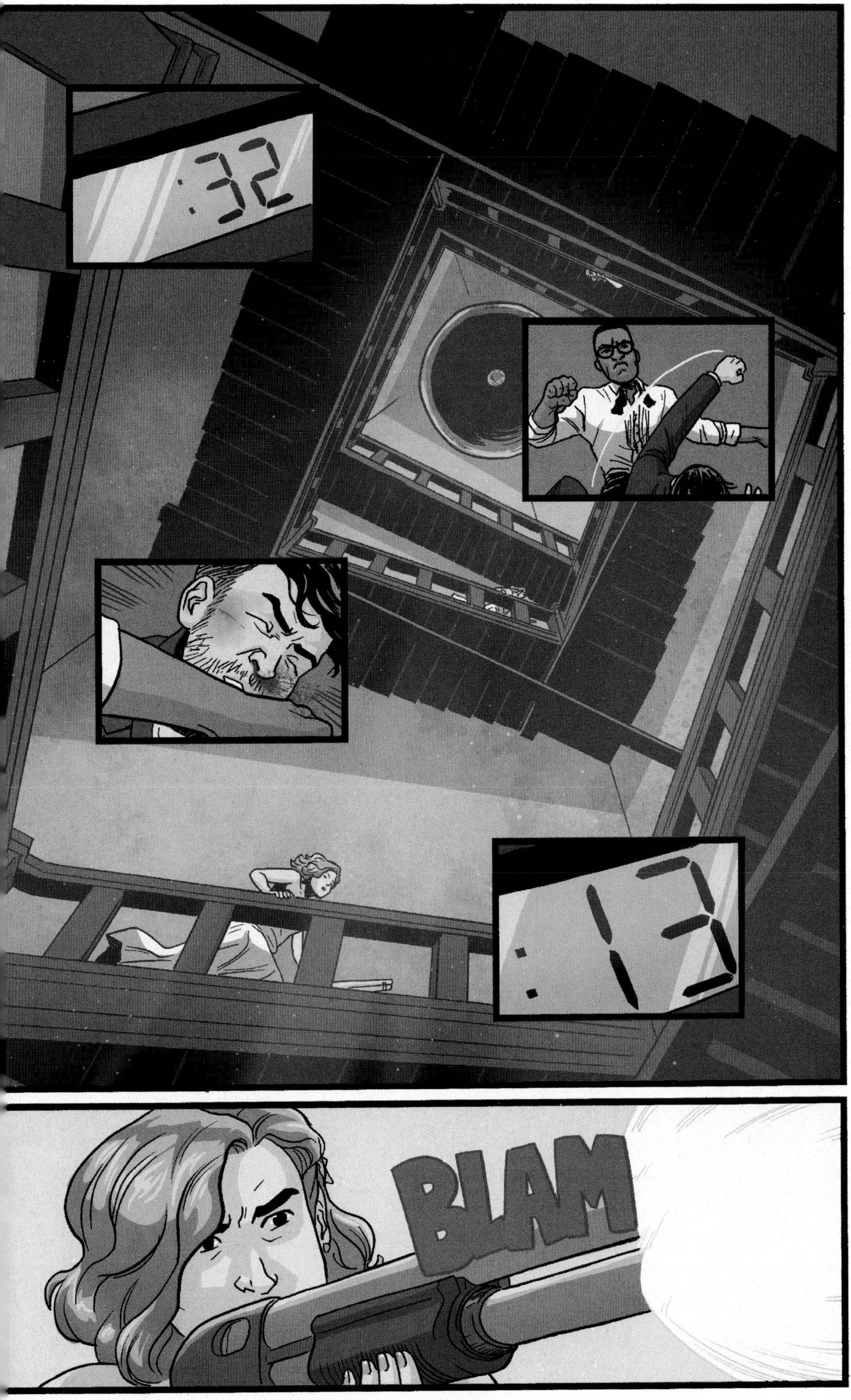

:32
:13
BLAM

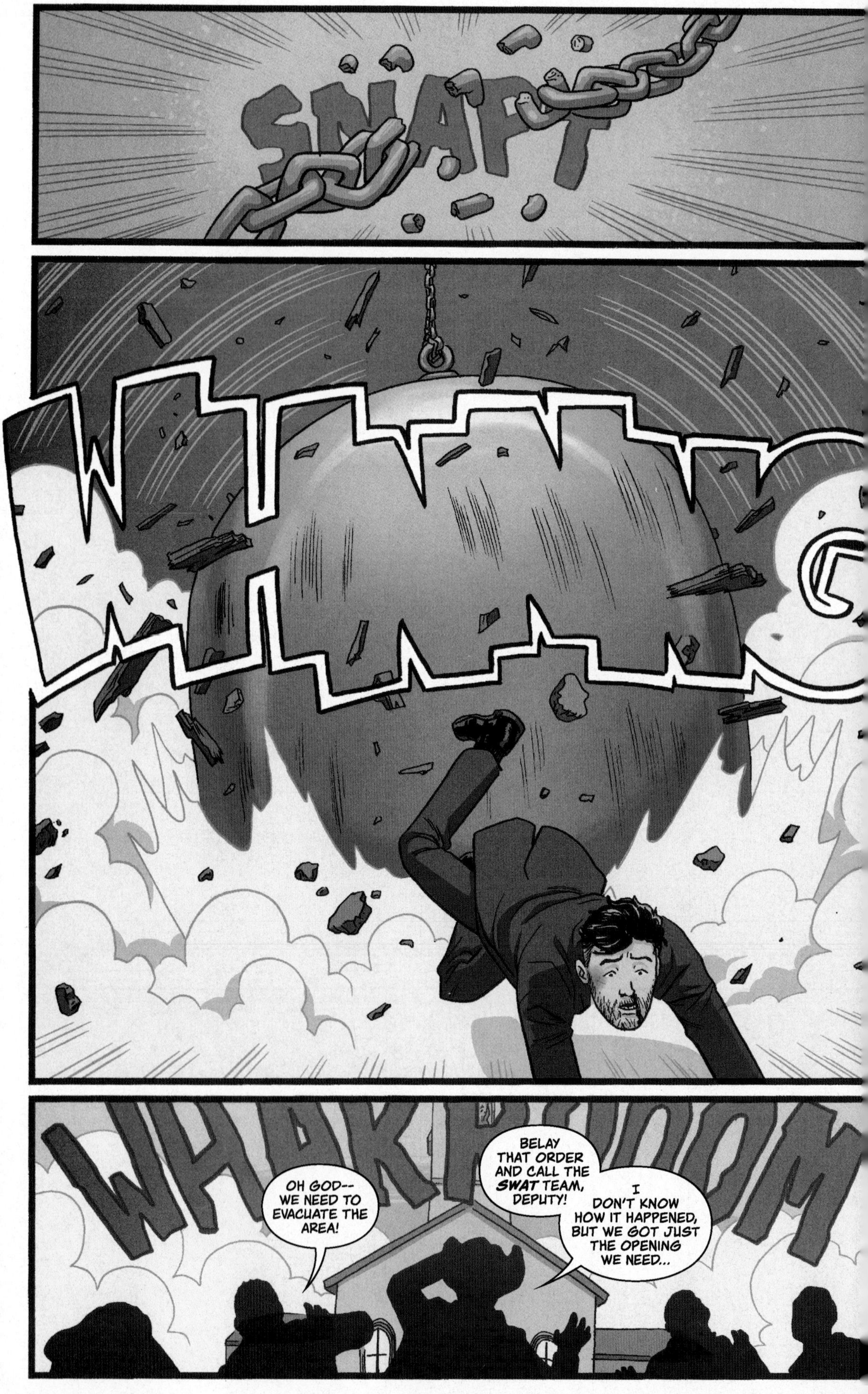
SNAP
WHANG
WHARROOOM
OH GOD-- WE NEED TO EVACUATE THE AREA!
BELAY THAT ORDER AND CALL THE SWAT TEAM, DEPUTY!
I DON'T KNOW HOW IT HAPPENED, BUT WE GOT JUST THE OPENING WE NEED...

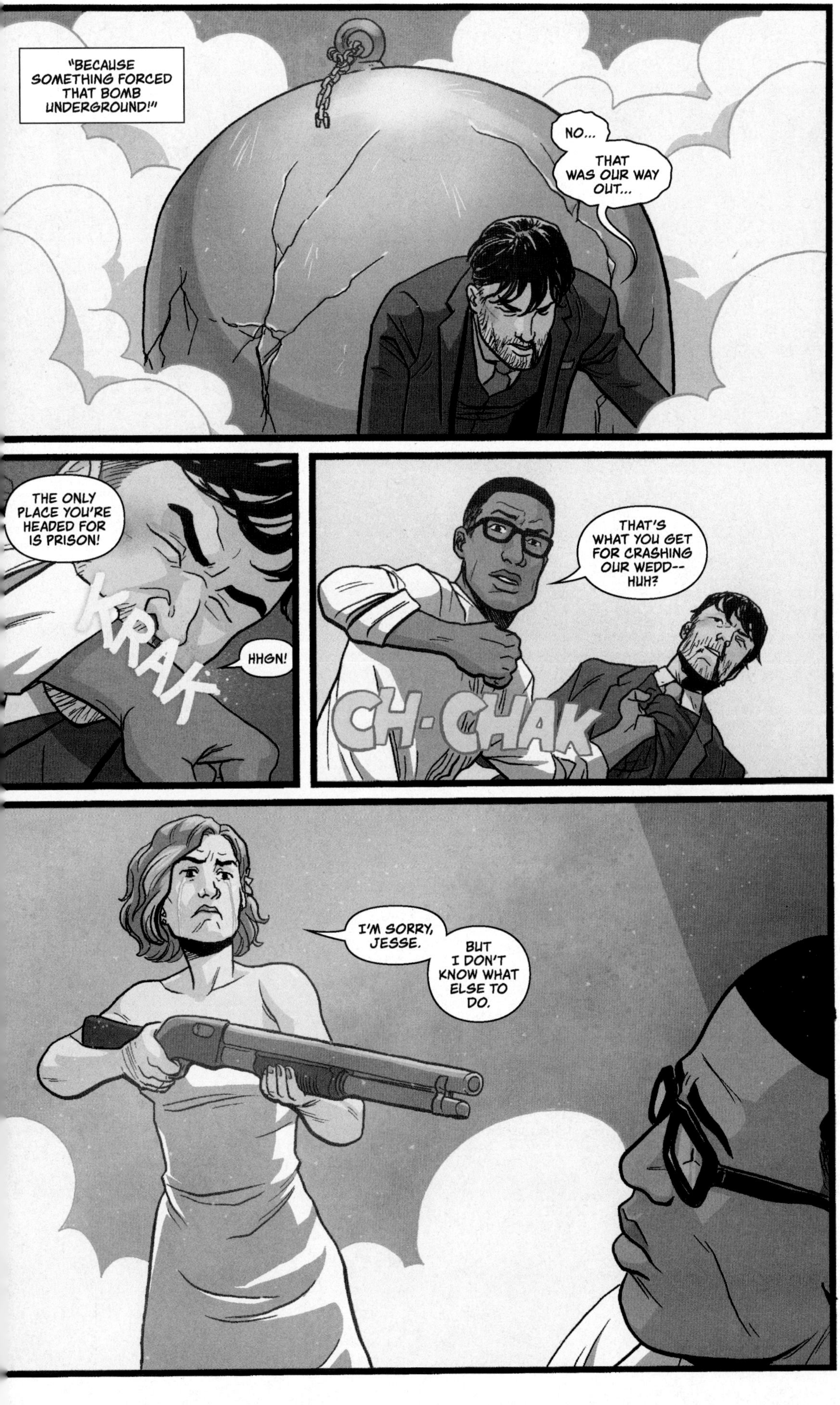
"BECAUSE SOMETHING FORCED THAT BOMB UNDERGROUND!"
NO...
THAT WAS OUR WAY OUT...
THE ONLY PLACE YOU'RE HEADED FOR IS PRISON!
KRAK
HHGN!
THAT'S WHAT YOU GET FOR CRASHING OUR WEDD-- HUH?
CH-CHAK
I'M SORRY, JESSE.
BUT I DON'T KNOW WHAT ELSE TO DO.

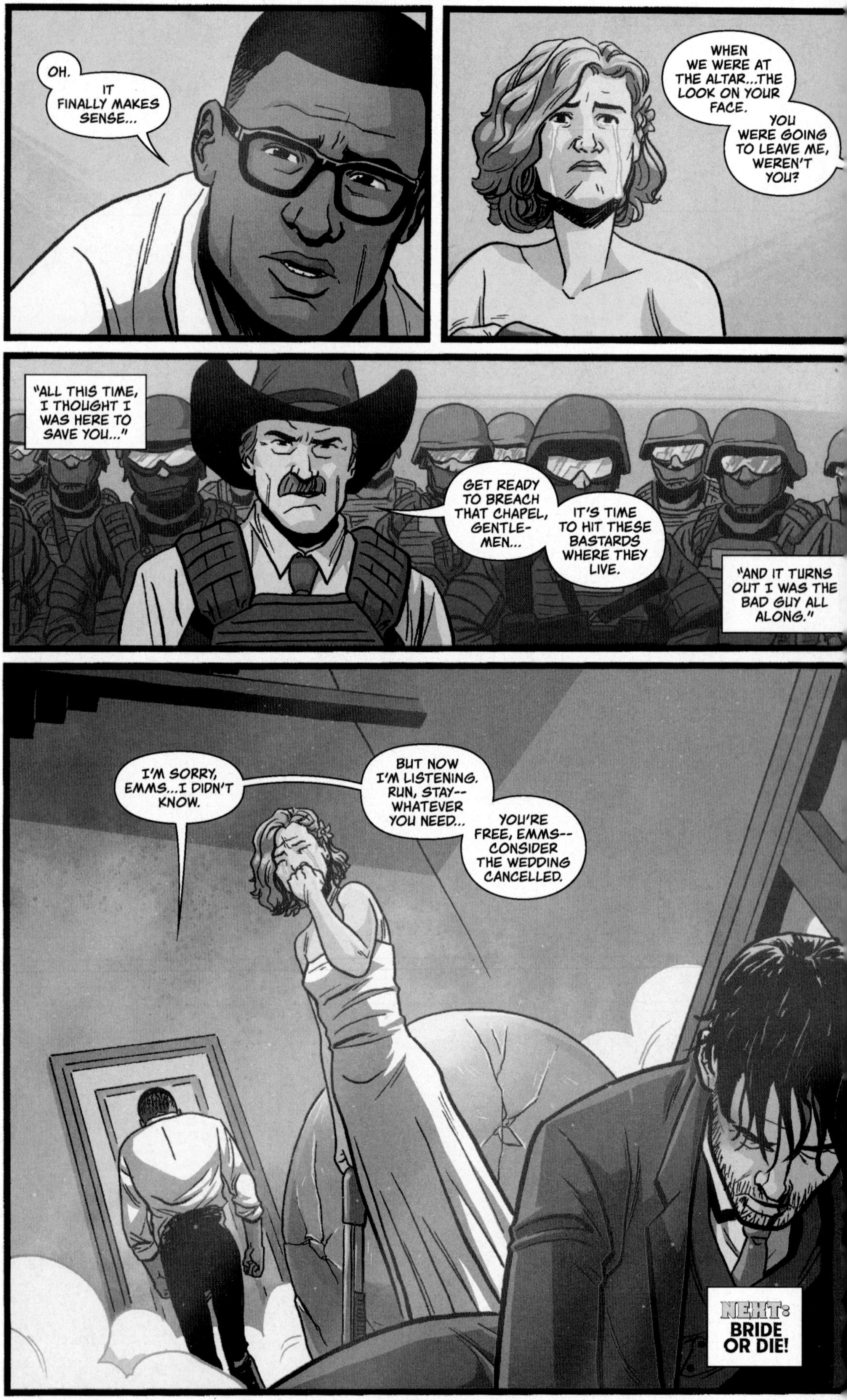
OH.
IT FINALLY MAKES SENSE...
WHEN WE WERE AT THE ALTAR...THE LOOK ON YOUR FACE.
YOU WERE GOING TO LEAVE ME, WEREN'T YOU?
"ALL THIS TIME, I THOUGHT I WAS HERE TO SAVE YOU..."
GET READY TO BREACH THAT CHAPEL, GENTLE-MEN...
IT'S TIME TO HIT THESE BASTARDS WHERE THEY LIVE.
"AND IT TURNS OUT I WAS THE BAD GUY ALL ALONG."
I'M SORRY, EMMS...I DIDN'T KNOW.
BUT NOW I'M LISTENING. RUN, STAY-- WHATEVER YOU NEED...
YOU'RE FREE, EMMS-- CONSIDER THE WEDDING CANCELLED.
NEXT: BRIDE OR DIE!

CHAPTER FOUR

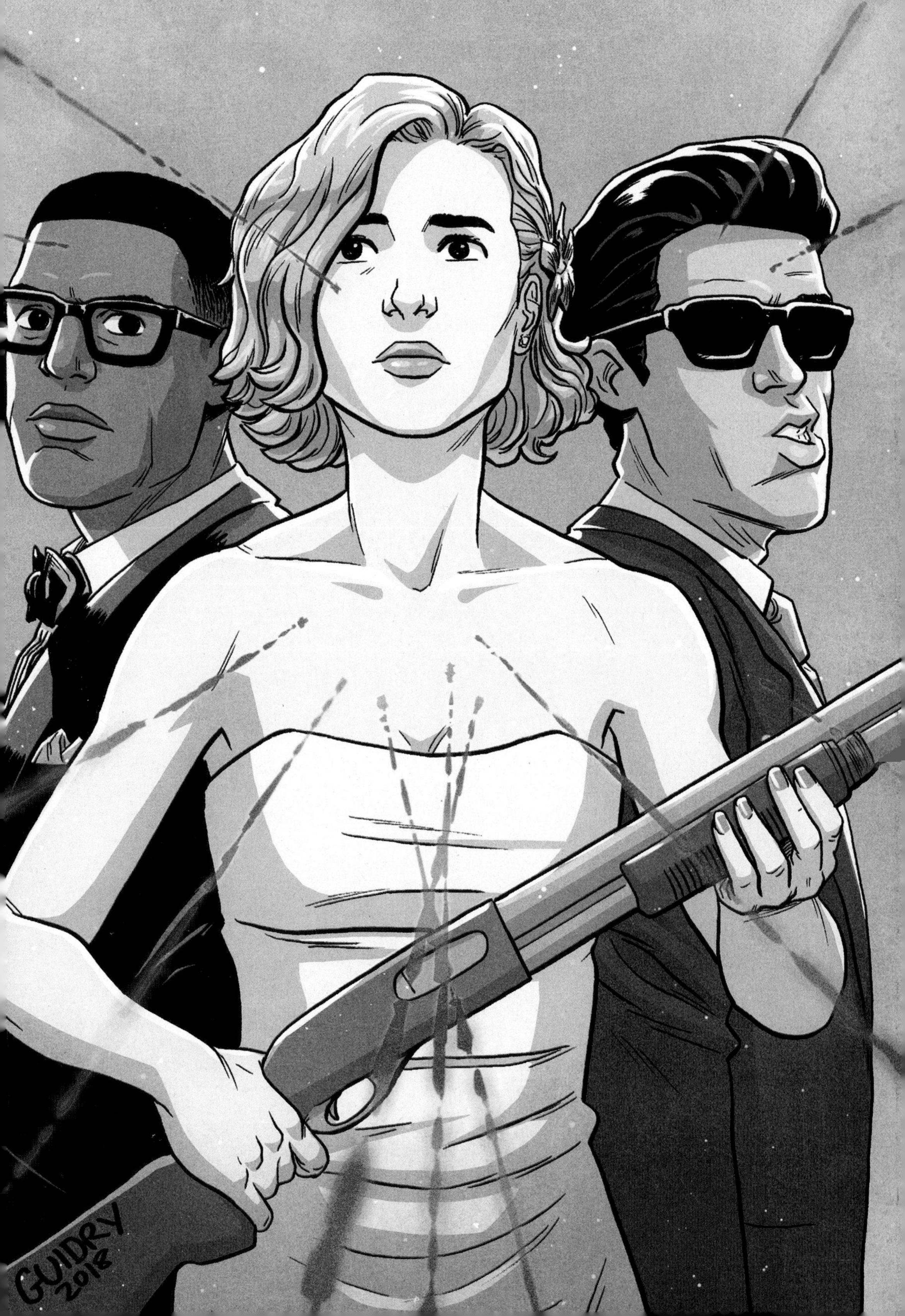
GUIDRY
2018

Going to the CHAPEL

4

Written by
DAVID PEPOSE

Art by
GAVIN GUIDRY

Colors by
ELIZABETH KRAMER

Lettering by
ARIANA MAHER

Covers by
JOHANNA THE MAD, MAAN HOUSE AND GAVIN GUIDRY

Chapel Of Love
Words and Music by Phil Spector, Ellie Greenwich and Jeff Barry
Copyright (c) 1964 UNIVERSAL - SONGS OF POLYGRAM INTERNATIONAL, INC., TRIO MUSIC
COMPANY and MOTHER BERTHA MUSIC, INC.
Copyright Renewed
All Rights for TRIO MUSIC COMPANY Administered by BMG RIGHTS MANAGEMENT (US) LLC
All Rights for MOTHER BERTHA MUSIC, INC. Controlled and Administered by EMI APRIL MUSIC INC.
All Rights Reserved Used by Permission
Reprinted by Permission of Hal Leonard LLC

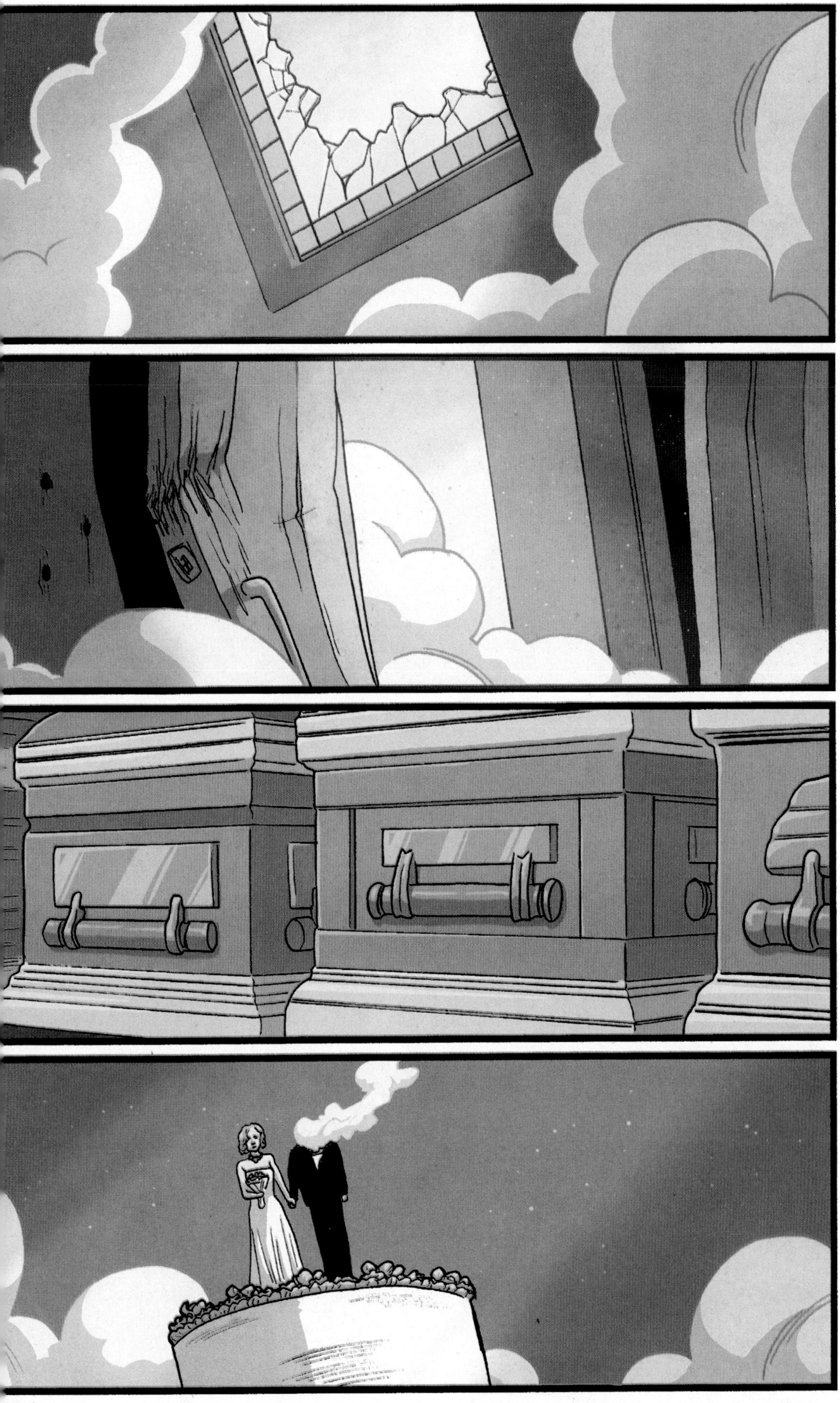

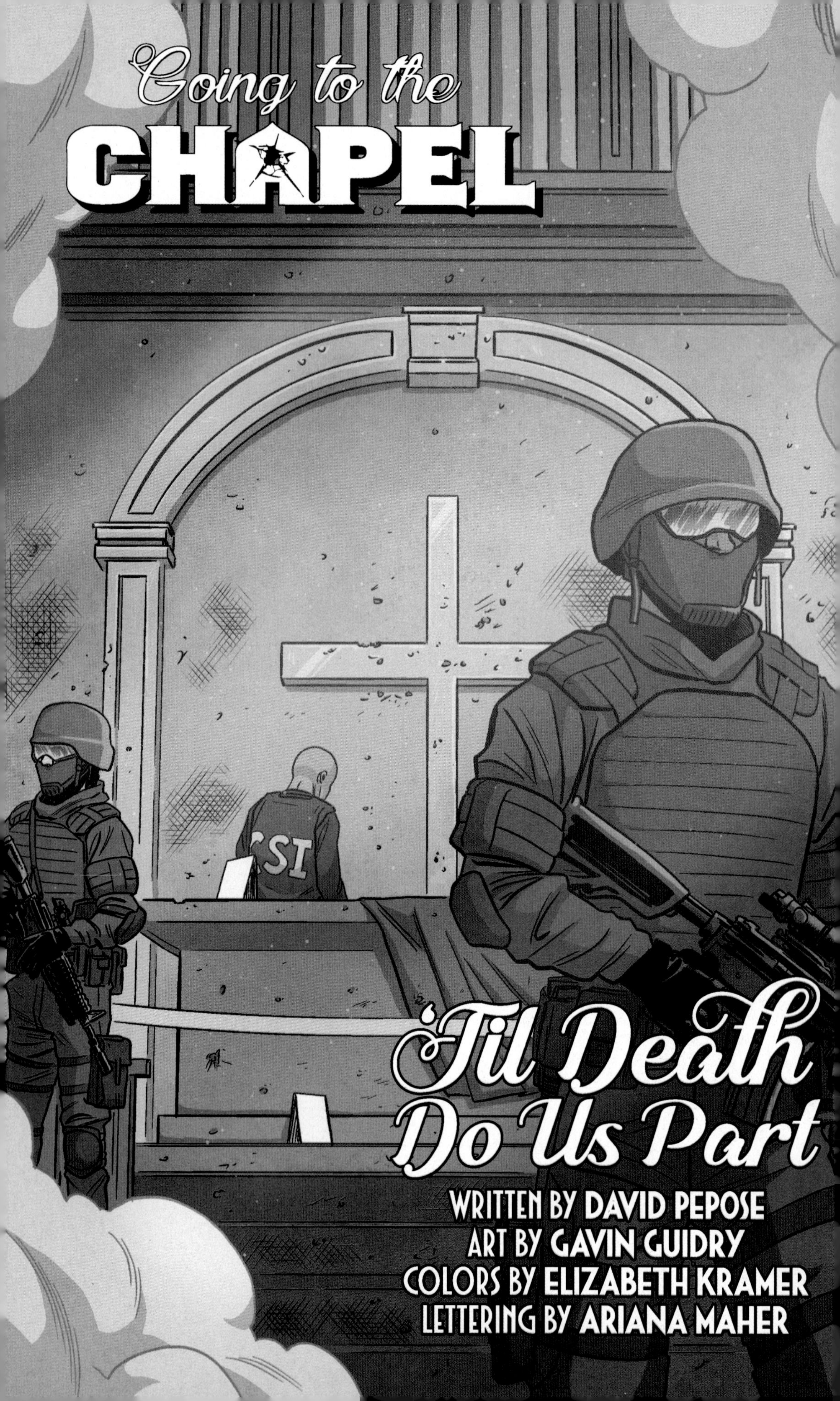

Going to the
CHAPEL
CSI
'Til Death Do Us Part
WRITTEN BY DAVID PEPOSE
ART BY GAVIN GUIDRY
COLORS BY ELIZABETH KRAMER
LETTERING BY ARIANA MAHER

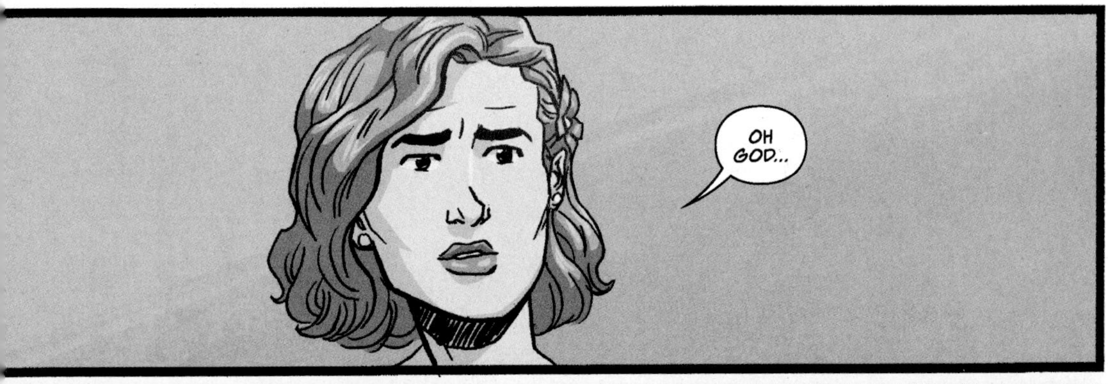
OH
GOD...

ONE HOUR AGO

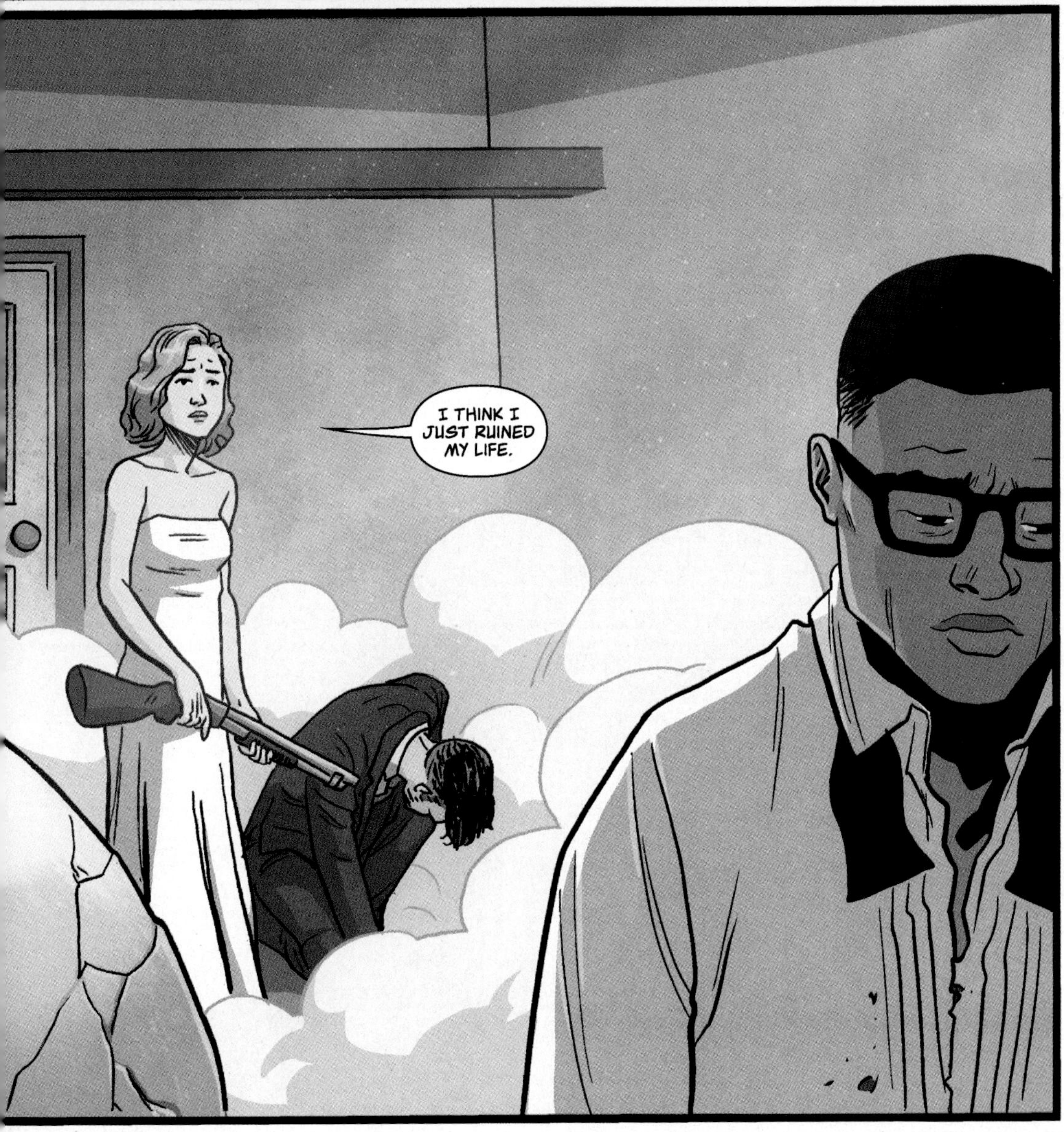
I THINK I
JUST RUINED
MY LIFE.

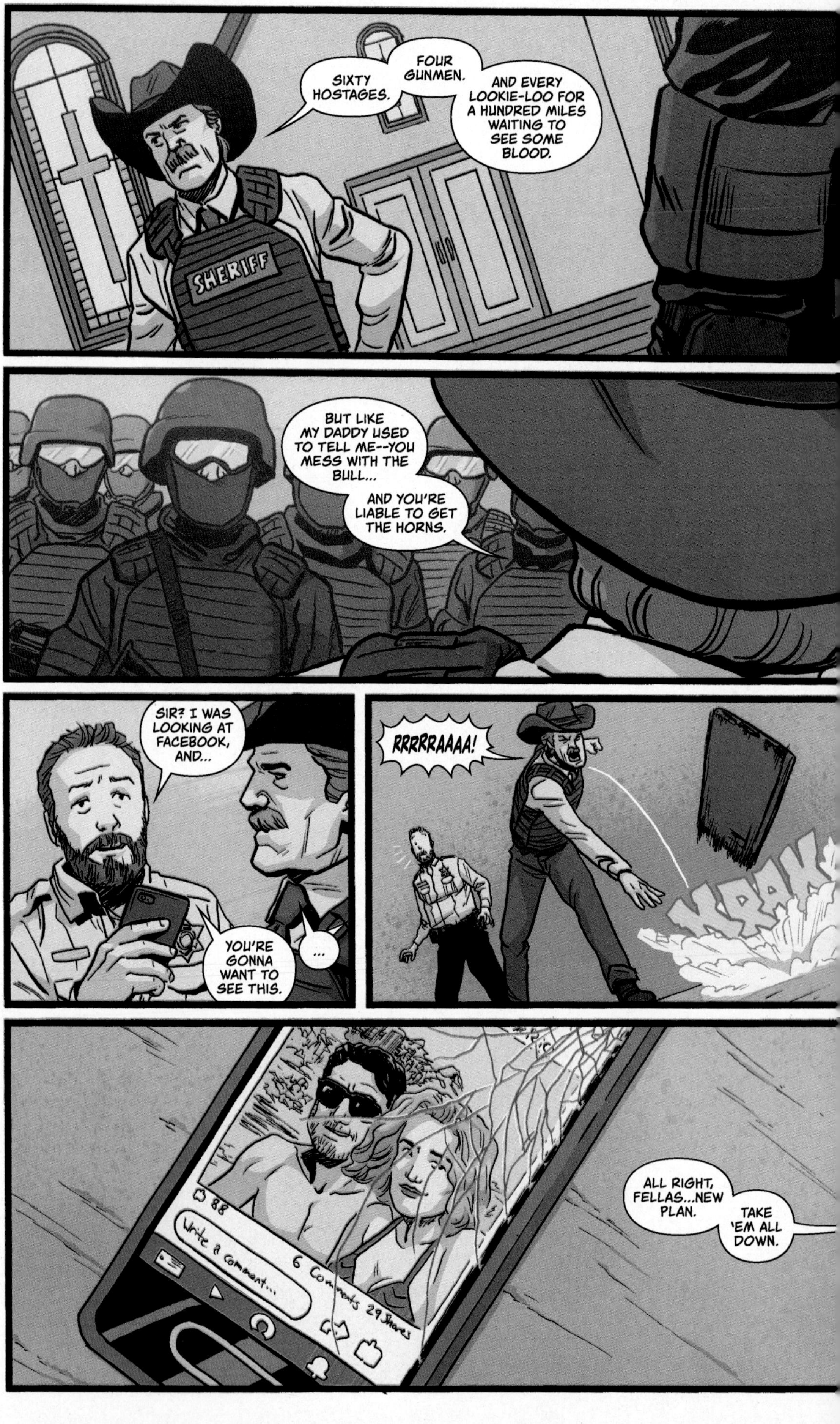
SIXTY HOSTAGES.
FOUR GUNMEN.
AND EVERY LOOKIE-LOO FOR A HUNDRED MILES WAITING TO SEE SOME BLOOD.
SHERIFF
BUT LIKE MY DADDY USED TO TELL ME--YOU MESS WITH THE BULL...
AND YOU'RE LIABLE TO GET THE HORNS.
SIR? I WAS LOOKING AT FACEBOOK, AND...
YOU'RE GONNA WANT TO SEE THIS.
...
RRRRRAAAAA!
88
Write a comment...
6 Comments 29 Shares
ALL RIGHT, FELLAS...NEW PLAN.
TAKE 'EM ALL DOWN.

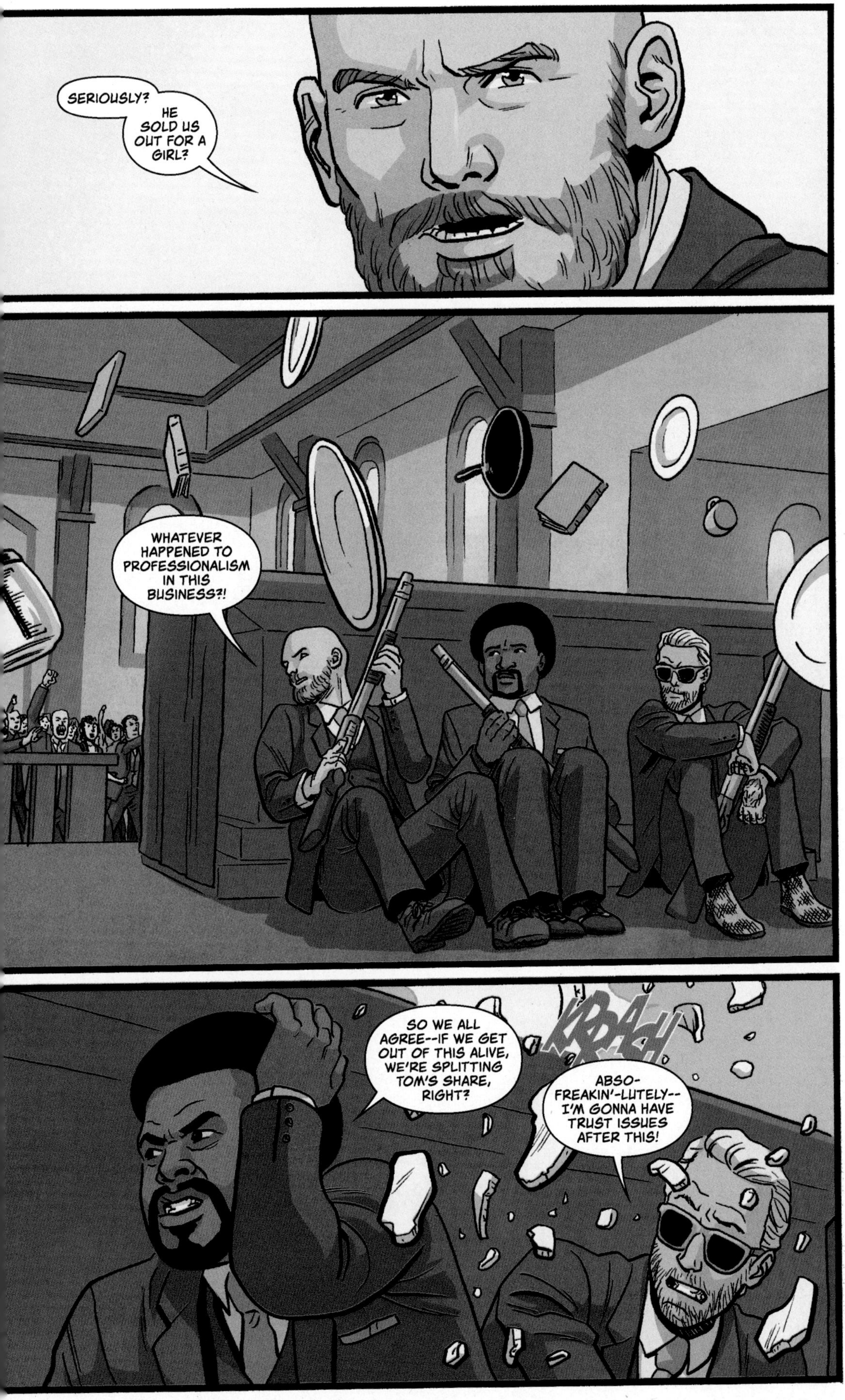
SERIOUSLY? HE SOLD US OUT FOR A GIRL?
WHATEVER HAPPENED TO PROFESSIONALISM IN THIS BUSINESS?!
SO WE ALL AGREE--IF WE GET OUT OF THIS ALIVE, WE'RE SPLITTING TOM'S SHARE, RIGHT?
KRASH
ABSO-FREAKIN'-LUTELY--I'M GONNA HAVE TRUST ISSUES AFTER THIS!

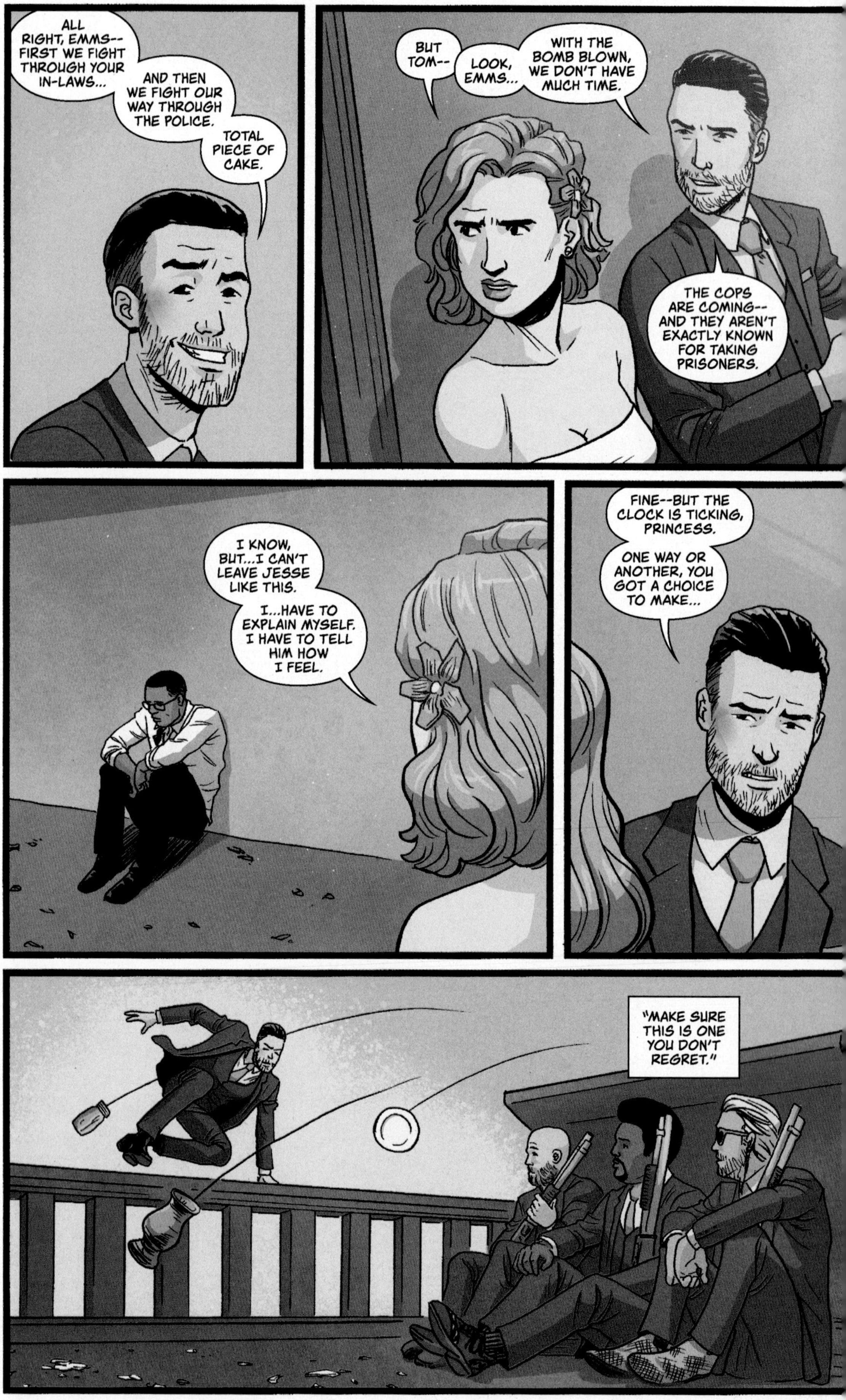
ALL RIGHT, EMMS-- FIRST WE FIGHT THROUGH YOUR IN-LAWS...
AND THEN WE FIGHT OUR WAY THROUGH THE POLICE.
TOTAL PIECE OF CAKE.
BUT TOM--
LOOK, EMMS...
WITH THE BOMB BLOWN, WE DON'T HAVE MUCH TIME.
THE COPS ARE COMING-- AND THEY AREN'T EXACTLY KNOWN FOR TAKING PRISONERS.
I KNOW, BUT...I CAN'T LEAVE JESSE LIKE THIS.
I...HAVE TO EXPLAIN MYSELF. I HAVE TO TELL HIM HOW I FEEL.
FINE--BUT THE CLOCK IS TICKING, PRINCESS.
ONE WAY OR ANOTHER, YOU GOT A CHOICE TO MAKE...
"MAKE SURE THIS IS ONE YOU DON'T REGRET."

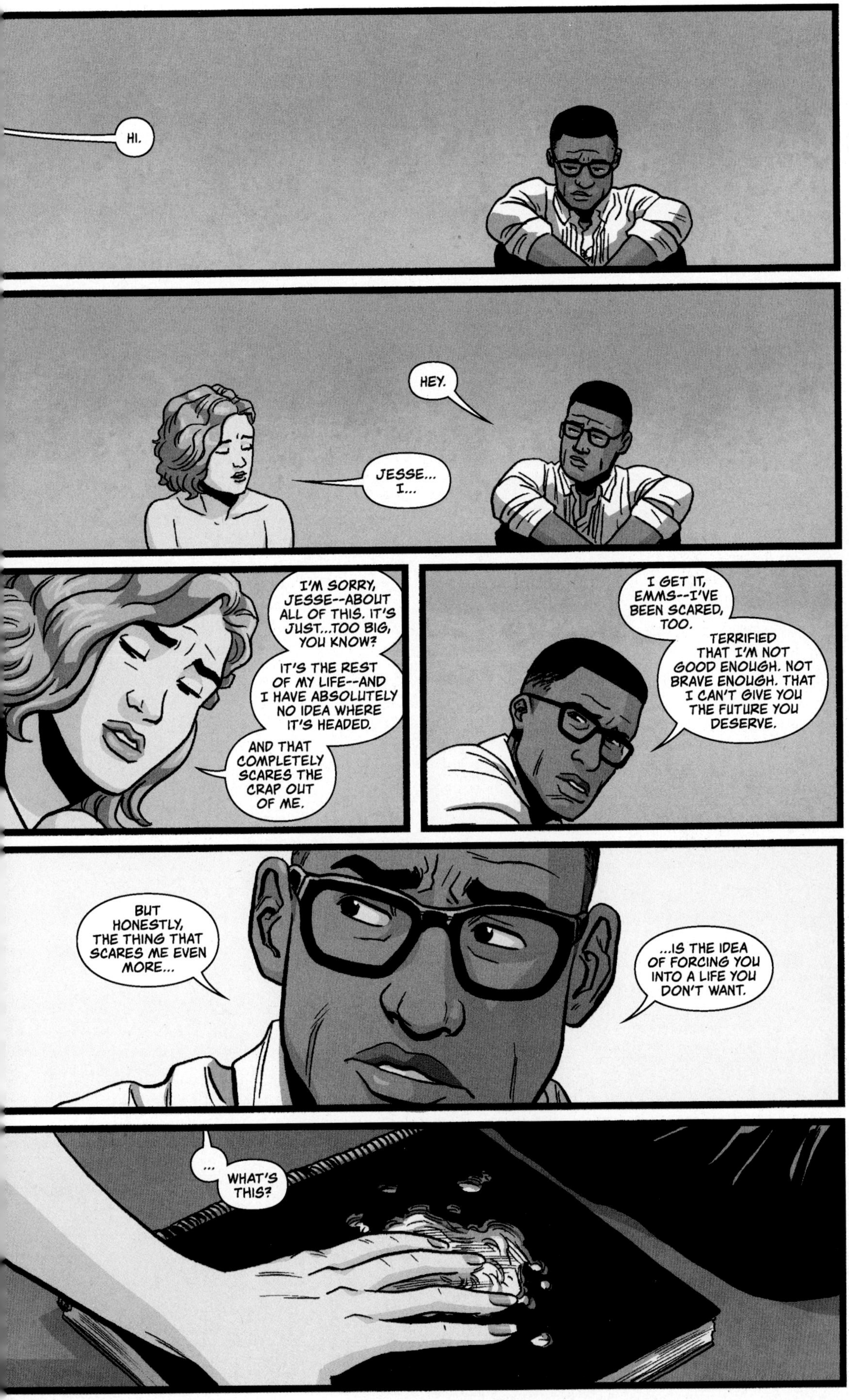
HI.
HEY.
JESSE... I...
I'M SORRY, JESSE--ABOUT ALL OF THIS. IT'S JUST...TOO BIG, YOU KNOW?
IT'S THE REST OF MY LIFE--AND I HAVE ABSOLUTELY NO IDEA WHERE IT'S HEADED.
AND THAT COMPLETELY SCARES THE CRAP OUT OF ME.
I GET IT, EMMS--I'VE BEEN SCARED, TOO.
TERRIFIED THAT I'M NOT GOOD ENOUGH. NOT BRAVE ENOUGH. THAT I CAN'T GIVE YOU THE FUTURE YOU DESERVE.
BUT HONESTLY, THE THING THAT SCARES ME EVEN MORE...
...IS THE IDEA OF FORCING YOU INTO A LIFE YOU DON'T WANT.
...
WHAT'S THIS?

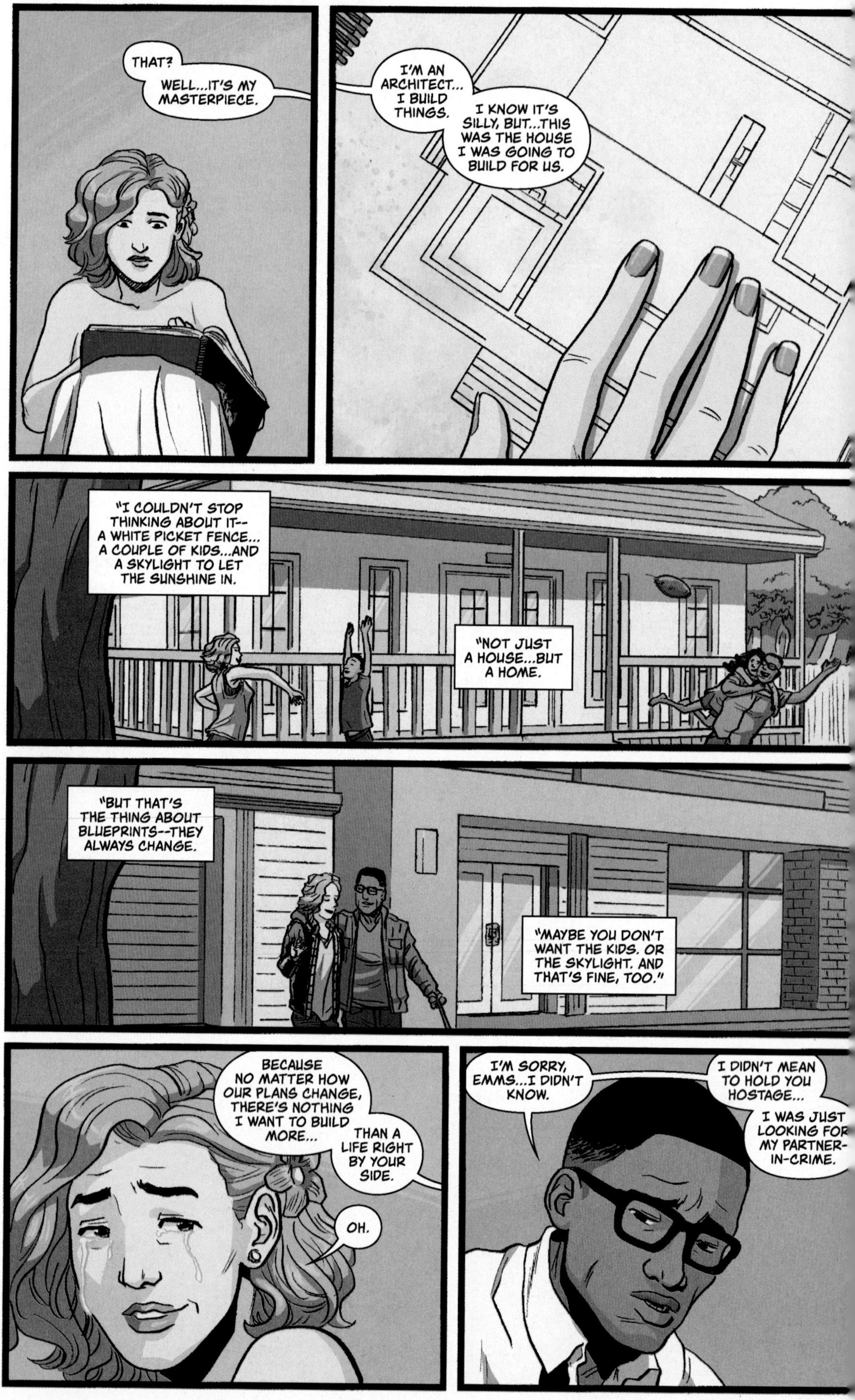
THAT?
WELL...IT'S MY MASTERPIECE.
I'M AN ARCHITECT... I BUILD THINGS.
I KNOW IT'S SILLY, BUT...THIS WAS THE HOUSE I WAS GOING TO BUILD FOR US.
"I COULDN'T STOP THINKING ABOUT IT-- A WHITE PICKET FENCE... A COUPLE OF KIDS...AND A SKYLIGHT TO LET THE SUNSHINE IN.
"NOT JUST A HOUSE...BUT A HOME.
"BUT THAT'S THE THING ABOUT BLUEPRINTS--THEY ALWAYS CHANGE.
"MAYBE YOU DON'T WANT THE KIDS. OR THE SKYLIGHT. AND THAT'S FINE, TOO."
BECAUSE NO MATTER HOW OUR PLANS CHANGE, THERE'S NOTHING I WANT TO BUILD MORE...
THAN A LIFE RIGHT BY YOUR SIDE.
OH.
I'M SORRY, EMMS...I DIDN'T KNOW.
I DIDN'T MEAN TO HOLD YOU HOSTAGE...
I WAS JUST LOOKING FOR MY PARTNER-IN-CRIME.

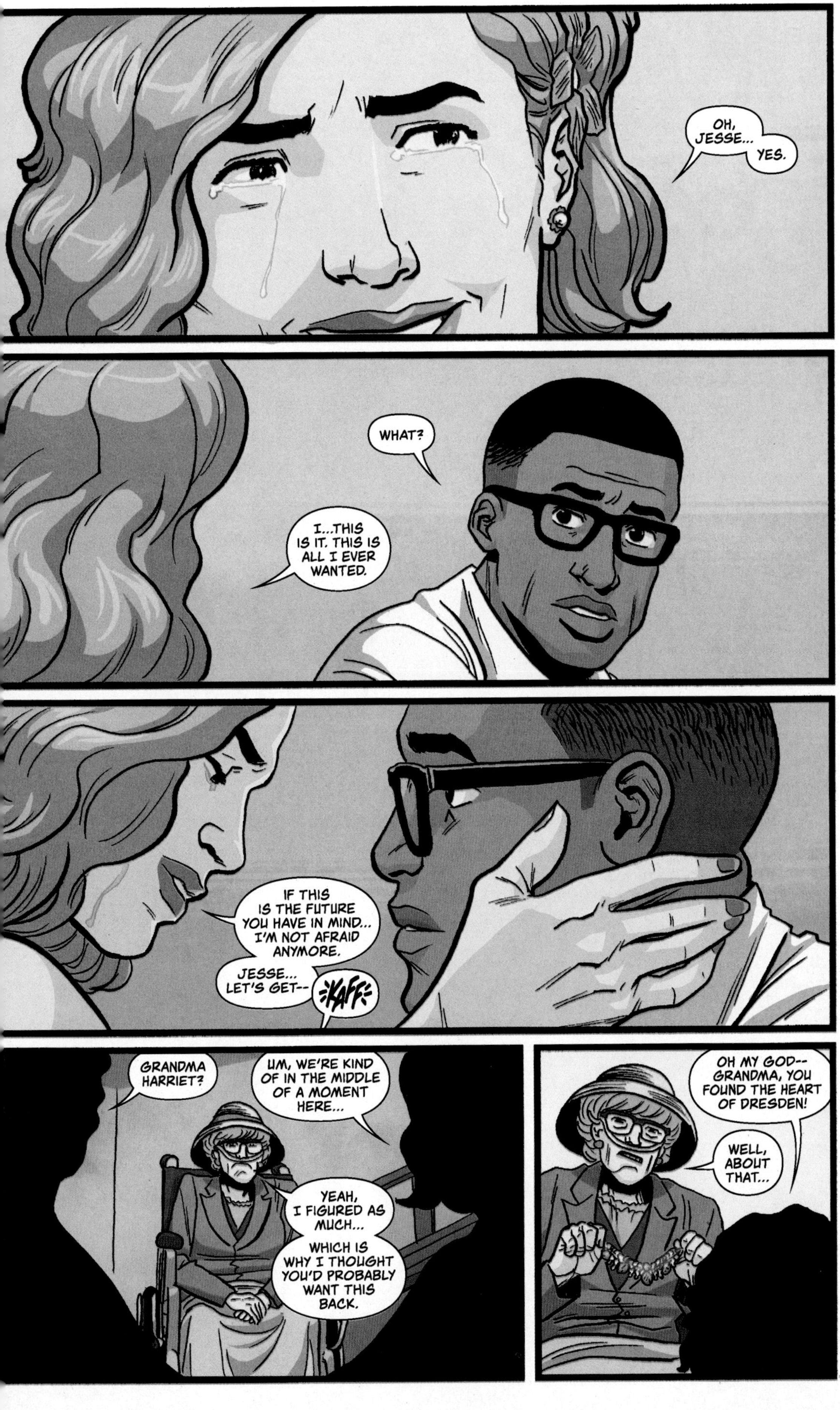
OH, JESSE... YES.
WHAT?
I...THIS IS IT. THIS IS ALL I EVER WANTED.
IF THIS IS THE FUTURE YOU HAVE IN MIND... I'M NOT AFRAID ANYMORE.
JESSE... LET'S GET--
KAFF
GRANDMA HARRIET?
UM, WE'RE KIND OF IN THE MIDDLE OF A MOMENT HERE...
YEAH, I FIGURED AS MUCH...
WHICH IS WHY I THOUGHT YOU'D PROBABLY WANT THIS BACK.
OH MY GOD-- GRANDMA, YOU FOUND THE HEART OF DRESDEN!
WELL, ABOUT THAT...

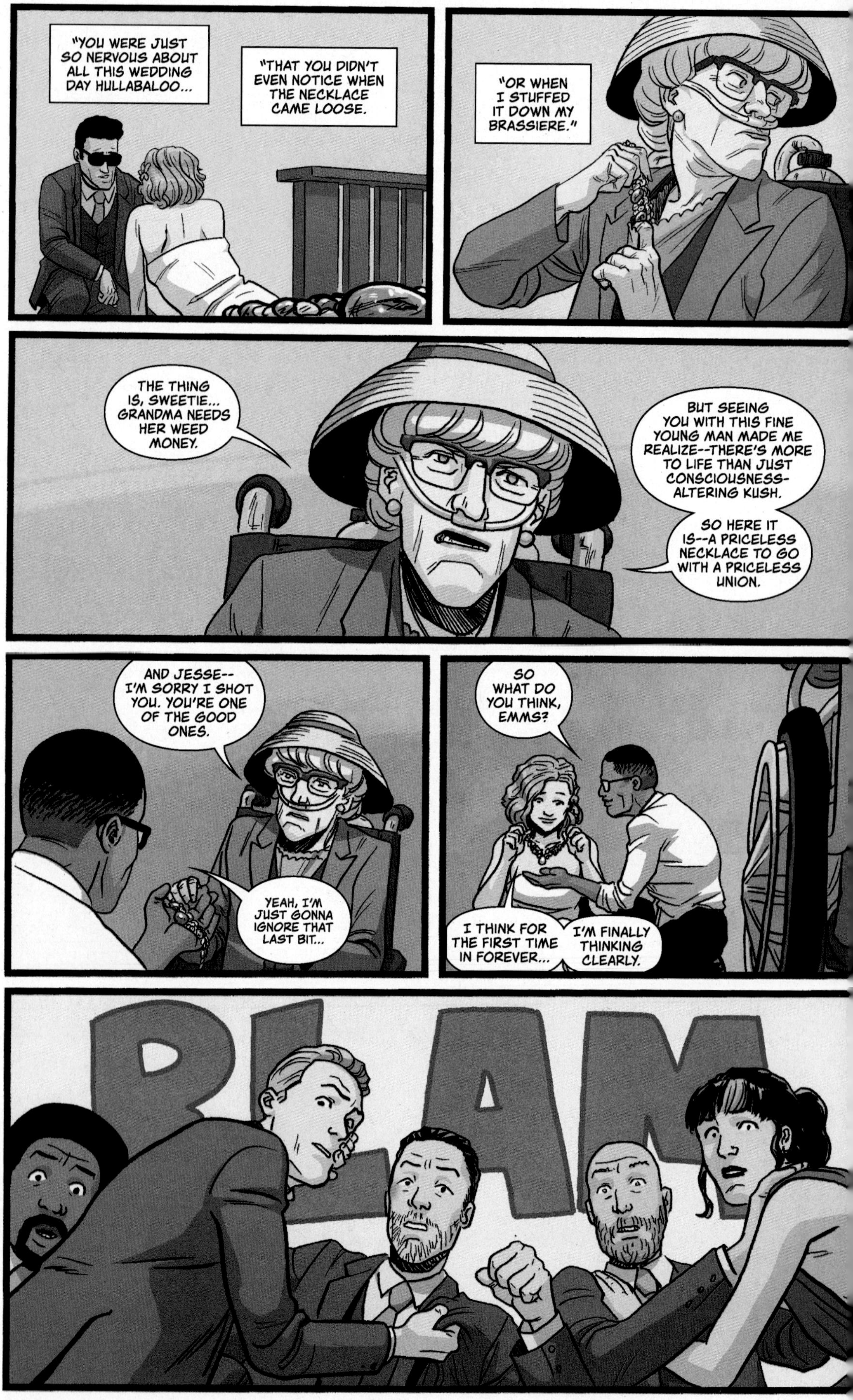

"YOU WERE JUST SO NERVOUS ABOUT ALL THIS WEDDING DAY HULLABALOO...
"THAT YOU DIDN'T EVEN NOTICE WHEN THE NECKLACE CAME LOOSE.
"OR WHEN I STUFFED IT DOWN MY BRASSIERE."
THE THING IS, SWEETIE... GRANDMA NEEDS HER WEED MONEY.
BUT SEEING YOU WITH THIS FINE YOUNG MAN MADE ME REALIZE--THERE'S MORE TO LIFE THAN JUST CONSCIOUSNESS-ALTERING KUSH.
SO HERE IT IS--A PRICELESS NECKLACE TO GO WITH A PRICELESS UNION.
AND JESSE-- I'M SORRY I SHOT YOU. YOU'RE ONE OF THE GOOD ONES.
YEAH, I'M JUST GONNA IGNORE THAT LAST BIT...
SO WHAT DO YOU THINK, EMMS?
I THINK FOR THE FIRST TIME IN FOREVER...
I'M FINALLY THINKING CLEARLY.
BLAM

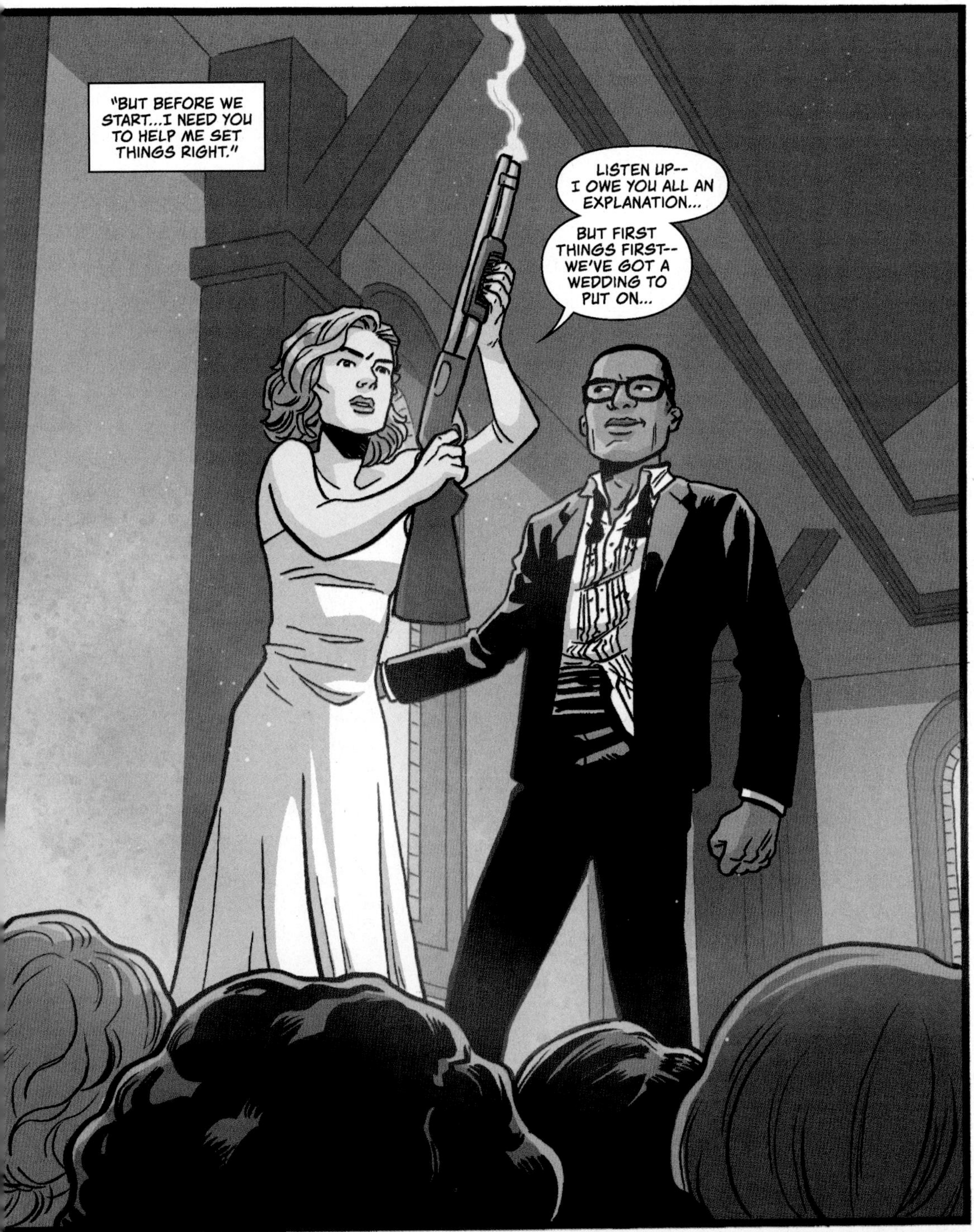
"BUT BEFORE WE START...I NEED YOU TO HELP ME SET THINGS RIGHT."
LISTEN UP-- I OWE YOU ALL AN EXPLANATION...
BUT FIRST THINGS FIRST-- WE'VE GOT A WEDDING TO PUT ON...

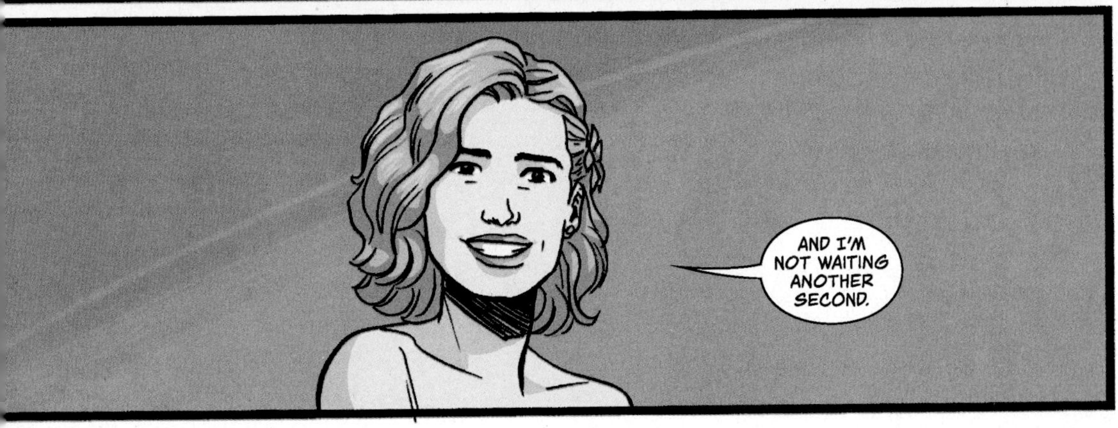
AND I'M NOT WAITING ANOTHER SECOND.

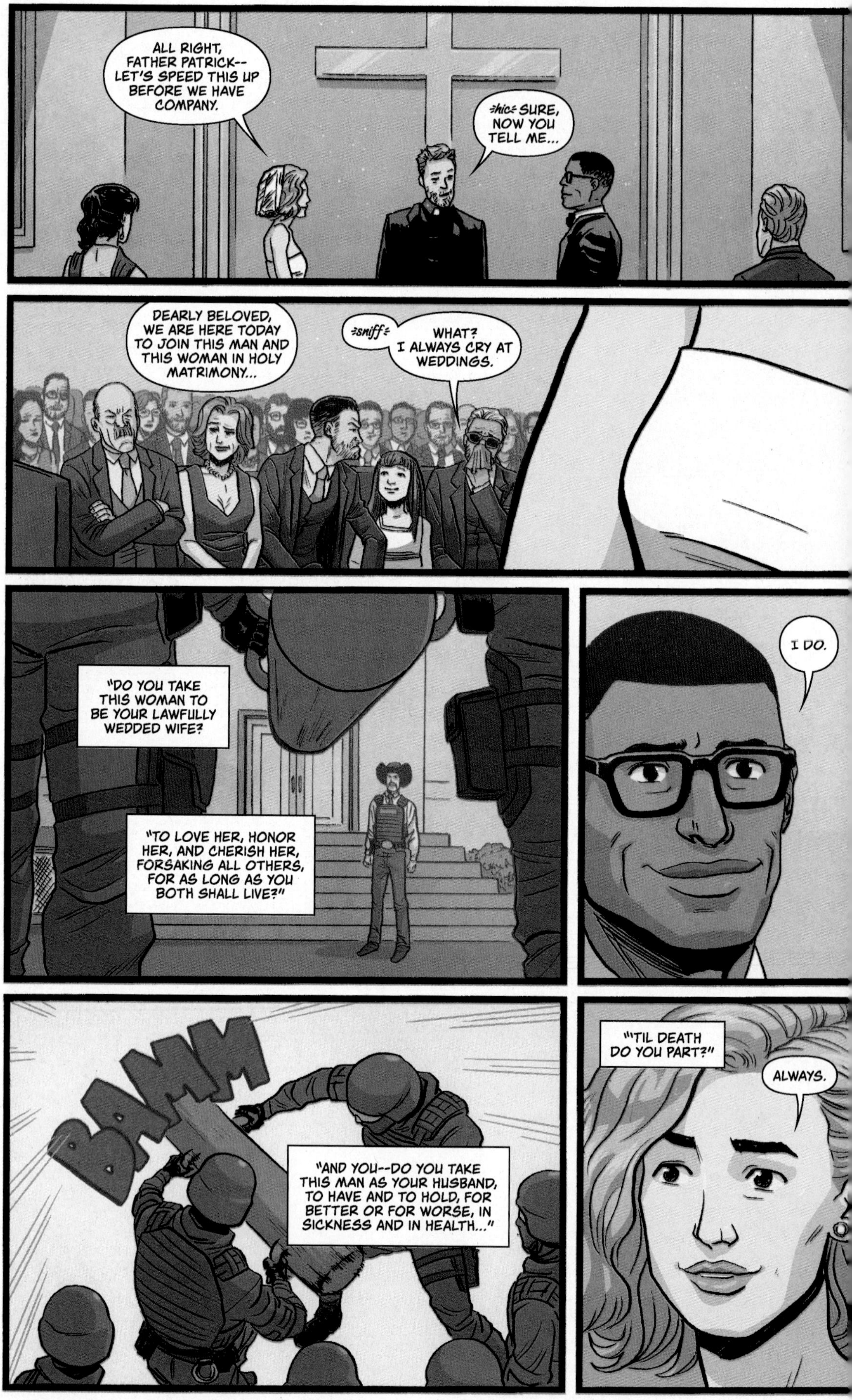
ALL RIGHT, FATHER PATRICK--LET'S SPEED THIS UP BEFORE WE HAVE COMPANY.
hic SURE, NOW YOU TELL ME...
DEARLY BELOVED, WE ARE HERE TODAY TO JOIN THIS MAN AND THIS WOMAN IN HOLY MATRIMONY...
sniff
WHAT? I ALWAYS CRY AT WEDDINGS.
"DO YOU TAKE THIS WOMAN TO BE YOUR LAWFULLY WEDDED WIFE?
"TO LOVE HER, HONOR HER, AND CHERISH HER, FORSAKING ALL OTHERS, FOR AS LONG AS YOU BOTH SHALL LIVE?"
I DO.
BAMM
"AND YOU--DO YOU TAKE THIS MAN AS YOUR HUSBAND, TO HAVE AND TO HOLD, FOR BETTER OR FOR WORSE, IN SICKNESS AND IN HEALTH..."
"TIL DEATH DO YOU PART?"
ALWAYS.

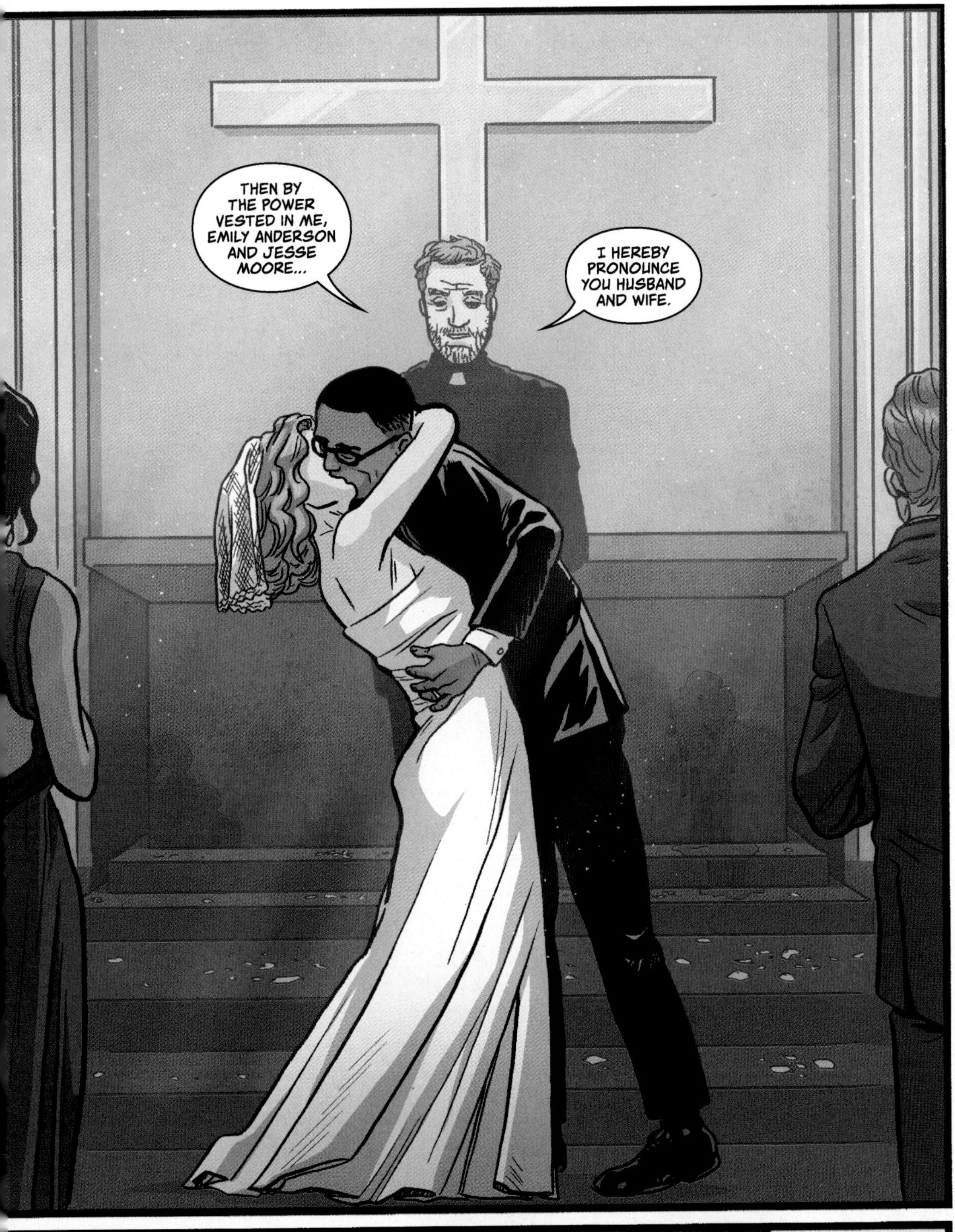
THEN BY THE POWER VESTED IN ME, EMILY ANDERSON AND JESSE MOORE...
I HEREBY PRONOUNCE YOU HUSBAND AND WIFE.

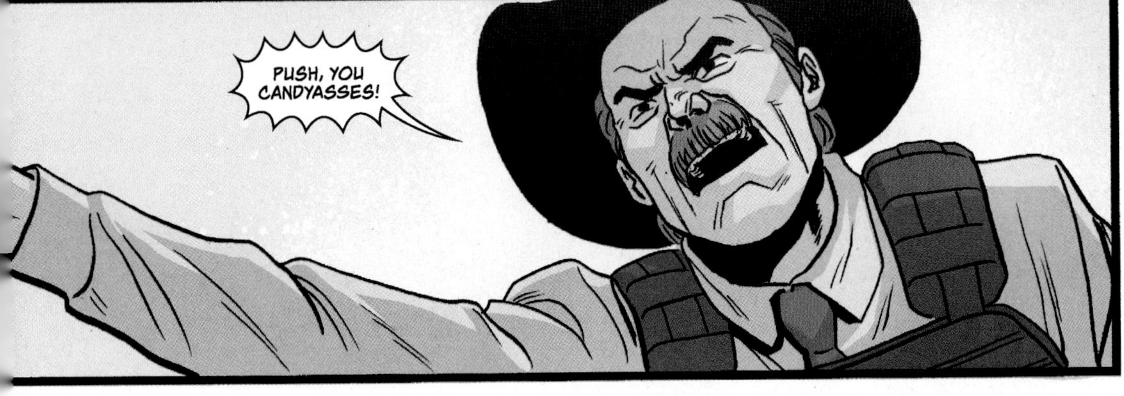
PUSH, YOU CANDYASSES!

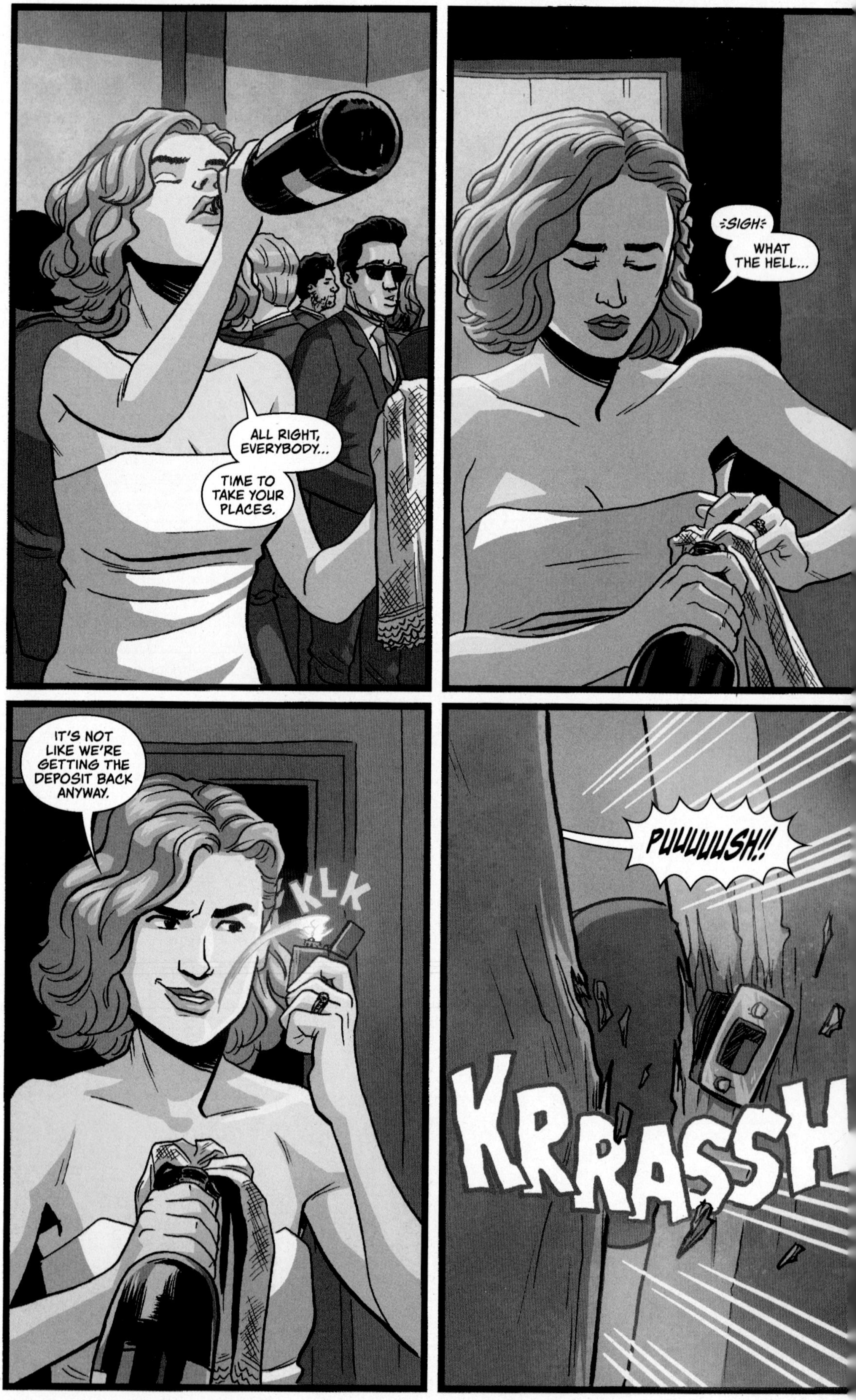

ALL RIGHT, EVERYBODY...
TIME TO TAKE YOUR PLACES.
SIGH
WHAT THE HELL...
IT'S NOT LIKE WE'RE GETTING THE DEPOSIT BACK ANYWAY.
KLK
PUUUUUSH!!
KRRASSH

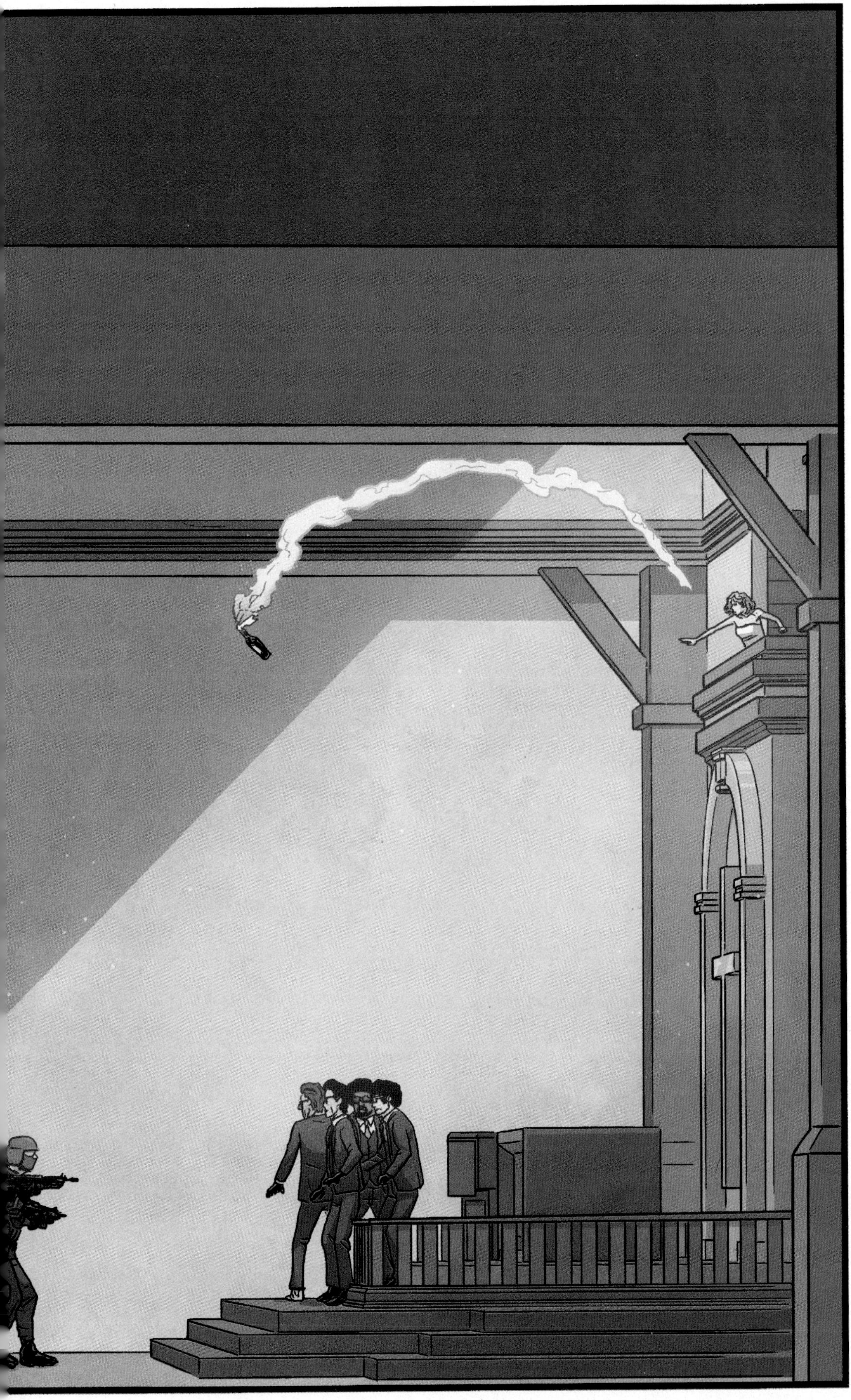

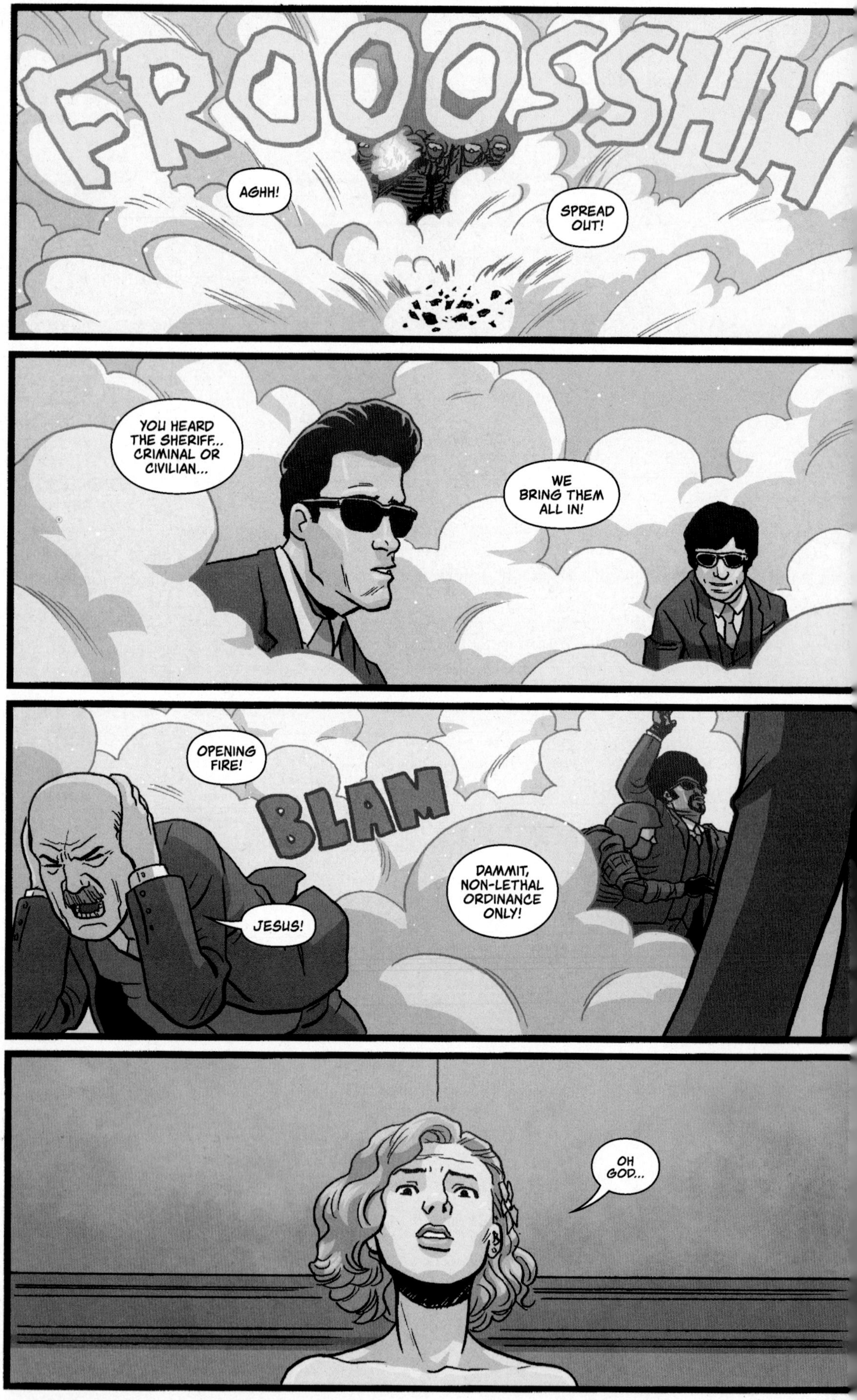
FROOOSSHH
AGHH!
SPREAD OUT!
YOU HEARD THE SHERIFF... CRIMINAL OR CIVILIAN...
WE BRING THEM ALL IN!
OPENING FIRE!
BLAM
JESUS!
DAMMIT, NON-LETHAL ORDINANCE ONLY!
OH GOD...

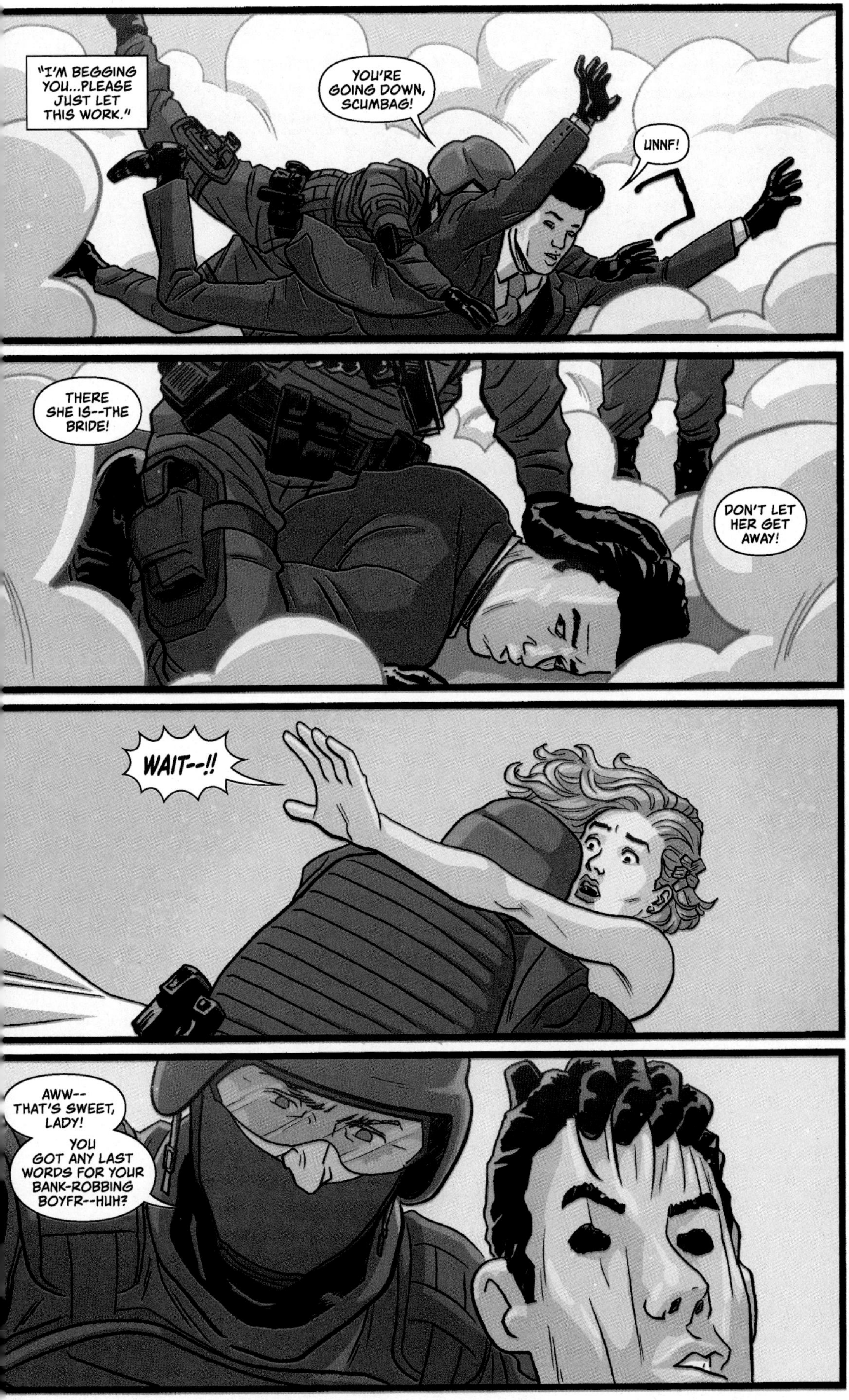
"I'M BEGGING YOU...PLEASE JUST LET THIS WORK."
YOU'RE GOING DOWN, SCUMBAG!
UNNF!
THERE SHE IS--THE BRIDE!
DON'T LET HER GET AWAY!
WAIT--!!
AWW-- THAT'S SWEET, LADY!
YOU GOT ANY LAST WORDS FOR YOUR BANK-ROBBING BOYFR--HUH?

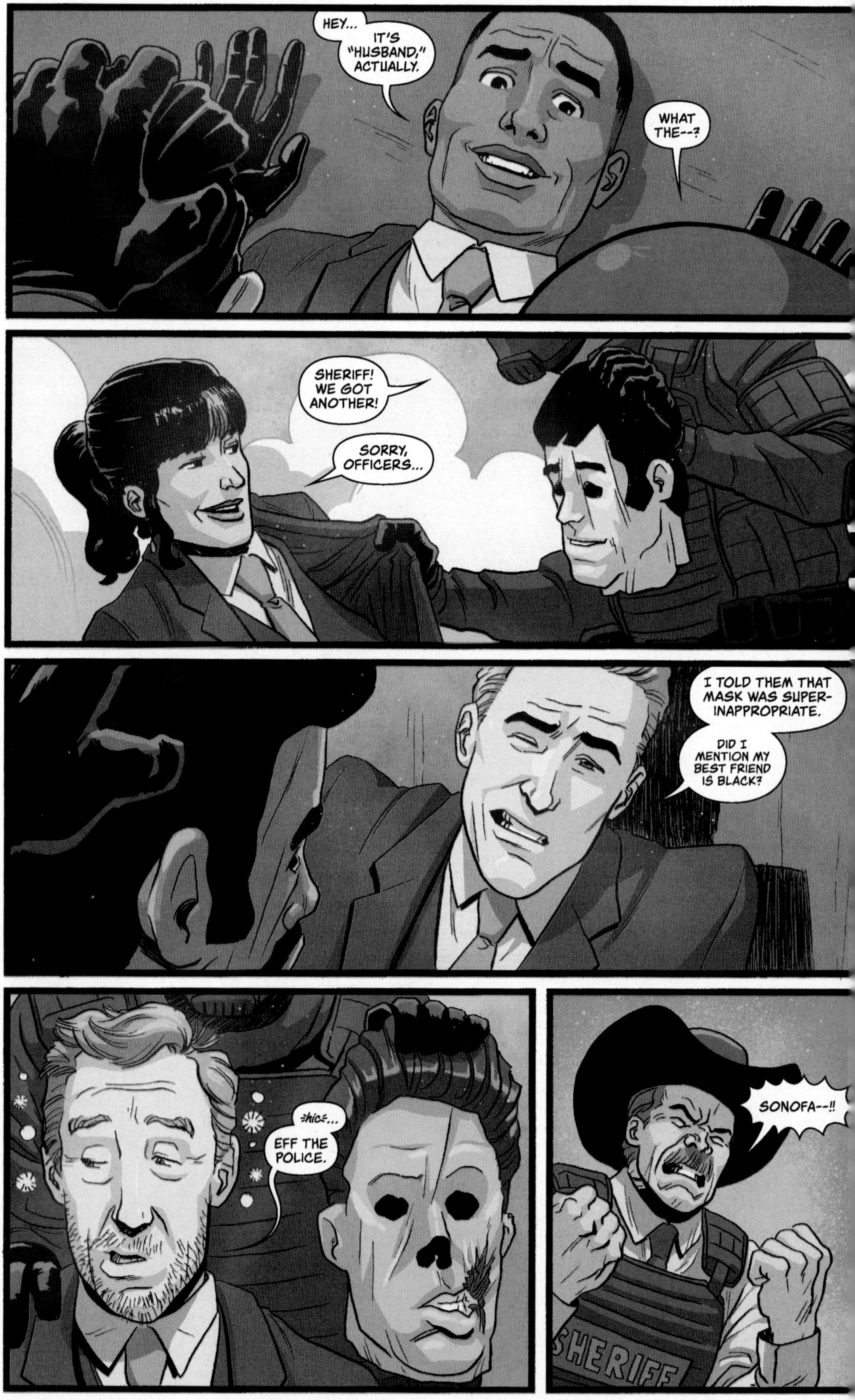
HEY... IT'S "HUSBAND," ACTUALLY.
WHAT THE--?
SHERIFF! WE GOT ANOTHER!
SORRY, OFFICERS...
I TOLD THEM THAT MASK WAS SUPER-INAPPROPRIATE.
DID I MENTION MY BEST FRIEND IS BLACK?
hic...
EFF THE POLICE.
SONOFA--!!
SHERIFF

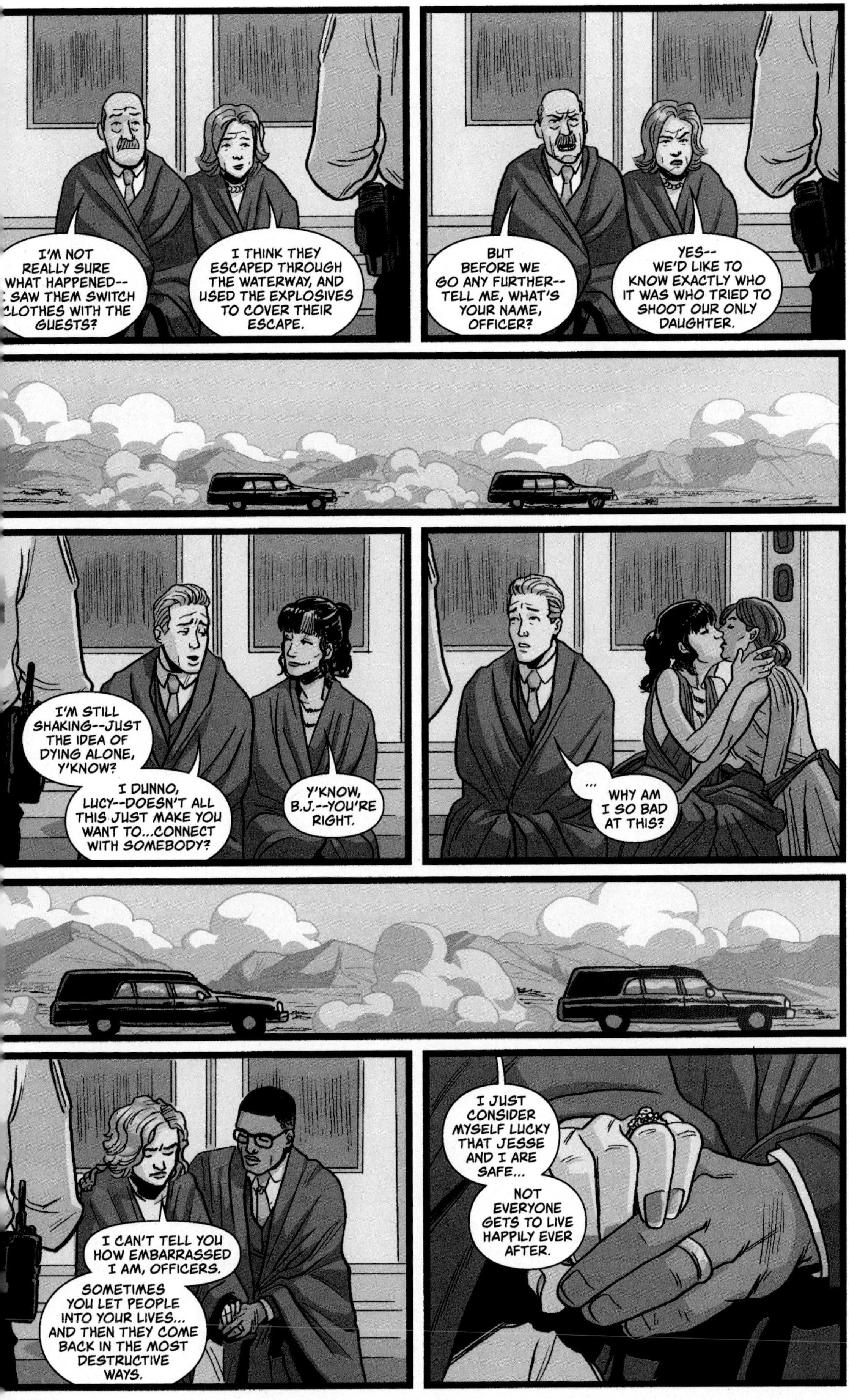
I'M NOT REALLY SURE WHAT HAPPENED-- I SAW THEM SWITCH CLOTHES WITH THE GUESTS?
I THINK THEY ESCAPED THROUGH THE WATERWAY, AND USED THE EXPLOSIVES TO COVER THEIR ESCAPE.
BUT BEFORE WE GO ANY FURTHER-- TELL ME, WHAT'S YOUR NAME, OFFICER?
YES-- WE'D LIKE TO KNOW EXACTLY WHO IT WAS WHO TRIED TO SHOOT OUR ONLY DAUGHTER.
I'M STILL SHAKING--JUST THE IDEA OF DYING ALONE, Y'KNOW?
I DUNNO, LUCY--DOESN'T ALL THIS JUST MAKE YOU WANT TO...CONNECT WITH SOMEBODY?
Y'KNOW, B.J.--YOU'RE RIGHT.
...
WHY AM I SO BAD AT THIS?
I CAN'T TELL YOU HOW EMBARRASSED I AM, OFFICERS.
SOMETIMES YOU LET PEOPLE INTO YOUR LIVES... AND THEN THEY COME BACK IN THE MOST DESTRUCTIVE WAYS.
I JUST CONSIDER MYSELF LUCKY THAT JESSE AND I ARE SAFE...
NOT EVERYONE GETS TO LIVE HAPPILY EVER AFTER.

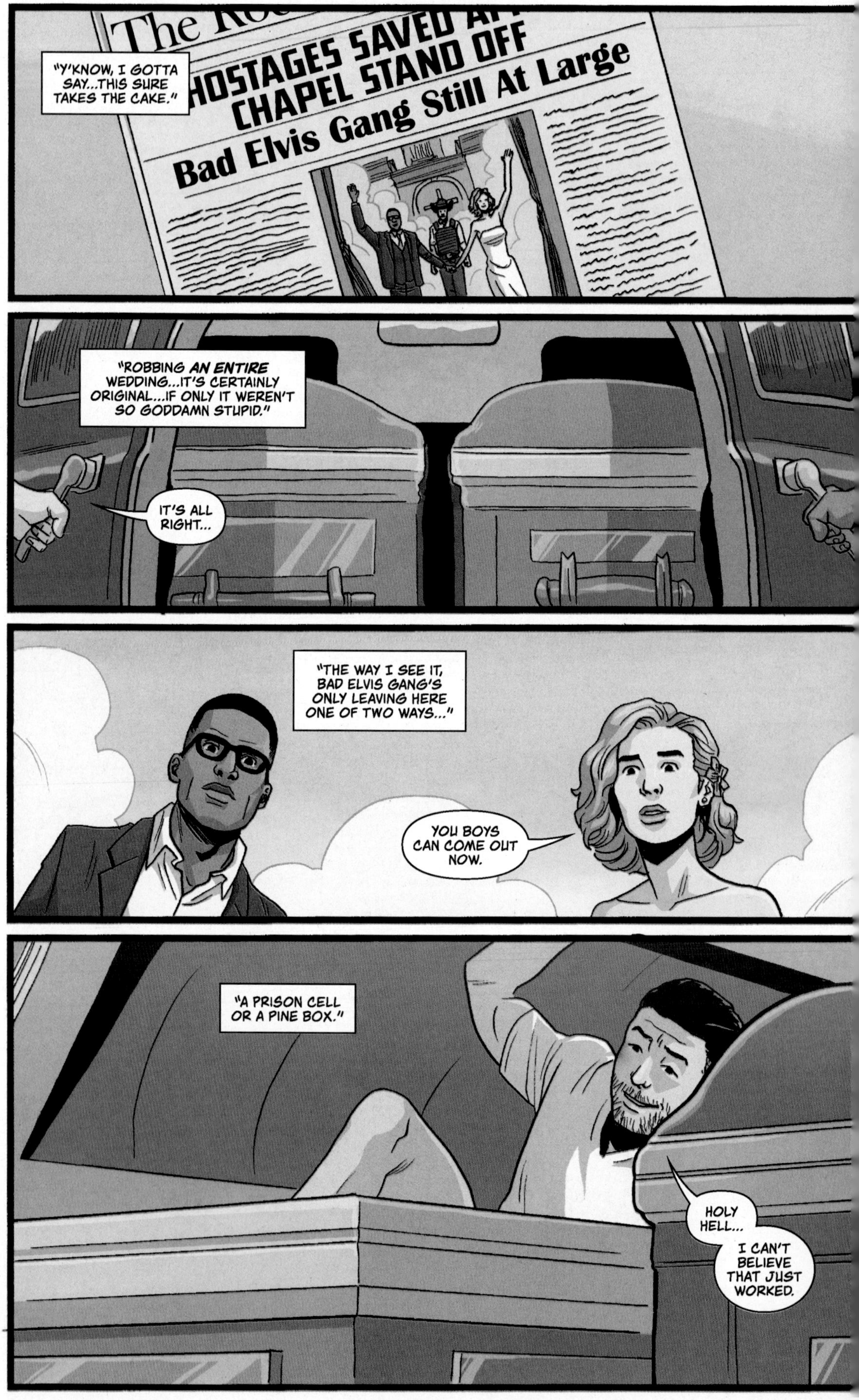

The Ro
HOSTAGES SAVED AT
CHAPEL STAND OFF
Bad Elvis Gang Still At Large
"Y'KNOW, I GOTTA SAY...THIS SURE TAKES THE CAKE."
"ROBBING AN ENTIRE WEDDING...IT'S CERTAINLY ORIGINAL...IF ONLY IT WEREN'T SO GODDAMN STUPID."
IT'S ALL RIGHT...
"THE WAY I SEE IT, BAD ELVIS GANG'S ONLY LEAVING HERE ONE OF TWO WAYS..."
YOU BOYS CAN COME OUT NOW.
"A PRISON CELL OR A PINE BOX."
HOLY HELL...
I CAN'T BELIEVE THAT JUST WORKED.

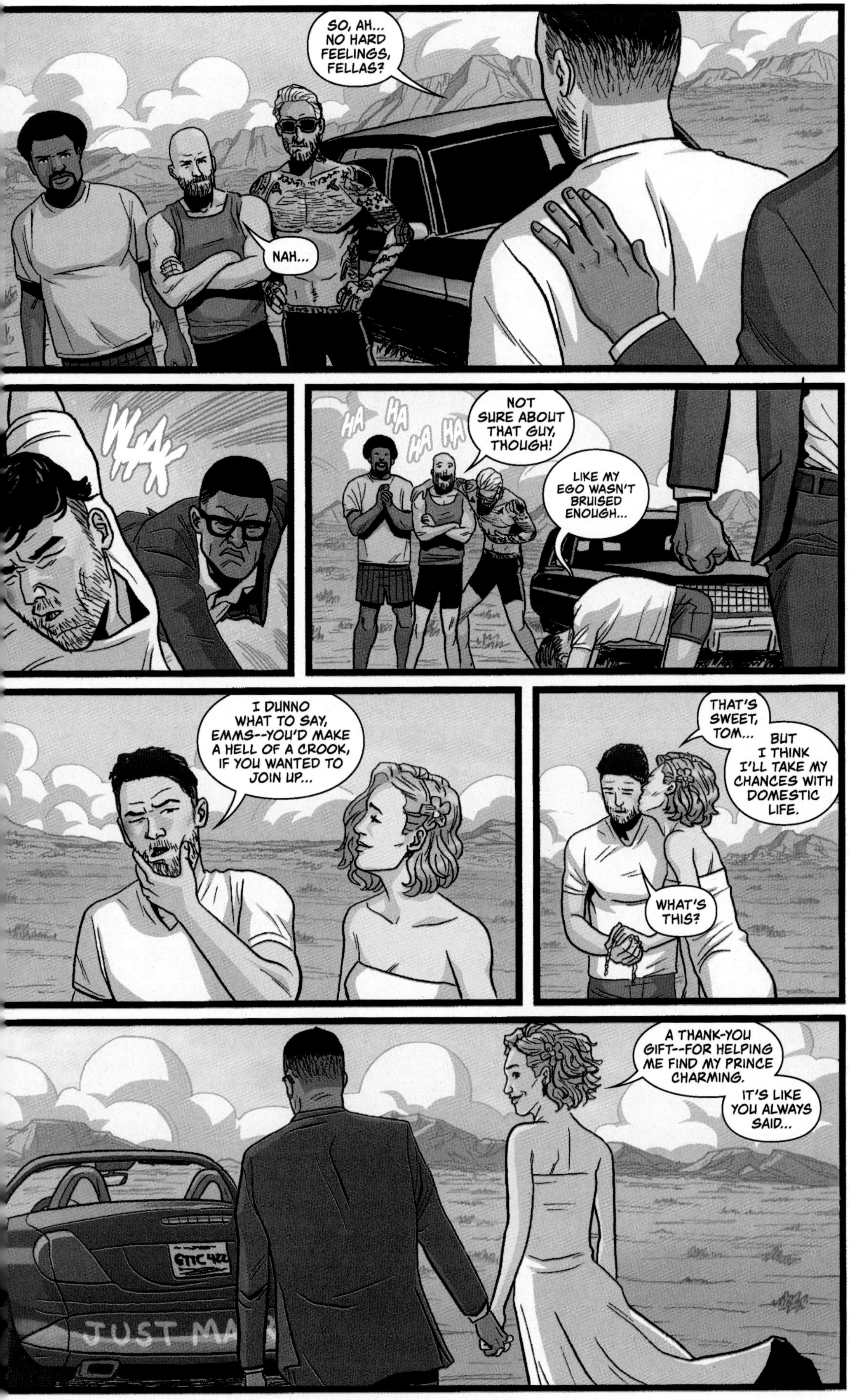

SO, AH... NO HARD FEELINGS, FELLAS?
NAH...
WHAK
HA HA HA HA
NOT SURE ABOUT THAT GUY, THOUGH!
LIKE MY EGO WASN'T BRUISED ENOUGH...
I DUNNO WHAT TO SAY, EMMS--YOU'D MAKE A HELL OF A CROOK, IF YOU WANTED TO JOIN UP...
THAT'S SWEET, TOM...
BUT I THINK I'LL TAKE MY CHANCES WITH DOMESTIC LIFE.
WHAT'S THIS?
A THANK-YOU GIFT--FOR HELPING ME FIND MY PRINCE CHARMING.
IT'S LIKE YOU ALWAYS SAID...
6TIC 422
JUST MA

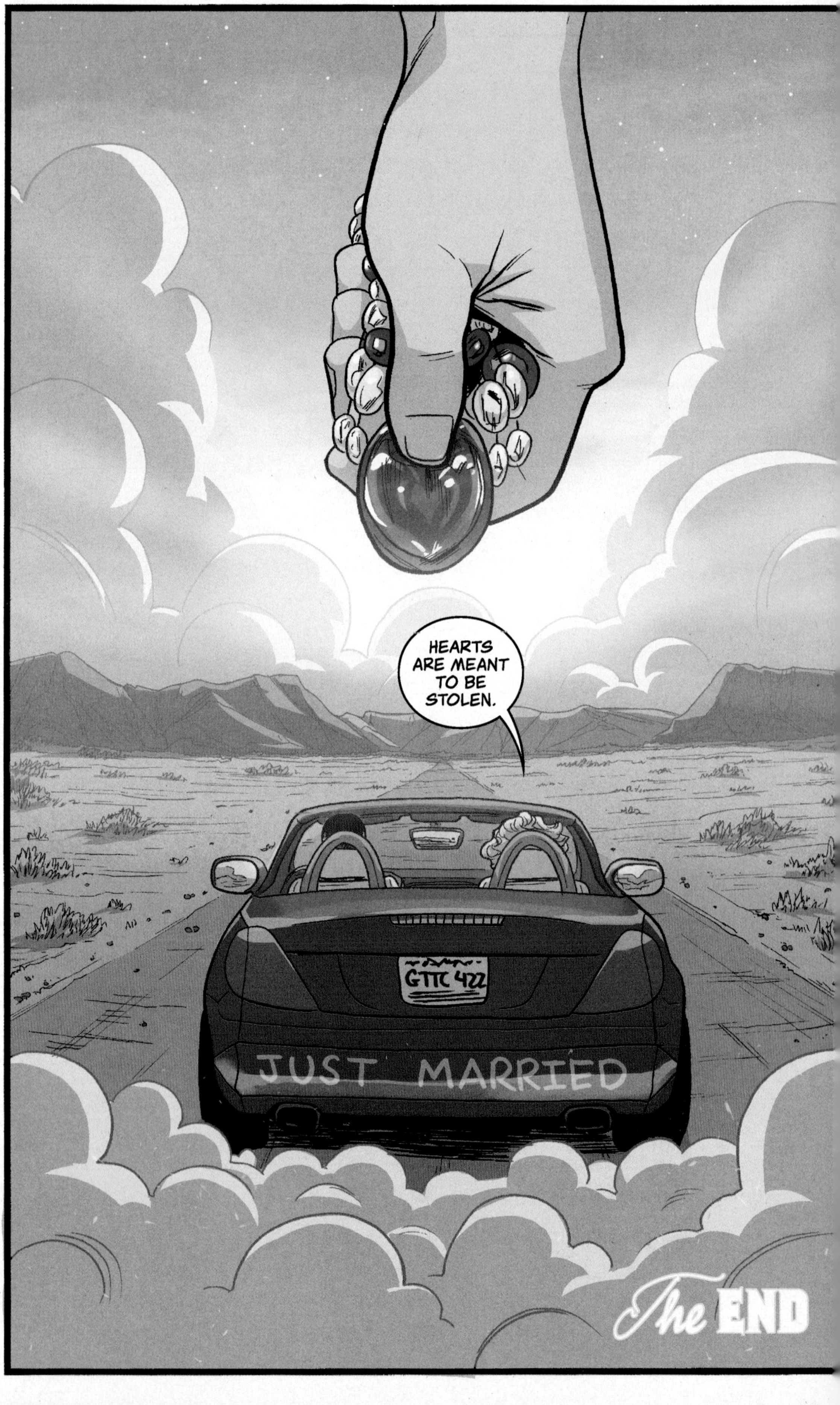
HEARTS ARE MEANT TO BE STOLEN.
GTTC 422
JUST MARRIED
The END

ISSUE #1 COVER BY LISA STERLE

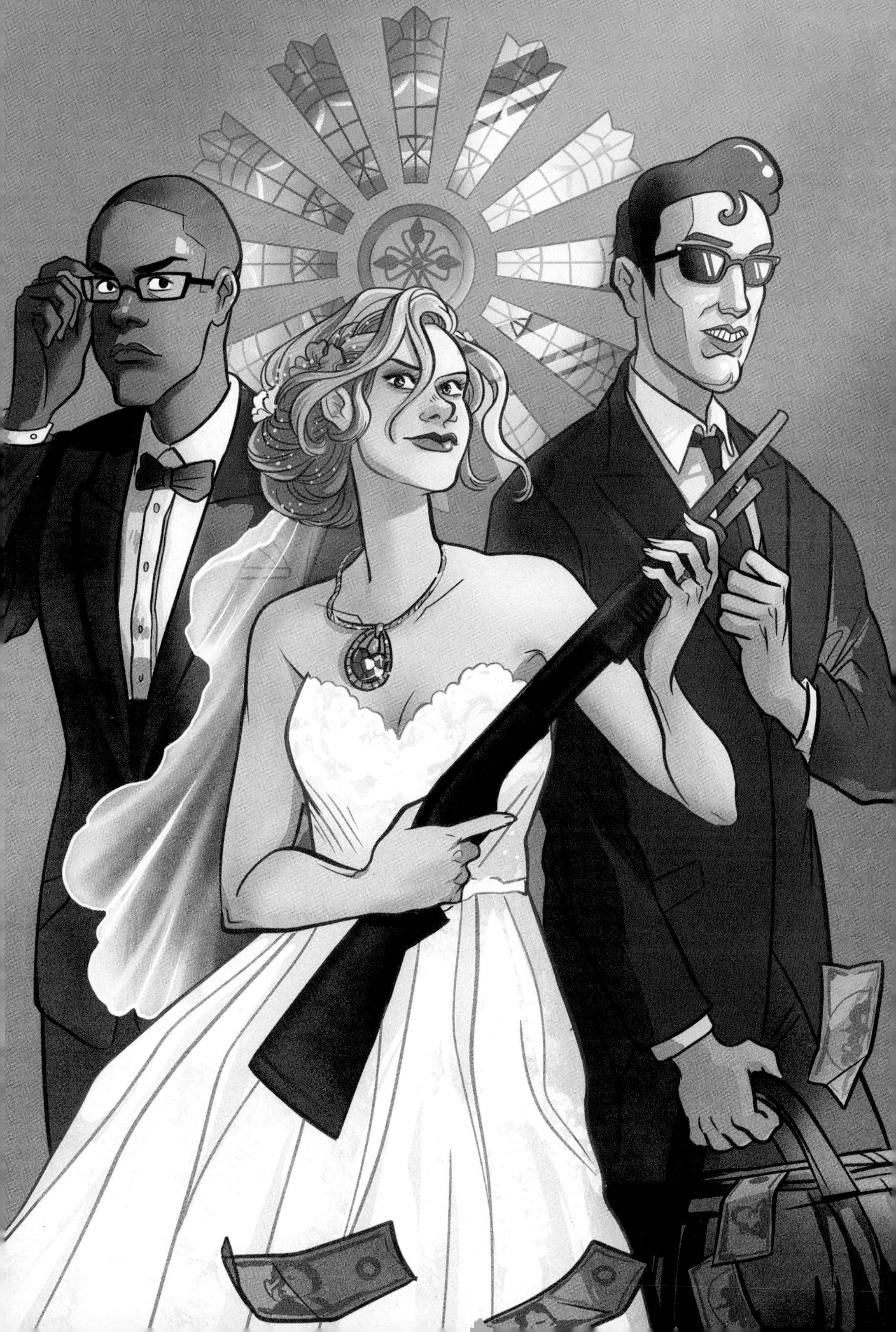

ISSUE #1 COVER BY MAAN HOUSE

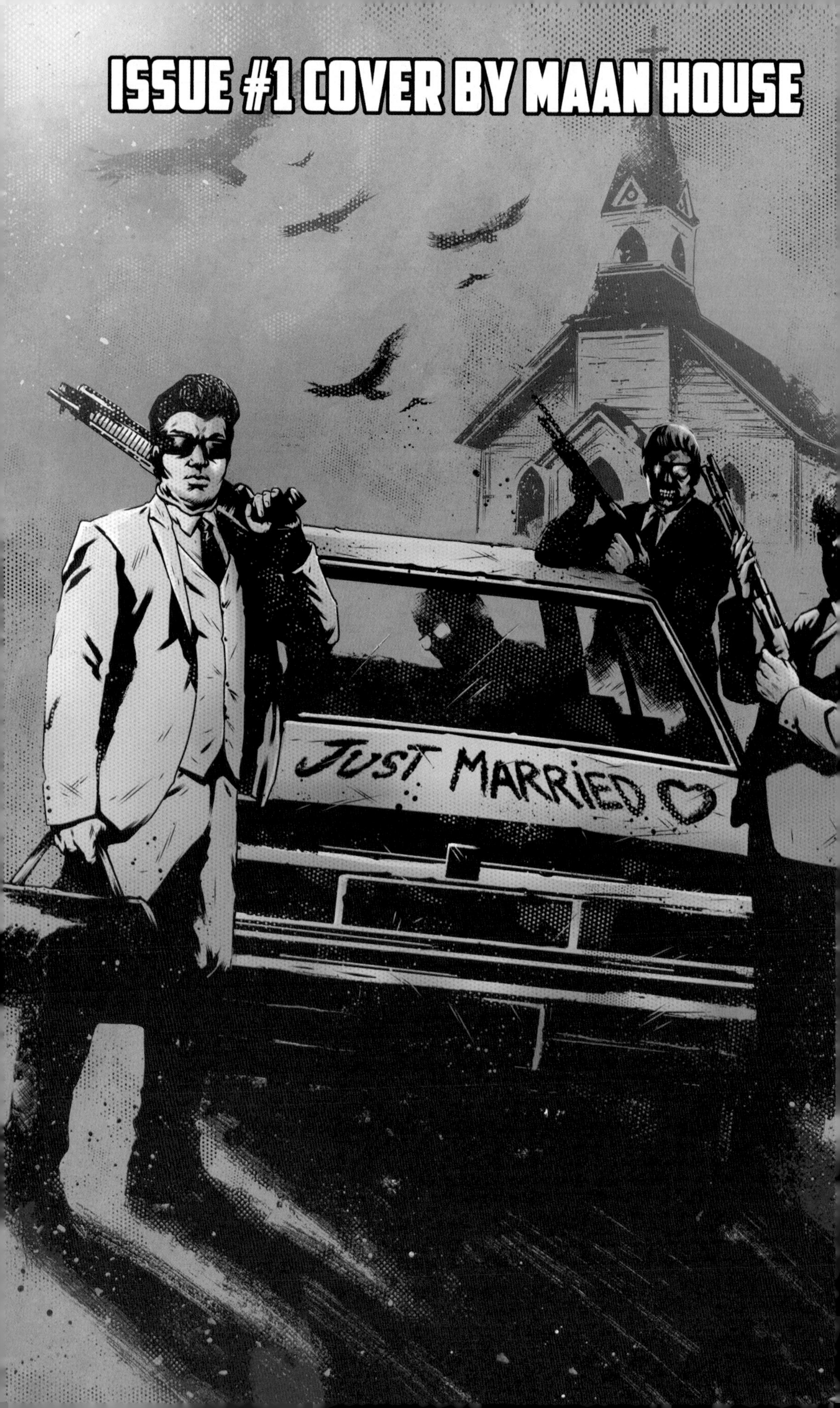
JUST MARRIED

ISSUE #2 COVER BY SWEENEY BOO

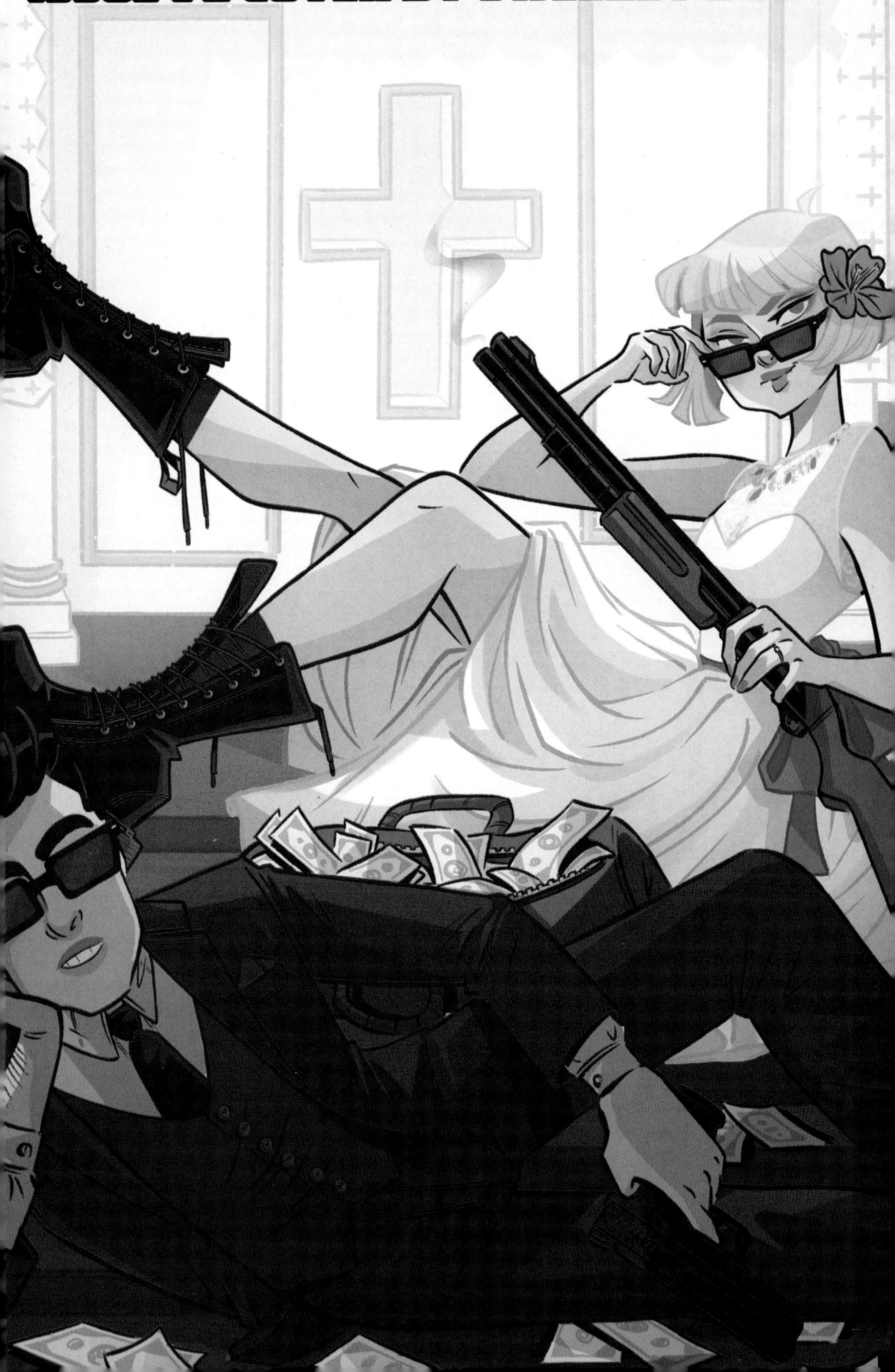

ISSUE #2 COVER BY MAAN HOUSE

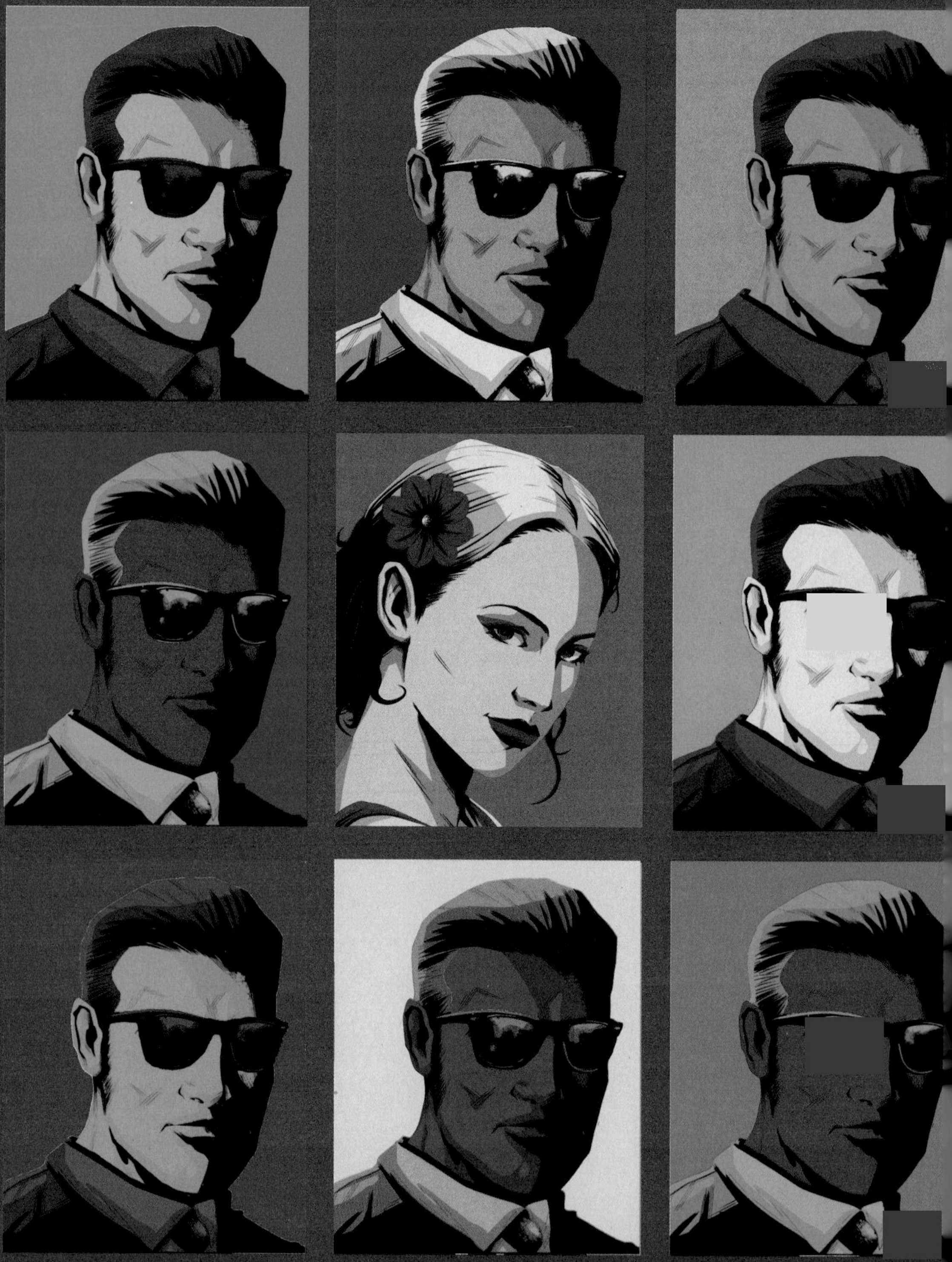

ISSUE #3 COVER BY EMILY PEARSON

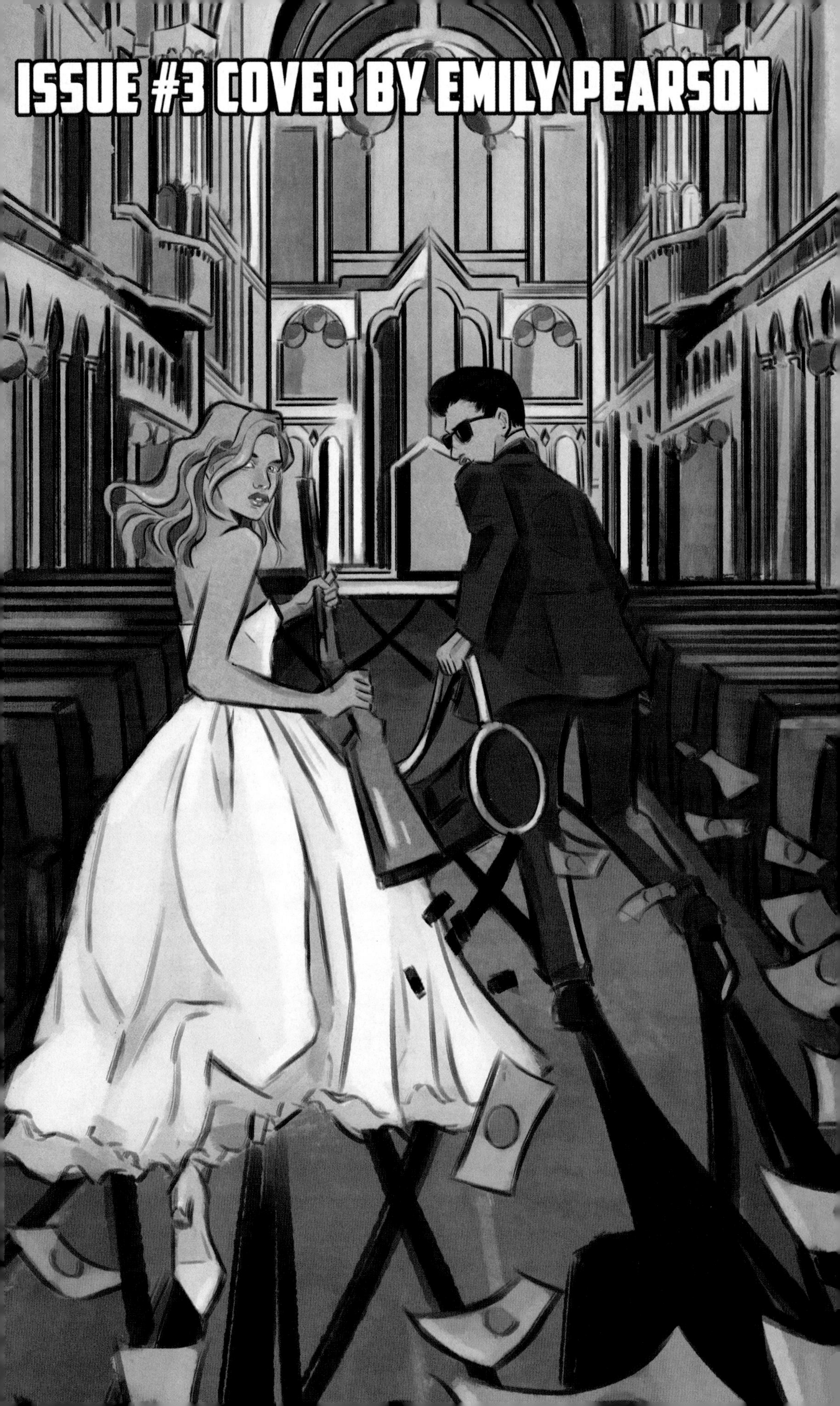

ISSUE #3 COVER BY MAAN HOUSE

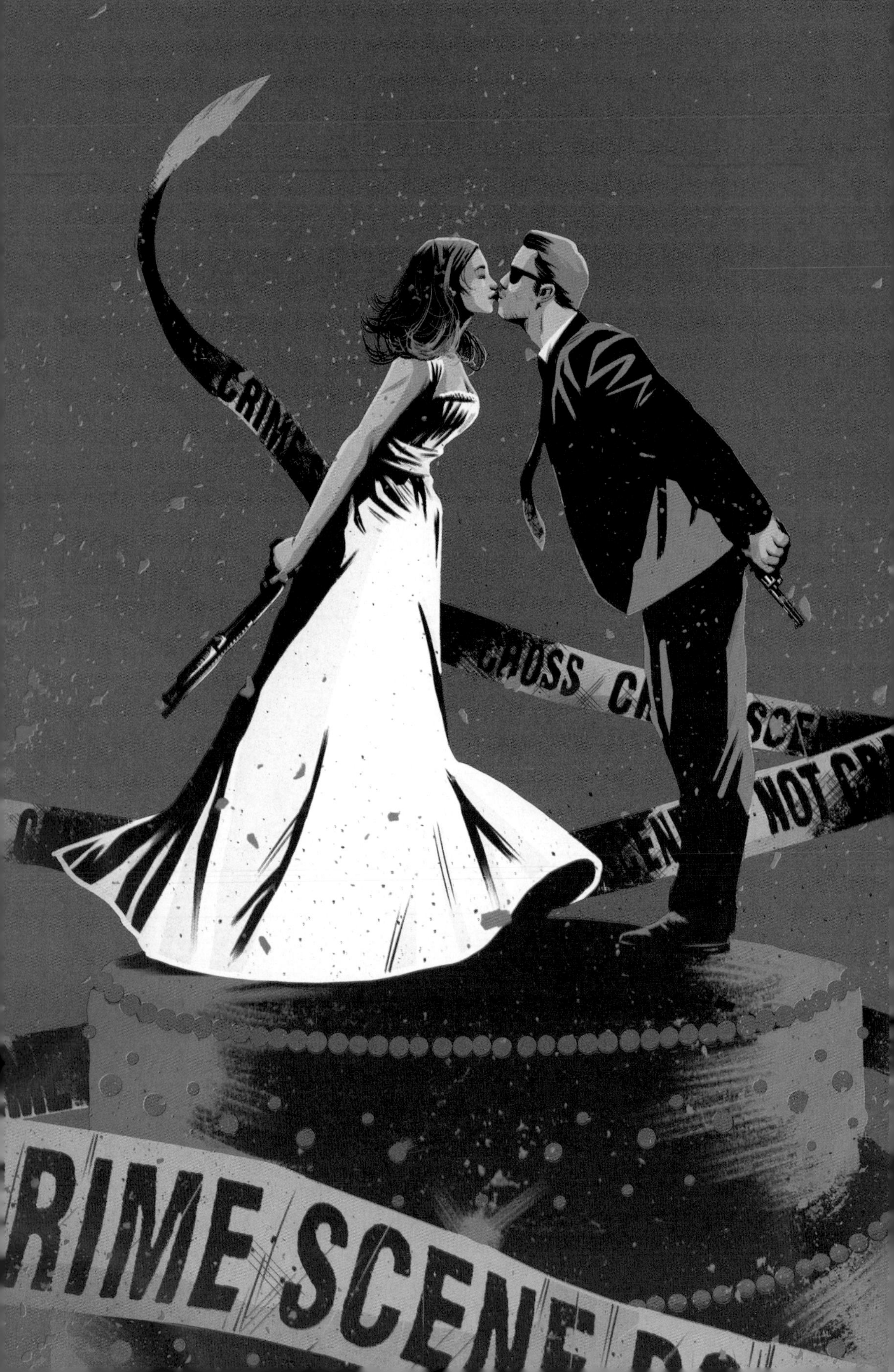
CRIM
CROSS
NOT
RIME SCENE

ISSUE #4 COVER BY JOHANNA THE MAD

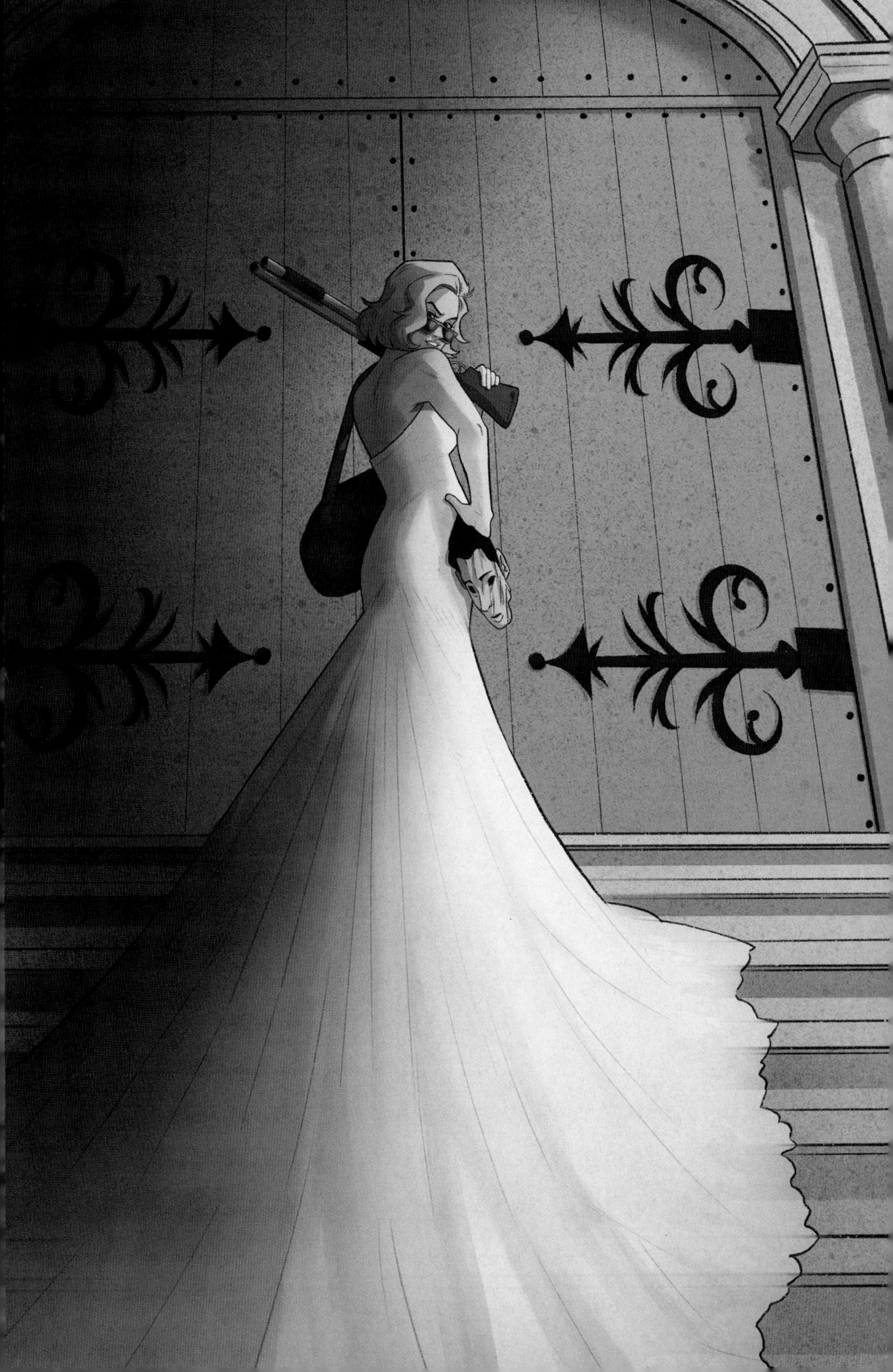

ISSUE #4 COVER BY MAAN HOUSE

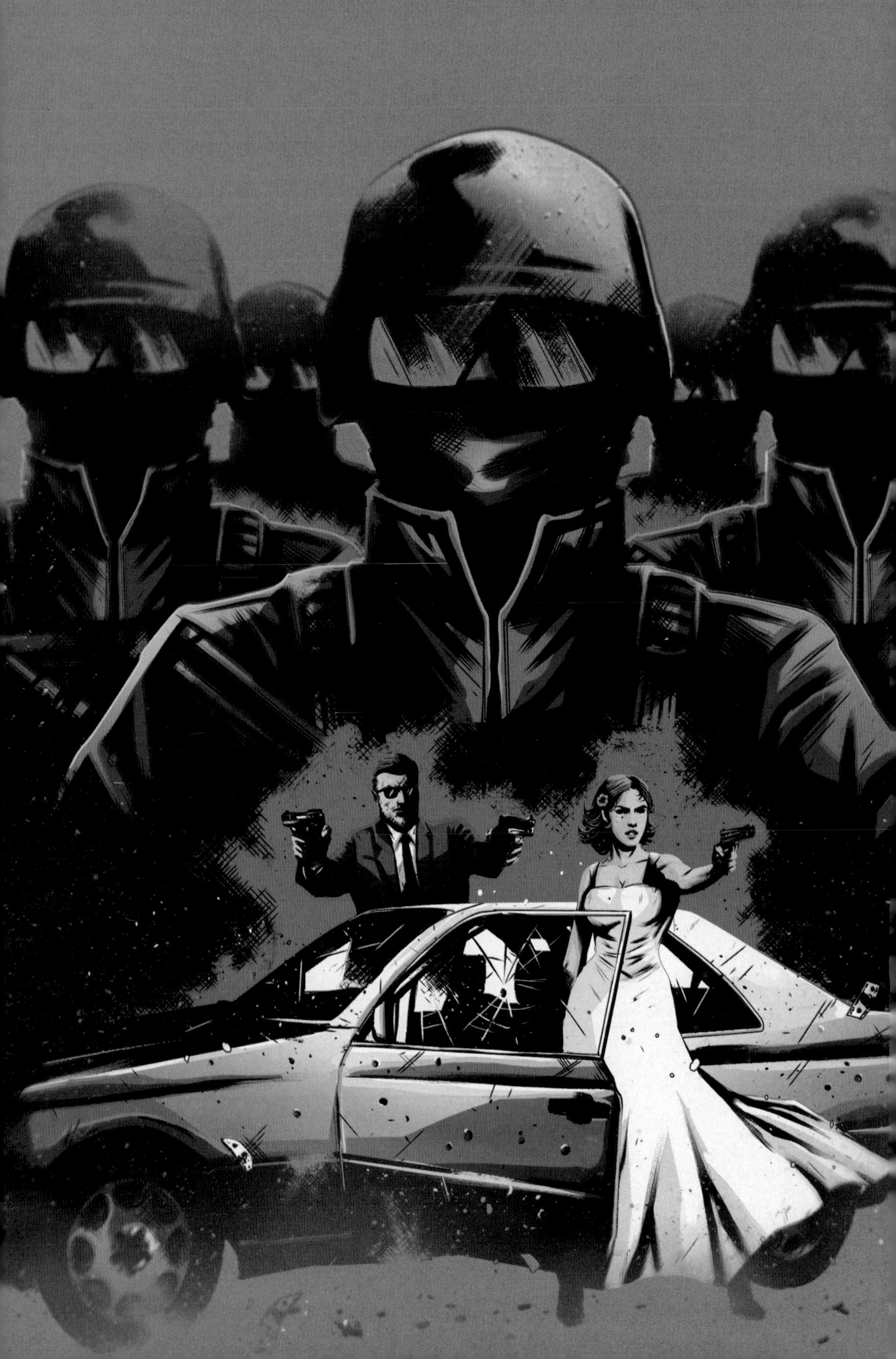